THE ASSIZE OF
NOVEL DISSEISIN

THE ASSIZE OF NOVEL DISSEISIN

BY

DONALD W. SUTHERLAND

OXFORD
AT THE CLARENDON PRESS
1973

Oxford University Press, Ely House, London W. 1

GLASGOW   NEW YORK   TORONTO   MELBOURNE   WELLINGTON
CAPE TOWN   IBADAN   NAIROBI   DAR ES SALAAM   LUSAKA   ADDIS ABABA
DELHI   BOMBAY   CALCUTTA   MADRAS   KARACHI   LAHORE   DACCA
KUALA LUMPUR   SINGAPORE   HONG KONG   TOKYO

Printed in Great Britain
at the University Press, Oxford
by Vivian Ridler
Printer to the University

TO MY PARENTS

PREFACE

THIS book is about an institution of the English law which flourished for three hundred years or so, from the twelfth century to the fifteenth. Since the times which it served were far from static and since the assize itself underwent many changes in those times, we are writing of an institution which meant different things in different stages of its long life. Its history is set forth, therefore, in one sense as a series of essays, each of which may do a little to illumine the life and thought of the particular age of which it has to tell. But such was the respect shown in the Middle Ages for the integrity—we almost say the transcendence—of rules of law, that medieval English legal institutions were, in Maitland's words, 'living things', with their individual characters, careers, and fortunes. The history of the assize possesses, then, the kind of unity that may mark a biography: whatever times the assize passed through and whatever it became, it must be understood in terms of its own continuous life.

For support in the preparation of the work I am beholden in the first place to the University of Iowa, which, besides providing through the years an academic home always friendly to research, has afforded me three several grants of released time for study and writing. In 1964–5 the American Council of Learned Societies and the Social Science Research Council joined in giving fellowships which made possible the initial collection of materials, and in 1971–2 a fellowship of the National Endowment for the Humanities and a travel grant from the American Philosophical Society added indispensable support for the completion of the research and writing.

For help in matters that concern the assize of nuisance I am grateful to Janet S. Loengard, who has allowed me to study and to cite her unpublished Ph.D. dissertation on that subject, presented in Columbia University in 1970. Anne L. Spitzer of Iowa City has given me access to the important thirteenth-century *Summa* of Gilbert of Thornton by graciously permitting me to use both the edition which she is preparing and her photocopies of the manuscripts. She has also read my whole book in draft and made a number of valuable comments.

In consulting manuscripts I have been aided by the staffs and governors of the British Museum, the John Rylands Library, the Library of Lincoln's Inn, the Bodleian Library in Oxford, and the Public Record Office in London. I am grateful to the Masters of the Bench of Lincoln's Inn, to the Librarian of the John Rylands Library, to the Harvard University Law Library, and to the Keeper of Western Manuscripts in the Bodleian Library for leave to include citations and quotations from manuscripts in their custody. The transcripts and translations of Crown-copyright records in the Public Record Office appear by permission of the Controller of H.M. Stationery Office.

Lastly I wish to acknowledge the help of my wife Judith. She has been a patient helper, a good counsellor, and a source of inspiration.

D. W. S.

Iowa City, Iowa
August 1972

CONTENTS

ABBREVIATIONS

Ass.	Liber Assisarum
B.M.	British Museum
BNB	*Bracton's Note Book*
C. 60/–	Chancery: Fine Rolls
C.P. 40/–	Court of Common Pleas: Plea Rolls
CRR	*Curia Regis Rolls*
Derby Assizes	*Calendar of the Cases for Derbyshire from Eyre and Assize Rolls*
Eyres of Beds i	Roll of the Justices in Eyre at Bedford, 1202 (Publications of the Bedfordshire Historical Record Society, i)
Eyres of Beds iii	Roll of the Justices in Eyre at Bedford, 1227 (Publications of the Bedfordshire Historical Record Society, iii)
Eyres of Beds ix	Roll of the Justices in Eyre, 1240 (Publications of the Bedfordshire Historical Record Society, ix)
Eyre of Bucks 1227	*Calendar of the Roll of the Justices in Eyre, 1227* (Records Branch of the Buckinghamshire Archaeological Society)
Eyres of Glos, Warw, Staffs	*Rolls of the Justices in Eyre for Gloucestershire, Warwickshire, and Staffordshire, 1221, 1222*
Eyres of Lincs and Worcs	*Rolls of the Justices in Eyre for Lincolnshire (1218–19) and Worcestershire (1221)*
Eyre of Yorks 1218–19	*Rolls of the Justices in Eyre for Yorkshire in 3 Henry III (1218–19)*
FNB	Fitzherbert, *La Nouvelle Natura Brevium*
J.I. 1/–	Justices Itinerant: Eyre Rolls, Assize Rolls, etc.
K.B. 26/–	Court of King's Bench: Curia Regis Rolls
K.B. 27/–	Court of King's Bench: Placita Coram Rege
Lincs Assize Rolls	*The Earliest Lincolnshire Assize Rolls, A.D. 1202–9*
MS. Y	British Museum Additional Manuscript 35116
Northants Pleas	*The Earliest Northamptonshire Assize Rolls, A.D. 1202 and 1203*
Northumb Assize Rolls	*Three Early Assize Rolls for the County of Northumberland*
P. & M.	Pollock and Maitland, *The History of English Law*
Pleas 1198–1202	*Pleas before the King or his Justices, 1198–1202*

Pleas 1198–1212	*Pleas before the King or his Justices, 1198–1212*
Procedure w/o Writ	*Select Cases of Procedure without Writ under Henry III*
PRS xiv	*Three Rolls of the King's Court in the Reign of King Richard I, A.D. 1194–5* (Pipe Roll Society, vol. 14)
PRS xxiv	*A Roll of the King's Court in the Reign of King Richard the First* (Pipe Roll Society, vol. 24)
Sel. Cases in K.B.	*Select Cases in the Court of King's Bench*
SR	*Statutes of the Realm*
Wilts Civil Pleas 1249	*Civil Pleas of the Wiltshire Eyre, 1249*
Wilts Crown Pleas 1249	*Crown Pleas of the Wiltshire Eyre, 1249*
Y.B.	Year Book
Yorks Assize Rolls	*Three Yorkshire Assize Rolls for the Reigns of King John and King Henry III*

I

THE FOUNDATION

THE assize of novel disseisin was an institution of the English common law, a form of courtroom procedure by which a plaintiff might sue to recover land or other real property. It was falling out of use around the year 1500 and had become wholly obsolete by about 1650. Dead now for these three hundred years and more, it has passed into total oblivion. The individual words that make up its name, words drawn from French and never completely assimilated, have ceased to carry meaning in modern English; and even the handful of specialist scholars who can always be found to take an interest in any subject under the sun have in this case evinced no more than a limited concern for a few aspects of the old assize, chiefly its early history, leaving much the better part of its tradition to slumber undisturbed in the pages of ancient lawbooks.

Given such a state of desuetude it needs a special effort of imagination to reconstruct now the life that was once in the assize. For upwards of two hundred, indeed for nearly three hundred, years from the late twelfth to the early fifteenth century, it was an extraordinarily vital institution. In every generation of those centuries it was familiar in an everyday way to thousands and thousands of Englishmen both rich and poor, who knew it at least as well as we nowadays know trial by jury or the rituals of our public meetings, and who relied on it even more. In those days the name held no mysteries, at any rate not to men of the upper classes to whom French was likely to come as easily as English. To them 'assize of novel disseisin' was a series of perfectly plain words, as plain as the words 'proceeding on a recent ejectment', which translate them into modern English, would be to us. Even to humble contemporaries whose linguistic horizons did not extend beyond English, the institution itself apart from its name was perfectly straightforward. It meant that if a freeholder of land was ejected from his property he could require the sheriff to set up a jury of

twelve, have them go look at the land, and bring them before
the king's justices when they next came to hold court in the
county. The justices asked the jurors whether the freeholder
had been illegally put out of his holding, as he complained, and
if they said that he had then the court would restore the land
to him at once. The plaintiff could be anyone at all, from an
earl to a cottager, provided only that he held his land freely.
The defendant, who was accused of making the illegal ejectment, might be man or woman, noble or commoner, free or
serf, layman or cleric: any person alive, in fact, except the king
and his agents acting under his express command.

This institution was designed and set in operation in the
reign of King Henry II (1154–89). Along with the grand assize
and the assize of mort d'ancestor it figured then as one of the
three principal measures by which King Henry sought to
provide a more rational civil justice through substituting trial
by jury for trial by battle. Novel disseisin was the first of the
three reforms, older by several years than the others, and in the
long run it was much the most successful. The grand assize
worked a salutary reform in the proceeding called the 'action
of right', but in the century or so after the grand assize was
instituted the action of right itself fell out of use. The assize of
mort d'ancestor, which protected the right of an heir to enter
into his heritage without obstruction, was extremely popular
for about a hundred years. Towards the end of the thirteenth
century and in the fourteenth it declined. But the assize of
novel disseisin went from strength to strength. It was a simpler
proceeding than the other two and this quality, attractive
in itself, also made it both faster and more versatile. Mort
d'ancestor passed out of use, in fact, because it was discovered in the end that novel disseisin could do its work more
efficiently.

The result was that novel disseisin became the staple form of
legal proceeding on which freeholders relied for the protection
of their rights. To generations of freeholding Englishmen it was
largely synonymous with security under law. The rights that it
protected, property in lands and tenements, were the most
important in the world for medieval men, for in those days
ownership of land more than anything else determined both
men's physical well-being and their standing in society. How

well the assize functioned was the principal measure of how secure the freeholder was in all this.

The assize provided a quick means of recovery for a freeholder who had been thrown out of his property. These unpleasant but common incidents in which an occupant was ejected—'disseised', as they said—might represent simple lawlessness, where the owner was ousted by a mere thief of land, perhaps by a local magnate bullying his lesser neighbour. But far more often they developed out of genuine disputes about property rights. The 'disseisor', who made the ejectment, would have a pretty good colour of title and could argue that he had only been taking over what was his own. In many cases it might appear, indeed, that the disseisor was right about this and that the land really did belong to him, or that he had at any rate a good right to be occupying it, as a guardian for example, or as a leaseholder whose term had not yet expired. When that happened the court that heard the assize of novel disseisin had to make a painful decision: whether to leave the land to the disseisor on the grounds that he was entitled or to restore it to the plaintiff on the grounds that he had been disseised without any process of law.

No society is likely to find a simple solution to this dilemma. An important piece of social policy is involved. Shall the state (or the king, or whatever) have an exclusive right to enforce justice? Or, on the contrary, may private individuals sometimes right their own wrongs, taking back their own property on their own initiative? A society that leans heavily toward the former view is likely to find that private rights, because they can never be upheld except through the action of the government, are treated as creations of the government, gracious and presumably revocable gifts. A society that goes far in the latter direction, allowing men to right their own wrongs, invites anarchy. Neither alternative was much to the liking of medieval Englishmen.

Through the assize of novel disseisin and through other law co-ordinated with it, England gradually worked out its solution to this common human problem. Justices handling cases of novel disseisin generally left the possession of land with the man who was entitled to it, even if he had gained possession as a disseisor. In the thirteenth century there were a good many exceptions to this policy, cases where the assize would undo a disseisin simply as such and regardless of title in the disseisor. In the fourteenth century the exceptions were mostly eliminated and by Richard II's reign a man with a sound title to land was nearly always allowed to go in and put out an adverse occupant.

This permissive policy was coupled, however, with another body of law, enforceable through other procedures, which limited the methods that a man might lawfully employ to disseise an adversary. One might not kill the opponent, for instance; it would be felony to do so. The rules went much further than simply to prohibit homicide, and as time went on and the assize became more uniformly permissive, these other rules became, complementarily, stricter than ever. In the end, by Richard II's time, the right of the true owner to eject an adversary, now almost invariably admitted, was balanced by such tight prohibitions upon his methods that it was wholly impossible for him in fact to put out an opponent who resisted without falling foul of the law. The right to take one's own was nearly universal but it was reduced to a ceremonial thing.

In the earlier period, in the thirteenth century, men with just claims had a limited but, within the limits, an effective power to take the law into their own hands. There were some measures that could legitimately be employed to compel the opponent to give way, and in most cases the assize of novel disseisin would not restore the land to the opponent if his disseisor really had a better title. It was a compromise, giving some room for private force, insisting for the rest on social control. By the end of the fourteenth century this compromise had been replaced by a subtle synthesis. The right to oust an opponent, fully conceded, was a right to make a solemn demonstration against him, never a right actually to force him out of the property. After making the demonstration one had to sue at law to get the land. But the owner who sued under these circumstances was not calling on the king to judge and then enforce his title to the property. He was asking the king to come in as an auxiliary, lending his aid to remove an obstacle to the party's own enforcement of his right, the obstacle of the adverse holder who would not withdraw but who stubbornly stood in his way. The king's court would have to review the owner's title in order to judge whether it ought to afford him the aid that he asked for. But that review was, in strict logic, an incidental matter. The law had attained a fine ideological balance; it established the autonomous character of property rights but made no room at all for anarchy. This synthesis remained for ever after a classic part of the common-law heritage.

It bore a practical dividend too. The owner who sued for the removal of those who obstructed his right could use the assize of novel disseisin as the vehicle of his suit. He had been in the property—in possession, then, 'seised' of it—when he made his ceremonial demonstration of taking it over; so he had been ejected, 'disseised', when his adversary refused to make way and let him occupy it as he was entitled. The courts accepted this reasoning because the assize was an unusually efficient proceeding, so that making it available wherever possible served to speed the course of justice. There were, however, other courtroom procedures that were even more efficient for the same purposes: actions of trespass in particular, where the owner who had made his demonstration of entering the holding charged that his adversary was 'trespassing' by refusing to make way for him. In the fifteenth and sixteenth centuries these alternative procedures gradually replaced the assize in everyday use, relegating it at last to history.

Its accomplishments did not pass away. It had given freeholders a security under the king's law which they never afterwards lost and it had led in defining once and for all, in the land law as the most vital area of men's interests, the English solution for the antithesis of private autonomy and social control.

The assize was created in the reign of Henry II, but beyond that basic fact almost nothing about its origin is agreed on any more. Eighty years ago Maitland believed that he could see its beginnings pretty clearly.[1] He thought that it was founded by an ordinance, now lost, made early in 1166 or perhaps a little before, which set out the essentials of the assize as it was known for ever after: a suit of party against party, authorized by a writ which the plaintiff purchased from the king, the 'writ of novel disseisin', under which the sheriff empanelled jurors and brought them into court to pronounce whether the plaintiff

[1] P. & M. i. 145–6.

had been wrongfully disseised of his freehold. Of late years every item of this account has been called in question. It has been doubted whether there was any ordinance, written or un-written.[1] Other critics who believe in an enactment have argued that the legislation provided nothing more than a temporary investigation of illegal disseisins, proceeding *ex officio* through juries of presentment, not at the suit of private parties and not under writs of novel disseisin.[2] In any case, it is argued, the assize as it was known in later times was a gradual growth in Henry's reign, not a single invention.

But we must protest that Maitland was right, or as close to the truth as hardly matters, on every point. There was, to begin with, an ordinance: the assize of novel disseisin was founded by a legislative act. The word itself, 'assize', is ambiguous, for it bore many meanings only loosely related to one another, but it may imply a legislative origin inasmuch as one of its senses is 'ordinance, statute'; the other sense of 'proceeding, action at law' may derive from this, the action being the content, the creation, of an enactment called an assize. Many years later Henry of Bracton, writing his lawbook in the 1250s, said that the assize of novel disseisin had been 'thought out and invented through many wakeful nights'.[3] A London custumal of about 1205 says that at a certain time in the past an 'assize was estab-lished in the realm by the lord king for the holding of recog-nitions concerning disseisin'.[4] The lawbook called Glanvill, written about 1188, says of Henry II's petty assizes in general that they were created 'by virtue of a constitution of the realm called an assize' and describes the good work of novel disseisin as 'the benefit of this constitution'.[5] In 1176 the amending legislation of Northampton spoke of 'disseisins committed against the assize'.[6] In 1166 the financial records of the royal government, the pipe rolls, begin all at once to tell of pecuniary

---

[1] Jolliffe, *Angevin Kingship*, pp. 46–7.

[2] Van Caenegem, *Royal Writs*, pp. 283–94; Milsom, 'Introduction', p. xxxix, and *Historical Foundations*, p. 117. Much of this rethinking of the origins of the assize was led by Lady Doris Stenton's remarks in the *Cambridge Medieval History* v. 586–7, but she subjects the developments of her ideas to an exacting critique in her *English Justice*, pp. 36–49.

[3] fo. 164b: 'multis vigiliis excogitatam et inventam.'

[4] *Borough Customs* i. 232 = *Munimenta Gildhallae Londoniensis* i. 114.

[5] Book XIII chapters 1, 32.

[6] *Select Charters*, p. 180.

penalties laid against subjects 'for disseisin', 'for wrongful disseisin', 'for disseisin against the king's writ', and 'for disseisin
against the king's assize'.[1]

No text of the original ordinance has been preserved and we
cannot say with any precision when it was enacted. Since the
first evidence of its enforcement comes from the financial
records of 1166 Maitland supposed that it was probably made
early in 1166 when King Henry held a great court at Clarendon
and issued the important legislation known as the Assize of
Clarendon.[2] It is true that the text of the Assize of Clarendon
as we have it says nothing at all about disseisins. But that text
is of questionable authority and we may well suppose if we like
that it omits some of the legislation that was enacted at Clarendon.[3] Certainly, when the work done at Clarendon was 'recalled'
and amended ten years later, at Northampton in 1176, one of
the matters then taken up was the modification of the assize
against disseisin.[4] Even if it never formed any part of the
document which we call the Assize of Clarendon, the assize
against disseisin may still have been made at the session at
Clarendon in 1166 and promulgated as a separate text.

The ordinance is just as likely, however, to have been made
some years earlier. Evidence of its enforcement first appears in
1166, but that may be only because general eyres began to be
held in that year, enabling the king's justices for the first time
to enforce systematically an ordinance which, for all we know,
might have been issued a good while before. Indeed, one of the
entries in the pipe roll of 1166 which records an amercement
'for a disseisin against the king's assize', collectable in Rutland,
places this item with the old business and not among Rutland's
'new cases' (nova placita) for 1166.[5] But there is more positive
evidence of an earlier date. In two writs that seem to belong to
the latter part of 1162 Henry II commanded the bishop of
Norwich to restore seisin of certain properties to the monastery

---

[1] *Pipe Roll 12 Henry II*, pp. 4, 7, 10, 14, 65.

[2] This council may have been held late in 1165 rather than, as has been supposed,
in the early months of 1166: Richardson and Sayles, *Governance*, p. 443 n.

[3] Ibid., pp. 438–44; Doris Stenton, *English Justice*, pp. 39–42; but see J. C. Holt in
Bullough and Storey, edd., *The Study of Medieval Records*, pp. 85–97.

[4] *Select Charters*, pp. 180–1.

[5] *Pipe Roll 12 Henry II*, p. 65. If this really represents a penalty laid before 1166
for violation of the assize, it need not be alone, for the early pipe rolls contain many
notes of penalties whose cause is not specified.

of St. Benet's Holme 'notwithstanding my assize'.[1] And even earlier the king had directed the archbishop of Canterbury that under certain conditions he was to restore possession of a parish church to one Osbert, a parson whose lord had put him out 'since the king's departure and against his edict'. This order was given some time in the years 1156–61.[2] The 'edict' of which it speaks was evidently directed against disseisins done since the king's latest departure from England,[3] which must be his crossing to the Continent either in January 1156 or in August 1158.[4] Most likely it was issued about the end of 1155 or in the summer of 1158, in anticipation of either the one departure or the other.

None of this evidence of an earlier date can, however, yield any certainty. The 'assize' of the writs of 1162, the 'edict' of the order of 1156–61 may be other, earlier acts of legislation and not the assize that we see being enforced in 1166. The Rutland amercement, recorded in 1166, may have been new in that year even though the pipe roll did not enter it among the new cases. All we can say for certain is that King Henry made his assize against disseisin some time between the last months of 1155 and the first months of 1166.

He laid it down as a permanent new law. From the time when we first find evidence of its enforcement in the pipe roll of 1166 new cases continue to appear in the successive pipe rolls, year after year and for every year. There is, it is true, one period of exception to this: no new cases were recorded for the three years 1172, 1173, and 1174. This gap has led Professor van Caenegem to conclude that the original assize was a tem-

---

[1] 'et non remaneat pro assisa mea.' *Register of St. Benet's Holme*, nos. 36, 39. The editor dates these writs 1162–8 and 1162–6 respectively. But both are witnessed at Rouen and both warn the addressee that if he does not comply with the order then Thomas Becket, archbishop of Canterbury, will take action. The only period when Henry was on the Continent and Thomas Becket in occupation of his see of Canterbury was June 1162–January 1163. R. C. van Caenegem prints a third similar writ which may also belong as early as 1162, *Royal Writs*, pp. 423–4.

[2] After he became king, Henry first departed England in January 1156. The writ was addressed to Archbishop Theobald, who died in 1161.

[3] The words 'since the king's departure' would not have been included in the writ merely to specify an accidental circumstance. They were put in because the matter was of legal significance, and the significance was, almost certainly, that the 'edict' did not apply to disseisins committed before the king's departure. This use of the king's movements as limiting-dates was already common, and remained a feature of the assize as we know it in Henry II's later years: below, pp. 9–10, 25.

[4] Eyton, *Itinerary*, pp. 16, 40.

porary measure calling on the justices itinerant to make a single round of investigations of disseisin throughout the kingdom, a task which, in the event, they completed in 1171; only through new legislation at Northampton in 1176 was the assize renewed for the making of a second series of investigations and only through the importunities of suitors did it become, some years after 1176, a permanent institution.[1]

The three-year hiatus in the enforcement of the assize is much more easily explained, however, by the fact that eyres were in abeyance during the years 1172 to 1174 and by the fact that in 1173 and 1174 the country was greatly disturbed by the revolt of Henry the Young King. The assize had not lapsed, only justice was for the time being not readily available under it. The Northampton legislation of 1176 does not obviously include a re-enactment of the assize against disseisin, and in any case events did not await that legislation: already in 1175 the pipe roll again shows new penalties being laid for breach of the assize, and its enforcement is attested for every year after that without any more exceptions.[2]

Permanent as it was, however, the legislation was always an assize of *novel* disseisin: it would correct only disseisins that had been committed in the recent past. Some recent event was appointed to mark a cut-off point, and as the years went on this limit was moved up from time to time. We first learn about this from the amending legislation of 1176, whose purpose was not to re-enact the assize but to advance the limitation-date: 'the justices shall cause recognitions to be made of disseisins done in violation of the assize since the time when the king first returned to England after peace was made between him and the king his son.'[3] They are, it is implied, *not* to try disseisins committed before that time.

King Henry II had made peace with his son Henry the Young King in September 1174. His return to England followed in May 1175,[4] and it was that date to which actions under the assize against disseisin were now to be limited. It has been supposed that the intent was to exclude from action disseisins committed during the time of revolt and war in 1173 and 1174,

---

[1] *Royal Writs*, pp. 284–92. Cf. the criticisms of Mr. G. D. G. Hall in *English Historical Review* lxxvi. 317–19.

[2] Van Caenegem, *Royal Writs*, p. 295.

[3] *Select Charters*, p. 180.   [4] Ramsay, *Angevin Empire*, pp. 182, 186.

when all was in disorder, a time concerning which inquiries by ordinary legal process would be difficult, a time to which ordinary rules of law ought not to apply.[1] But the fighting in England had for practical purposes been ended by August 1174; formal peace was made with the Young King in September 1174 and with the King of Scots in December of the same year,[2] while the new limitation on the assize was the king's return to his realm several months later in May 1175.

When that limitation was first enacted at Northampton its term lay only eight months in the past (May 1175–January 1176). Glanvill, who provides our next information about the limitation of actions of novel disseisin, shows that when he wrote in 1188 or thereabouts the action was limited to the period since the king's last crossing from England to Normandy.[3] In those last years of his reign Henry crossed frequently to Normandy: in April 1185, again in February 1187, finally in July 1188.[4] The limitation shown by Glanvill was, therefore, very short, just like that which was imposed by the legislation at Northampton in 1176; and, again like the limit declared at Northampton, that of Glanvill's day was defined in terms of the king's movements. Some time probably about the end of 1155 or in the summer of 1158 King Henry had issued some sort of assize, possibly the very one that concerns us, to punish disseisins committed after his departure from England.[5] Evidently it was a principle observed all through his reign that actions under his new laws against disseisin should always be straitly limited, available only for disseisins committed during the past year or two. Evidently it was a habit, usual if not invariable, to define the limit in terms of the king's movements in and out of the realm. If that is so then it is highly probable that the original assize, whenever it was enacted in 1155–66, bore a similar limitation, fixed at some date in what was then the very recent past.[6]

[1] Richardson and Sayles, *Governance*, p. 198. The authors state, erroneously, that the new limit was the time when peace was made, September 1174, rather than Henry's return to his realm in the following May. The mistake is set right in the same authors' *Law and Legislation*, p. 99.

[2] Ramsay, *Angevin Empire*, pp. 180–4.   [3] Book XIII chapters 33, 35–7.

[4] Ramsay, *Angevin Empire*, pp. 226, 232, 239.   [5] Above, p. 8.

[6] The guesses hazarded by R. C. van Caenegem, H. G. Richardson, and G. O. Sayles, that the original assize, being enacted in 1166, may have applied to disseisins committed since the beginning of Henry's reign in December 1154, seem

The central concern of the assize was with disseisins of lands. It prohibited men from ejecting one another from fields and buildings, woods and meadows, and generally from lands held in demesne.[1] But it included a good deal else besides. It probably covered common of pasture. Glanvill says so in clear terms,[2] and his evidence of c. 1188 is anticipated by that of the chronicler of Meaux abbey, who tells that common of pasture was recovered against his house by a writ of novel disseisin: his story can be dated c.1176.[3] When the pipe roll for 1168 records that a man was amerced 'for having a hedge constructed over a pasture',[4] it seems probable that this was an offence against the assize, which from its beginning, then, protected common rights in pasture. Other common rights, as in estovers or turbary, may also have been included.[5]

Perhaps putting up a hedge as did the offender of 1168 was not, strictly speaking, a disseisin. It might be considered to amount rather to 'raising a nuisance', that is, working in such a way as to interfere with another landholder's enjoyment of his rights. But that made no difference, for the assize was directed from the first against nuisances as well as against disseisins. Even if it was not intended to shut them out of a part of the land, a hedge through a pasture made it difficult for the commoners to use their grazing rights in the area now divided in two by the barrier. In other circumstances a newly erected bank or hedge might block a right of way that a neighbouring landowner had always used as incidental to his holding.[6] Raising the level of one's millpond would be a nuisance if the water backed up and covered a neighbour's land.[7] Nuisance

therefore not to be well directed. Van Caenegem, *Royal Writs*, p. 286, Richardson and Sayles, *Governance*, p. 198. The term 'novel disseisin' does not appear, however, until 1181: van Caenegem, *Royal Writs*, p. 294.

[1] *Pipe Roll 14 Henry II* (1168), p. 137: 'assisa de terra quam Rogerus Martel tenuit.'   [2] Book XIII chapter 37.

[3] *Chronica de Melsa* i. 175. For the date, see the documents in *Early Yorks Charters* ii. 389–92.

[4] *Pipe Roll 14 Henry II*, p. 44: 'pro sepe quam fieri fecit super pasturam.' The pipe roll does not say that his offence was a violation of the assize, but it probably was so, for in the previous year a subject had been amerced 'pro fossato facto . . . super assisam': *Pipe Roll 13 Henry II*, p. 157.

[5] Below, p. 135 n. 1.

[6] *CRR* v. 33–4 (1207), *BNB* nos. 1196 (1236–7), 1253 (1238–9).

[7] So also if a wholly new mill-and-pond encroached on another's land: *PRS* xiv. 74 (1195–6), *Pleas 1198–1202* ii. 606 (1201), *CRR* iii. 155 (1204).

could equally well be committed by entering another's demesne land and doing there something that injured him: as if a landholder maintained a bank to mark and defend the boundary of his enclosure, and someone came and tore it down.[1]

Glanvill detailed just these cases—the building or abating of banks and hedges and the raising of millponds 'to the nuisance' —as matters that were remediable by the assize, and he implied that there were others.[2] Besides the case already mentioned of the hedge across the pasture in 1168, we read in the early pipe rolls of a penalty against one Peverel who in 1166 had 'broken a pond against the king's assize',[3] of Ralph fitz Adam who in 1167 built a bank on another's land 'against the assize',[4] of men who in 1168 had 'broken a boundary against the king's assize',[5] and of others who 'wrongfully constructed a bank' and 'wrongfully constructed a bank in the abbot of Chertsey's land'.[6] Whatever other nuisances may also have been covered, it is clear that all those resulting from ponds, banks, and hedges, built and destroyed, were included from the beginning.[7]

The assize extended its protection to free tenements only; it restrained disseisins of free tenements and of common of pasture appurtenant to them; it corrected nuisances against free tenements. It did not apply to serfs and their holdings, for in 1170 the abbot of Peterborough's men of Quadring (Lincolnshire) were amerced 'because they invoked the assize as freemen whereas they were serfs'.[8] By the time Glanvill wrote, about 1188, land held as security for the repayment of a debt, land held 'in gage' as they said, was not covered;[9] and from just a

---

[1] CRR ii. 48 (1201), iii. 155 (1204), BNB nos. 806 (1233), 1953 (1221), Eyres of Beds iii. 6 (1227), J.I. 1/1217 m. 3 (1271), Bracton fos. 114b, 235.

[2] Book XIII chapters 34–6.

[3] Pipe Roll 12 Henry II, p. 128, and 13 Henry II, p. 156. The editor of the earlier pipe roll has identified Peverel as a hundred, but there is no hundred or other community by that name. In the latter pipe roll Peverel paid the debt in full and is marked 'quietus', with the masculine-singular form of the adjective. In Regesta Stephani nos. 627, 630, 631, Peverel appears again as the name of an individual. For later examples of breaking of ponds as nuisance, see CRR iii. 132, 214–15 (1204), v. 70–1 (1207), and Bracton fo. 232b.   [4] Pipe Roll 13 Henry II, p. 157.

[5] Pipe Roll 14 Henry II, p. 107.   [6] Ibid., pp. 43, 219.

[7] For the matters actionable as nuisance under the assize in the thirteenth century, see below, p. 63.

[8] Pipe Roll 16 Henry II, p. 149.

[9] Book X chapter 11. This doctrine is confirmed by the earliest plea rolls, PRS xiv. 67 (1194–5).

few years later the plea rolls, beginning in 1194, show that
termors, who held land for fixed periods whether as gage for
debts or otherwise, and feudal guardians were also excluded.[1]
The plaintiff must be one who held at least for his own full
lifetime, or who held hereditarily; none other had a 'free tenement'. This rule may have been original with the assize, but we
cannot tell, for there is no substantial evidence from before
Glanvill.[2]

   As for the enforcement of its prohibition against disseisin, the
assize in its original form probably directed some use of juries
of presentment. The pipe roll of 1168 records a collective
amercement 'for concealing a disseisin' against Lifton hundred
in Devon and several similar mulcts 'for concealing a disseisin
which they later presented' against the Wiltshire manors of
Gore, Orcheston, Winterbourne, Berwick, and Tilshead. These
juries of presentment are puzzling, and the mystery only
deepens when we read of an individual of Wiltshire, Robert
fitz Ralph, who was amerced for failing to present a disseisin.[3]
The assize of novel disseisin as we know it from later times was
always an action brought at the suit of the party and never
employed the procedure by presentment; nor does there appear
any evidence that juries of presentment were ever used under
the assize after 1168. Still, the entries for 1168 are presumably
to be connected with the assize, though none of them mentions
it directly.

   From the evidence of their use at this early date Professor
van Caenegem has argued that the original assize was a
'criminalistic' measure relying entirely on presentment for its
execution, and that only later did individual victims of disseisin, seeing its usefulness, seek and gain the king's permission

---

[1] The evidence is chiefly negative: no cases ever appear in which tenants of
these estates recover by the assize. But from an early date we can see them using
other remedies in the king's court, evidently because they may not have the assize:
the gageholder, *Rotuli Curiae Regis* i. 82 (1194–5); the termor, *PRS* xiv. 48 (1194),
CRR ii. 118 (1202); the feudal guardian, *BNB* no. 1709 (1226).

[2] An entry of 1175, *Pipe Roll 21 Henry II*, p. 56, may imply that lands held in gage
were not protected by the assize at that date, for in that record a subject made a
special payment of 40s. 'ut placitet saisitus de vadio suo'.

[3] *Pipe Roll 14 Henry II*, pp. 133, 164 f., and cf. *Pipe Roll 16 Henry II*, p. 138 (1170),
amercement of Rushmonden hundred, Sussex, 'pro dissaisina concelata'. This
penalty was first laid in 1168, *Pipe Roll 14 Henry II*, p. 196, and *15 Henry II*, p. 58
but it is not until 1170 that the records specify the reason for it.

to bring private actions under its terms.[1] But the evidence for
private prosecutions does not come later than that of presentments. The same pipe roll of 1168 which first tells of penalties
against communities, and against an individual, for failure to
present disseisins also records that 'Richard fitz William Des-
penser owes five marks for having the assize of the land that
Roger Martel held'.[2] In 1170 Alan Malet was amerced 'for
failure of a claim touching the assize',[3] William Fulkelin agreed
to pay one mark 'to have the assize for one carucate of land in
Eynsworth',[4] and, as we have already noticed in another connection, the abbot of Peterborough's men of Quadring owed
one mark 'because they invoked the assize as freemen whereas
they were serfs'.[5] There are several entries in the pipe roll for
1175 that tell the same story.[6] The original assize somehow
combined procedure by presentment with opportunity for
private prosecution. Men who had been disseised could complain, and prosecute, and see the assize enforced at their suit
against their disseisors. It was this procedure, 'civil' as Glanvill
calls it, which alone survived to come into the full light of history as the assize of novel disseisin.

The full light of history begins with Glanvill about 1188.[7]
He tells that the procedure for one who wanted to sue an assize
of novel disseisin was to go to the king's chancery and obtain a
writ in the following form:

> The king to the sheriff, greeting. N. has complained to me that
> R. has wrongfully and without a judgment disseised him of his free
> tenement in such-and-such a township since my last crossing to
> Normandy. Therefore I command you that, if N. will give you
> security for prosecuting his claim, you see to it that the chattels that
> were seized in that tenement are restored to it and that the tenement
> and the chattels remain in peace until the Sunday after Easter. In
> the meantime you are to see to it that the tenement is viewed by
> twelve free and lawful men of the neighbourhood, whose names are
> to be endorsed on this writ. Summon them by good summoners to

---

[1] Van Caenegem, *Royal Writs*, pp. 284–8.

[2] *Pipe Roll 14 Henry II*, p. 137.   [3] *Pipe Roll 16 Henry II*, p. 148.

[4] Ibid., p. 160.   [5] Above, p. 12.

[6] *Pipe Roll 21 Henry II*, p. 31: 'pro habenda assisa'; p. 175: 'pro habenda terra
sua in pace de qua Hugo Clericus voluit habere assisam'; and several other new
debts 'for a recognition', pp. 78, 98 (*bis*), 124, which should be interpreted in the
light of Alan la Zuche's fine in *Pipe Roll 23 Henry II*, p. 191.

[7] Book XIII chapters 32–9.

be before me [*or my justices*] at that time, ready to make the recognition. Attach the aforesaid R., or his bailiff if he cannot be found, by the security of gage and reliable pledges to be there then to hear the recognition. Have there the summoners and this writ and the names of the pledges. Witness [etc.].

The same form was used, *mutatis mutandis*, when the complaint was about common of pasture or a nuisance.

The directions contained in the writ were all meant to be followed literally. On the appointed day there should, consequently, appear in the king's court the plaintiff, the alleged disseisor or his bailiff, and a group of twelve neighbours who had inspected the tenements and were prepared to be sworn as a jury to decide by their verdict whether the defendant had illegally disseised the plaintiff. If the verdict spoke for the plaintiff, the defendant, convicted of disseisin, was amerced[1] and the plaintiff got his land back by judgment[2] together with the chattels that were on the estate when he was disseised and the profits that had accrued while the defendant held the land.

This procedure, or something much like it, seems to have been laid down from the beginning in the original enactment.[3] This has been doubted of late, partly because of the unwarranted belief that the assize in its original form provided only for

[1] Glanvill, Book XIII chapter 38: 'semper victus, sive fuerit appellans sive appellatus, in misericordia domini regis remanet propter violentam dissaisinam ... Pena autem ... est misericordia ... tantum.' The pipe rolls from 1166 record many amercements for violation of the assize: see the references collected by van Caenegem, *Royal Writs*, pp. 294–5.

[2] Glanvill does not say this directly, but that is probably because it seemed to him to go without saying. From the beginning private parties had prosecuted actions under the assize, as we have seen, and they would hardly have done so except in the hope of recovering their land. Van Caenegem, *Royal Writs*, p. 462, prints a writ of 1164–6 in which the king commands one Osbert of Brai to put the monks of Lire in seisin of a certain church, 'sicut recognitum fuit apud Walengeford sacramento iuratorum coram iusticia mea et adiudicatum eis'. This may be a restoration of land by judgment under the assize, as Professor van Caenegem takes it, pp. 286–7, but it is not certain that the assize of novel disseisin was the legal basis of these proceedings.

[3] It is not to be supposed that any public announcement or published text set forth the details of the assize, for Henry II's legislation seems always to have been promulgated in the briefest possible form: Richardson and Sayles, *Law and Legislation*, p. 104. But the very brevity of the published texts shows that more detailed plans for carrying the new laws into execution must have been concerted among the king and his officers when new laws were made. Such plans may fairly be regarded as parts of the legislation itself, and it is in such plans that the particulars of the assize of novel disseisin would probably have been spelt out.

proceedings on presentment and not for private suits, but also because Glanvill postpones his discussion of novel disseisin to the very end of his Book XIII after he has dealt with all the other petty assizes, a fact which may be, as Mr. Hall suggests, 'surprising if we think of 1166 as the date of its origin but less so if we accept the view that regular civil litigation by means of this writ was a very recent development when the treatise was written'.[1] But really it need not surprise, for Glanvill's arrangement of his material has nothing to do with age. He discusses mort d'ancestor, which was created in 1176, first of all among the petty assizes, and later he deals with *Utrum*, which dates from 1164. What controlled his arrangement was one of those procedural elements inconsequential to modern eyes but capable of looming very large in the Middle Ages: the number and kinds of essoins, or excuses for non-attendance, that the court would allow the defendant in each type of lawsuit before proceeding against him by default. Glanvill's whole treatise was devoted primarily to the law of the king's court. All the actions in the king's court described in his first twelve books admitted three essoins, as did also the most important of the others, actions in feudal or county courts, that he spoke of there. Then when he came in Book XIII to write about the petty assizes he wrote first of mort d'ancestor and of five others, all of which allowed two essoins. Novel disseisin followed, the last of the petty assizes in order of discussion because here the defendant could have no essoin at all; and then in Book XIV the author continued and concluded his treatise with criminal pleas, which similarly admitted no essoins when they were prosecuted at the king's suit.

So there is no reason at all for supposing that the procedure in novel disseisin as Glanvill describes it was devised late rather than early. There is, on the contrary, some positive reason for believing that it was original. Its central feature was a trial by jury, that is, in the terminology of the time, a recognition. Now from as early as 1176 we have direct word of some sort of recognitions being held under the assize, from the amending legislation which we have quoted before:

the justices shall cause recognitions to be made of disseisins done

[1] Note to Glanvill, Book XIII chapter 32.

in violation of the assize since the time when the king first returned to England after peace was made between him and the king his son.[1]

In the immediately preceding section the legislation of Northampton had founded the assize of mort d'ancestor, to guarantee to heirs immediate possession of their ancestors' holdings, in these terms:

If the chief lord of a fee denies to the heirs of a deceased tenant, when they demand it, the seisin which the decedent had, the justices of the lord king shall cause . . . recognitions to be made by twelve lawful men, what seisin the decedent . . . had on the day when he was alive and dead, and according as it shall be recognized the justices shall restore seisin to his heirs.

The key words repeat like a refrain in these two successive paragraphs: 'the justices of the lord king shall cause recognitions to be made what seisin the decedent had . . .', and then 'the justices shall cause recognitions to be made of disseisins. . . .' It would be extraordinary if the recognitions referred to in the one section and in the other were not of the same type. But those of the earlier paragraph, the original assizes of mort d'ancestor, must be recognitions at the suit of private parties, for they are to be held 'if the chief lord . . . denies seisin . . . to the heirs'. So the 'recognitions of disseisins' of the second paragraph must be of the same sort.[2] The legislation of 1176 is describing the principal characteristic of the assize of novel disseisin as Glanvill explained it about a dozen years later.

Apart from this specific evidence there is a more general consideration. The details of procedure under the assize as they appear from Glanvill and from the earliest plea rolls of the years around 1200 were all remarkably well adapted for a single

---

[1] Above, p. 9.

[2] Professor van Caenegem agrees, *Royal Writs*, pp. 319-20, that in 1176 the assize against disseisin must have used the same procedure as was then instituted in the new assize of mort d'ancestor. But because he believes that at that time the assize against disseisin was still a 'criminalistic' measure enforced by *ex officio* inquiries through juries of presentment, he infers that the procedure in the assize of mort d'ancestor in the first years of its being was in the same form, and that it was only some while later that mort d'ancestor, like novel disseisin, became a civil action at the suit of the party. But there is not a single piece of evidence to show that justices ever received any presentments under the assize of mort d'ancestor. When we get our first information about the enforcement of this new assize, from 1179, it takes the form of payments to the king by suitors who desire to prosecute under its terms: Doris Stenton, *English Justice*, pp. 44-5.

purpose, namely, to make this action work rapidly. They might
have been hit upon item by item through the years, from
experiment to experiment in the chancery and by justices who
consistently favoured dispatch in the handling of lawsuits. But
they do not look like that. They look like a deliberately co-
ordinated design, thought out as a whole. But if so, then they
must have been legislated into effect all at once. The creative
enactment was presumably the one which we know occurred
some time in the years 1155–66.

I know that many thoughtful people discountenance similar
arguments that the design of Nature, or the structure of living
substances, are proof of a creator God. But it should need less
to convince them of the probability of a legislating king. Let us
look at the evidence of a purposive design intended to expedite
litigation.[1]

The writ of novel disseisin called for the jurors to inspect the
land beforehand and to appear in court already prepared to
render their verdict. The intent was, clearly, to have the justices
take the verdict and give judgment on the first day the case
came up. The defendant, who would most wish to create delay
if he could, was by no means to be allowed to do so. To bring
him to court, he was attached rather than summoned: attachment was a more compelling measure. If the sheriff could not
find him to attach him it was enough to attach his bailiff. If the
bailiff could not be found either the assize would proceed
nevertheless, hastened if anything rather than hindered by
their absence.[2] So also if one of them was attached but chose
contumaciously to stay away; the assize proceeded at once by
default. Neither could the defendant essoin himself even once,
for any cause.[3] If he came, he could not defer proceedings by
showing that he was under age, or that the plaintiff was under
age, for in bringing or defending this action the law was all the
same for minors and for adults. If the defendant had handed on
to a third party the land which he had taken from the plaintiff

---

[1] The details which follow are taken from Glanvill, Book XIII chapters 32–9,
except as other evidence is cited in the notes.

[2] Below, p. 67.

[3] Glanvill, Book XIII chapter 38: 'in hac autem recognitione nullum admittitur
essonium.' *Rotuli Curiae Regis* i. 411 (1199), *Eyres of Lincs and Worcs* nos. 365 (1219),
1532 (1221), *Eyre of Yorks 1218–19* nos. 315, 1133, *Eyres of Glos, Warw, Staffs* no.
20 (1221).

by disseisin, it mattered not: the assize lay against the disseisor as such, not against the holder of the property.[1] If the defendant had retained the land, he could not hold up the case by vouching to warranty anyone who was absent and who would have to be summoned for a later day. He could vouch an absent warrantor only if he first confessed the disseisin. In that case the action between the plaintiff and defendant would be settled at once on the basis of the confession without any verdict being rendered. The plaintiff won his suit, and any further proceedings on later court days would be entirely between the defendant and the man whom he had vouched.

If the defendant or his bailiff came, they would of course be given an opportunity to speak in defence. But we must think here only of arguments and pleadings that would take perhaps thirty minutes or an hour. In general the defence was not allowed to enter any plea that would call for an adjournment. The defendant could say that he was the plaintiff's lord and that he had disseised the man under a valid judgment of his feudal court, but he must straightway produce the suitors of his court to settle the matter at once by their witness.[2] He could plead that the plaintiff was a villein, but he must bring with him as proof relatives of the plaintiff's who acknowledged their villein status.[3] He could offer other pleas and arguments and

[1] This rule appears from *Pleas 1198–1202* ii. 430 (1201), *CRR* iii. 305, iv. 41 (1205), iv. 230 (1206), v. 65 (1207), and from the fact that in all the hundreds of cases in the earliest surviving plea rolls there is not a single example of a plaintiff who failed because the original disseisor, still living and charged as defendant, was no longer in occupation of the holdings. Even in the earliest records, however, it seems to have been common practice to join the current tenant who had come in after the disseisin as a co-defendant with the original disseisor: *PRS* xiv. 132 (1194–5), *CRR* i. 29 (1196), *Rotuli Curiae Regis* i. 369–70 (1199), *CRR* ii. 146, 149 (1203), iv. 201 (1206). Early in the thirteenth century the rule was changed, so that plaintiffs were required to charge as defendants both the disseisor and the current tenant, where these were different persons (below, p. 57); but the old rule is still applied in *Eyres of Glos, Warw, Staffs* nos. 1007, 1010, 1463 (1221–2), and *CRR* xiii. 404 (1228).

[2] *PRS* xiv. 40 (1194), *Rotuli Curiae Regis* i. 313–14 (1199), *Northants Pleas* no. 786 (1203), *Pleas 1198–1212* iii. 932 (1204). The same rule is probably reflected in *CRR* iii. 62 (1203), 161–2 (1204), *Eyres of Lincs and Worcs* no. 946 (1221). In *Northants Pleas* no. 809 (1203), an adjournment was allowed, but only for about twenty-four hours.

[3] *CRR* iii. 140 (1204), *Pleas 1198–1212* iv. 4072, 4102 (1209), *Eyres of Glos, Warw, Staffs* no. 540 (1221); Bracton fos. 199, 216, 290. In *BNB* no. 1812 (1227) the defendant was allowed an adjournment to bring the relatives, but he had to give pledges that he would produce them on the day that was assigned him.

submit them to the verdict of the jurors already assembled.[1] But though they perforce made some exceptions, the justices did everything they could to keep out pleas that would have to await another session of the court before they could be tried.[2]

Now all of these rules were unusual, and many of them were unique in novel disseisin. This was the only action where the defendant's bailiff could be called in his stead, the only party action where the defendant was allowed no essoins, the only action for lands where the current tenant need not be named as a defendant, the only one where no vouchers to warranty were permitted to delay judgment. Rules intended to expedite the case were woven into every stage, continually shaping the proceedings. On the whole it is probable that we have here a conscious design, the fruit of those 'many wakeful nights' through which Henry of Bracton said the assize was thought out. The midnight oil was probably burned at the very beginning, when Henry II's assize against disseisin was in the making, some time in the years about 1160.

The designers of the assize, though they deserve high praise for their work, did not invent any wholly new concepts or procedures. Both the general European tradition of legal scholarship and the practice of law and administration in England provided them with abundant materials. The canon law of the church had long recognized the principle that a bishop should not be deprived of the administration of his see unless a judgment had first been given against him in court. This rule was as well known in England as in other parts of the western

---

[1] Recovery by judgment of another court might sometimes be proved by the jurors of the assize if the suitors of the court were not at hand: *PRS* xiv. 69 (1195–6), *Rotuli Curiae Regis* ii. 194 (1200), J.I. 1/1182 m. 10 (1254). So could a plea of villeinage, if the relatives were not in court, *Rotuli Curiae Regis* i. 84 (1194), *CRR* iii. 143 (1204), *Pleas 1198–1212* iv. 4072, 4102 (1209), *BNB* no. 281 (1228), K.B. 26/123 m. 5 (1242), K.B. 27/3 m. 4 (1273), and cf. Bracton fos. 193, 199–199b; and other matters in defence, *Rotuli Curiae Regis* i. 422 (1199). But there was some doubt whether the jury's verdict could be allowed to establish a judgment in a feudal or county court, *CRR* iii. 98 (1204), *Eyres of Lincs and Worcs* no. 946 (1221), *BNB* no. 1767 (1227), Bracton fos. 205b, 218. No record ever shows judgments or final concords in the king's court being proven by verdict, and from later evidence it appears expressly that this was not allowed: Bracton fo. 218, Y.B. Pasch. 10 Ed. II no. 13, Trin. 10 Ed. II no. 6 (1317), Hil. 11 Ed. II no. 35 (1318), Mich. 11 Ed. III p. 261 (1337).

[2] See Note A, p. 214.

Christian community[1] and it had a tendency to slip over into secular law. In the *Leges Henrici Primi*, composed in England about 1114–18, we read, 'No one should plead at law while disseised, unless the case concerns the disseisin itself'.[2] In 1139 a papal legate invoked the rule on behalf of bishops whom King Stephen had put out of their sees: 'The king should restore the bishops to their own, as is required even where legal proceedings have been entered into, for otherwise according to the Law of Nations they need not plead at law while disseised.'[3] In 1199 it was cited and applied in a case in the king's court.[4] In the latter part of the twelfth century it could set men to thinking new thoughts. Traditionally stated as a rule only about bishops, and in their case requiring only that the deprived bishop must be restored before any legal proceedings could be taken against him, it was developed by the ecclesiastical lawyers of the late twelfth century to yield the *actio spolii*, a very close canonist equivalent of the assize of novel disseisin, by which any holder of a benefice in the church could sue for recovery on the simple ground that he had been 'despoiled'.[5] At the same time and in much the same ways, it must have played on the thoughts of the makers of the assize.

It is, however, a long way from the rule that a bishop ejected from his see must be put back before answering charges, to either the *actio spolii* or the assize of novel disseisin. The influence of Roman law probably aided in the development of

---

[1] It was incorporated in canons of the Pseudo-Isidorean collection, and received thence into Gratian's *Decretum*. Pope Alexander II invoked it in a letter to William the Conqueror: 'in pristinum locum debere restitui [episcopum] iudicavimus, deinde causam eius . . . retractandam et definiendam' (Mansi xix. 950). So also, in 1117, Pope Paschal II to King Henry I: 'electus . . . ad suam ecclesiam omnimodis revocetur; si quod autem quaestionis . . . nascitur, praesentibus utrisque partibus in nostra praesentia pertractetur' (Mansi xx. 1012). Other evidences are cited by van Caenegem, *Royal Writs*, p. 281 n. 2. For the subject as a whole, see Ruffini, *L'actio spolii*, pp. 143 ff.

[2] 'Nemo dissaisitus placitet, nisi in ipsa dissaisiacione agatur.' Liebermann, *Gesetze* i. 574, and cf. other statements in the same work, i. 548, 563, 574, 582.

[3] William of Malmesbury, *Historia Novella* ii. 553.

[4] *Rotuli Curiae Regis* i. 421. Other evidences of its application in secular courts in England are collected by van Caenegem, *Royal Writs*, p. 282 n. 1, and Joüon des Longrais, 'La portée politique', pp. 549–51.

[5] Ruffini, *L'actio spolii*, pp. 288–95. Before Gratian the old canonical rule had occasionally been applied to others than bishops, ibid., p. 235. The name *actio spolii* is modern, not medieval, ibid., p. 393. We may not take it, with Maitland (P. & M. ii. 48), that the *actio spolii* served as a model for novel disseisin, for it cannot have been much earlier than the assize and may have been later.

both of the new proceedings, for Justinian's *Corpus Juris Civilis* describes a group of legal processes, the so-called interdicts, which were admirably calculated to serve as model and inspiration. In particular, the interdict called *unde vi* seems to have guided the development of the assize.[1]

Learned men in England in the mid twelfth century certainly knew about *unde vi*,[2] and the assize and the interdict agree on so many points both in general and in detail that the resemblances are not likely to be coincidental. The interdict, like the assize, taught that it was against the law for the possessor of property to be put out by force. Like the assize, it applied to land and to property, such as buildings, that was fixed to land, but not to moveable goods. The interdict and the assize both proscribed all force and not only violence, force of arms, or dire threats: it was a violation of the interdict if the possessor was put out in almost any way without process of law and against his will, and this was exactly the concept, in England, of illegal disseisin.[3] To use the interdict the Roman must have been in actual possession, just like the Englishman who wanted to use the assize; it was not enough if a right accrued to him and he came to take possession and found himself shut out by an adversary, *deicitur enim qui amittit possessionem, non qui non accipitur*.[4] A slave or a *colonus*, even though he actually occupied the land on which he had been placed by his superior, could not recover by *unde vi* if he was ejected; the assize, similarly, was not for the villein. But a superior could use the interdict if a third party ejected his slave or *colonus*, the lord could use the assize if a stranger disseised his villein. And in the assize as in the interdict, if the defendant lost the case and had to give up the land the right was reserved him, as we shall see, to reopen the discussion by bringing a counter-suit in which he might win it back.[5] But if all this seems to strain the bounds of coin-

---

[1] For the influence of the Roman interdicts in the canonical development in the twelfth century, see Ruffini, op. cit., pp. 297–303. The interdict *unde vi* is set forth in Institutes iv. 15. 6, Digest xliii. 16, and Code viii. 4.

[2] For their knowledge of Roman and canon law in general, see van Caenegem, *Royal Writs*, pp. 365–70, and Richardson and Sayles, *Law and Legislation*, ch. IV. Vacarius's *Liber Pauperum*, written in England about 1150, includes in Book VIII title 12 a generous selection of material about *unde vi*.

[3] Below, pp. 145–7.   [4] Digest xliii. 16. 1. 26.

[5] Below, pp. 39–40.

cidence, two other points of resemblance surely break them. The interdict and the assize, each concerned as they were with lands and not with moveable goods, each provided nevertheless that when the complainant was successful in his action and got back possession of his land by judgment he should recover along with it the moveable property that had been on the estate when he was ejected and the income that the land had produced while he was kept out.[1] And they both went by the curious rule that one who was dispossessed by force in Rome, disseised in England, could recover his possession by suing the man who originally ejected him, as sole defendant, even if that person had subsequently given up or lost possession to a third party.[2]

If the influence of the Roman law thus seems to be clear, still it is influence of which we have to speak, not imitation, for there are differences as well as resemblances between *unde vi* and novel disseisin. It may not be a significant difference that the Roman interdict was available to the heirs of the man who had been ejected by force whereas novel disseisin was always restricted to the two original parties, the ejected tenant and his disseisor. An English heir was not the same thing as a Roman heir, who had, in fact, no very close equivalent in English law, and so it was wholly impossible for the assize to copy the interdict in this respect.[3] But there are undoubted differences. The interdict imposed no limitation on the time within which action might be brought. If the man who had been ejected waited for more than a year of *dies utiles* this would modify his right to recover moveable property and income but it would not bar his suit. In contrast, the assize of novel disseisin was always limited by some fixed event of the recent past, chosen anew from time to time to keep the limitation from growing too long with the passing years. The assize protected

[1] There was independent and purely English precedent for the restoration of chattels, for which see below, p. 26, but not for the recovery of profits.

[2] As to this point in the law of the assize, see above, pp. 18–19. As to the interdict, see Digest xliii. 16. 7, 'Cum a te vi deiectus sim, si Titius eandem rem possidere coeperit, non possum cum alio quam tecum interdicto [unde vi] experiri', a passage included by Vacarius in the *Liber Pauperum*, viii. 12. Cf. Digest xliii. 16. 12, which implies the same doctrine.

[3] The peculiar qualities of the *heres* in Roman law appear readily from Vacarius's *Liber Pauperum* vi. 15–23. Glanvill, vi. 1 and vii. 1, fully recognized the difference between a *dos* in Roman law and a *dos* in English law.

incorporeal properties, rights of common of pasture to begin with and later others such as rents,[1] and protected against nuisances, while the interdict always confined itself to land and other tangible fixed property.[2] There was no close analogy in Roman law to the recognition of twelve lawful men by which suits were determined in novel disseisin. Most significant of all, the terminology of novel disseisin owes nothing to those passages of Justinian's *Corpus* that deal with the interdict. 'N. has complained to me', 'wrongfully and without a judgment disseised him', 'free tenement', 'chattels' to be restored to the holding: none of these is an expression known to Roman law.[3] The designers of the assize used Roman law as a source of suggestions but not as a model to be copied.

They had other materials to go on as well. In twelfth-century England formal judicial proceedings in suits for lands and tenements followed the ponderous, dilatory, and often arbitrary pattern of the 'action of right'. There was no inspiration here, except by way of repulsion, for the designers of the assize. But the country was also long since familiar with other, informal procedures, more administrative than judicial, for sorting out doubts and disputes about men's holdings. A man who was aggrieved would approach his lord, or the king, or the sheriff, and tell him a definite story of wrong that he had suffered, perhaps at the hands of a stranger or perhaps from the superior himself to whom the appeal was made. His father had died, he might say, and someone else wrongfully took over the heritage; or, he was being denied the benefit of an agreement that he had made with his lord about how he should hold his tenement; or, he or his ancestor had been wrongfully put out of the property; and so forth. The superior might know that the complaint was justified, or affect to know this, and take direct executive measures to set it right. But often he did not know and had to investigate before he acted. In public, in one of his courts, he would inquire of witnesses, if witnesses there were

---

[1] Below, pp. 50–2.

[2] But Ruffini, *L'actio spolii*, pp. 260 ff., comments on a tendency among the medieval glossators of the Roman law to extend the interdicts to incorporeal properties.

[3] The *fructus*—income—which Glanvill says shall be restored to the successful plaintiff seem to recall the *fructuum ratio* of the interdict. Glanvill, xiii. 38; Digest xliii. 16. 1. 40–1.

whose testimony bore on the matter. There might be a show of documents, and argument about them. Commonest of all, and, in England, at least as old as the reign of William the Conqueror, was the practice of empanelling a group of peers and neighbours as a jury to tell the investigator what he needed to know; their verdicts possessed by the custom of the country a degree of provisional authority. As the findings of his inquiry led him to see the justice of the matter, the superior would either give or deny relief to the complainant.[1]

The writs that often issued from the royal administrative apparatus when this sort of proceeding was carried on upon an appeal to the king reveal too that the complaints of wrong were likely to specify the time of the alleged offence, and that when relief was afforded it was likely to take the form of a restoration of the complainant to his holdings 'as of' a certain time in the past: 'as he held on the day when he parted from the king at Windsor',[2] 'as he held before the bishop of Salisbury was captured at Oxford',[3] 'as he held on the day when William I was alive and dead'.[4] Sometimes the point that was specified was the day when the king last crossed the Channel from England: 'the day I crossed the sea',[5] 'the day the king crossed the sea',[6] 'the day King Henry last crossed the sea to go to Normandy'.[7]

---

[1] This informal procedure is best known from the writs that were often issued upon complaints laid before the king, documents brilliantly studied by Professor van Caenegem, *Royal Writs*, pp. 51–194, 261–335, with the extremely valuable collection of writs, pp. 439–66. The *Leges Henrici Primi* apparently refers to the procedure upon complaint when it speaks of 'a case [that] concerns disseisin itself' (quoted above, p. 21), and proceedings specifically in a feudal court are contemplated in the contemporary *Leis Willelme*: 'Si hom volt derehdner cuvenant de terre vers sun seinur, par ses pers de la tenure meimes, qu'il apelerad a testimonie, lui estuverad derehdner' (c. 23; Liebermann, *Gesetze*, i. 510). There is a report of lengthy proceedings in the feudal court of Archbishop Theobald of Canterbury in the late 1150s, cited below, pp. 40–1, and a document of *c.* 1150 speaks of a 'recognition' concerning rights in land held in a lord's manor court, F. M. Stenton, *First Century of English Feudalism*, pp. 42–3. The procedure survived in the thirteenth century and after in petitions of right to the king, inquisitions *post mortem* held both by the king and by feudal lords (e.g. *Sel. Cases in K.B.* iii. 15 (1287), K.B. 27/121 m. 37 (1289)), and informal requests to the sheriff that he lend his aid in restoring a petitioner who had suffered disseisin (below, p. 118).

[2] Van Caenegem, *Royal Writs*, no. 29 (1091–5), pp. 426–7.
[3] Ibid., no. 61 (1149–54), p. 442.
[4] Ibid., no. 64 (1087–94), pp. 444–5. Cf. *Regesta Stephani* no. 316.
[5] Van Caenegem, op. cit., no. 52 (1077), p. 439.
[6] Ibid., no. 59 (1116–18), pp. 441–2.
[7] Ibid., no. 83 (early Stephen), p. 454.

Sometimes the beneficiary was to be restored to all the holdings of which he had been deprived since a certain day in the past: 'since I returned to the bishop . . . his land',[1] 'since I fell ill',[2] 'since the quarrel broke out between us',[3] 'since the death of Henry [I]'.[4]

This English tradition contained all the principal elements of the assize of novel disseisin: the complaint of a wrong, the recognition by a jury, the limitation of relief to a certain fixed time in the past. When the king gave relief he sometimes specified that the complainant should get back along with his land all his goods that had been on the land,[5] just as novel disseisin later gave restoration of chattels. What puts the influence of the tradition beyond any doubt is that it provided two particular forms of words that found a place in the writ of novel disseisin. From the latter years of Henry I's reign writs issued in favour of men who complained to the king might use the phrase 'wrongfully and without a judgment disseised him',[6] while the opening phrase, 'N. has complained to me', appears in the first years of Henry II.[7]

The inventors of the assize were guided by all these materials, canon law and Roman law and English practice.[8] They used them with a free hand. Their assize gave a legal proceeding which was inspired only in the most general way by canonical principles, which unlike the Roman interdict was determined by the verdict of a jury, which unlike the old English proceedings on complaints was limited to cases of disseisin, standard-

---

[1] Van Caenegem, op. cit., no. 29 (1091–5), pp. 426–7.

[2] Ibid., no. 68 (1093–8), p. 447. [3] Ibid., no. 84 (1139), pp. 454–5.

[4] Ibid., no. 91 (1156, 1158), p. 459. Cf. p. 213 n. 1, and *Regesta Stephani* nos. 187, 885.

[5] Van Caenegem, op. cit., nos. 37, 66, 68, 74, 75, 76, 79, 86, 95; *Regesta Stephani* nos. 122, 135, 529. These writs range in date from 1093–7 to 1154–64.

[6] Van Caenegem, op. cit., pp. 276–7, 300, and nos. 80, 17, 44a, 61, 85, 86, 87, 89, 90, 91, 92, 94, 96, 98; *Regesta Stephani* no. 886. These documents range in date from *c.* 1130 to 1166. A little earlier the *Leges Henrici Primi* used the phrase in speaking of homicide: 'qui iniuste vel sine iudicio fuerint occisi'. Liebermann, *Gesetze* i. 591.

[7] Van Caenegem, op. cit., p. 301 n. 3.

[8] It is also possible that they may have been influenced by the Londoners' procedure later known as the 'assize of fresh force', which closely resembled the assize of novel disseisin and, according to the London custom-book of *c.* 1205, antedated the king's assize: above, p. 6 n. 4. But the book of customs is likely to have exaggerated the antiquity of the city's institutions, and in any case it suggests that the makers of the king's assize did not know of the London practice.

ized, and available only in the king's court. If our legislators were thus capable of drawing on tradition without being controlled by it, it must be because they approached tradition with their own problems formulated and their own purposes in mind. What were the problems they hoped to solve and the purposes they hoped to serve?

They wished in the first place to provide for the better keeping of the peace. As a king who came to the throne after years of civil war, Henry II was acutely conscious of his role as a peacemaker. As a ruler who had to be absent from his realm for long periods, tending to his Continental interests, he knew the constant danger that disorder might break out during his sojourns overseas. Personal animosities or the desire to rob and plunder could bring gross breaches of the peace; but in a country almost all of whose capital wealth lay in its land, far and away the most serious disputes, those that would most tempt men, and tempt the most powerful men, to violence, were inevitably disputes about lands. So in order to help keep the peace Henry II legislated against disseisin. If actions under the original assize were limited, as we have some reason to suspect, to the period after the king's latest departure from the realm, whenever that might be, then the assize bespoke its concern for the preservation of the peace by making sure that actions of novel disseisin would always be available for those times when the king was out of easy reach and the peace was especially fragile. The amercement of the convicted disseisor was sometimes very heavy,[1] and the terms in which Glanvill tells of these penalties testify to a desire to punish breach of the peace: 'The defeated party, whether he be the appellor or the appellee, is always in the king's mercy on account of disseisin, because it is violent.'[2]

[1] In 1167 Ralph fitz Adam was amerced £100 because he built a hedge in violation of the assize: *Pipe Roll 13 Henry II*, p. 157. In 1186 Lambert *medicus* owed £100 for a disseisin: *Pipe Roll 32 Henry II*, p. 94. And see the statistics collected by van Caenegem, *Royal Writs*, p. 295.

[2] Above, p. 15 n. 1. Professor van Caenegem believes that Glanvill meant to distinguish here between disseisin with violence and simple disseisin without violence. In the former case the plaintiff was an 'appellor', as though he were prosecuting a criminal appeal, and he was liable in the event that his prosecution failed to pay the same penalty, amercement, that would fall on the defendant, the 'appellee', if the prosecution had been successful—another feature of criminal law. *Royal Writs*, pp. 266–7. It is unlikely, however, that Glanvill meant to make any

It is entirely consonant with this policy of punishing and preventing breaches of the peace by disseisin that the assize should have provided for lands to be restored to the men who had been disseised. Maitland doubted this: 'If all that we want is peace and quiet, it may be enough to punish ejectors by fine or imprisonment.'[1] But to take the fruits of his wrongdoing away from the disseisor was probably thought necessary if disseisin was to be effectively discouraged, for in many cases the value of the holdings that might be acquired by disseisin would be greater than the burden of any purely personal penalties that could in justice be laid against a man for this kind of offence. Henry II devised or (more likely) developed in presentment for felony a procedure against theft and robbery that resulted in personal penalties only and that seldom gave back to the victim of crime the goods that had been stolen from him.[2] But here the personal penalties were extremely heavy, mutilation or death and total forfeiture. That kind of punishment could not reasonably be imposed for disseisin. In any case, the best way of bringing disseisins to light for trial and punishment was to encourage private suits. As indestructible, permanent sources of income, lands and tenements were so valuable that men who had been disseised could fairly be counted on to prosecute if only they were given a convenient procedure and, of course, the prospect of recovery. The expeditious procedure of the assize, the judgment of recovery in favour of the successful plaintiff, may have been given simply to encourage suits in order that breaches of the peace by disseisin might more surely be repressed.

The better keeping of the peace does not seem, however, to have been the principal object of the assize. The doctrines and precedents of the past which Henry's ministers studied so carefully were not much concerned with the good policing of a

such distinction. Certainly he says nothing about any contrasting case, where the disseisin is found not to be violent and the losing party is not amerced; instead, he says that the amercement is 'always' laid. And he goes on directly to use the word 'appellor' to describe every plaintiff in novel disseisin, for he says, 'If the appellor does not prosecute on the day assigned him then his pledges will also be in mercy', a provision that must surely apply to every plaintiff. Elsewhere in his treatise, ii. 3, Glanvill describes a suit for land by writ of right as an 'appeal'. Probably the author regarded every disseisin as violent in some sense, following Digest xliii. 16. 1. 24.

[1] P. & M. ii. 43. [2] Ibid. ii. 165–6.

realm but rather with the good protection of rights in property and offices. The bishop despoiled of his see, who might invoke the canonical rule that we have noticed, was generally put out by high governing authority, by a king or perhaps an archbishop, who then proceeded to take legal action against him. He had suffered no violence, but he had been denied due process of law, being subject to execution before judgment was given in the suit against him, and it was this denial of due process which the canonical rule was meant to correct. The Roman interdict *unde vi* was not principally a measure in restraint of violence. The writs that the Norman kings of England issued upon complaints of wrongs to lands and tenements, and the writs that continued the tradition under Henry II, show hardly a trace of concern for peace and quiet. Their object was to get the land back into the hands of the rightful owner. When it was a complaint of disseisin, they usually did not even inquire who the disseisor was, and they almost never showed any desire to punish him.[1] Their care was for property and not for police.

It would be surprising if the makers of the assize had studied all these materials as deeply as they did in order to come up with a police measure. Their main concern, in fact, was not to help keep the peace but rather to furnish better protection for property. We may be sure of this for the simple reason that the definitions they used, the extensions they granted, the limitations they imposed were never cast in terms of peace or breach of peace but always in terms of property. Their legislation was against disseisin as such, which was not always violent but which always crossed someone's claim to ownership of lands and tenements. Disseisins of common of pasture were included, which would seldom be violent: the offender was almost sure to be the owner of the pasture land, who disseised by refusing to admit the commoners' beasts or by impounding them if he found them there. Nuisances were included, which were not likely to be breaches of peace: as often as not they consisted in work by the defendant on his own land, as he put up a new hedge or raised the dam that created his millpond. But the

[1] But see van Caenegem, *Royal Writs*, no. 59 (1116–18), pp. 441–2: 'Ponantur per plegios omnes illi homines qui eam [navem] ceperunt, ut sint ad rectum regi quando eos habere voluerit.' No. 68 (1093–8), p. 447: 'Et illos qui eos disseisierunt et sua post predictum terminum ceperunt pone per bonos plegios.' No. 79 (1107–29), p. 452: 'Volo scire quare dissaisiti sunt et qui eos dissaisivit.'

villein was excluded from the benefits of the assize even if he had suffered violence, even if he had suffered it at the hand of a stranger and not of his lord; and so, presently if not originally, the gageholder was also excluded. The assize was for freeholders. Where freehold was affected it would operate even if there had been no violence, but where freehold was not affected it would not operate even if there had been violence. The protection of freehold property rights must have been the primary purpose, the keeping of the peace only secondary.

Professor Milsom has argued lately that the assize may have been established in principle as a remedy specifically for tenants against their feudal lords, when their lords disseised them wrongfully and without judgment at law, and may have been available only incidentally against other disseisors.[1] There can be no doubt that the assize was consciously directed against lords who disseised their tenants. The protection of common rights in pasture proves as much, for the owner of the pasture land, who might shut out the commoners and so disseise them, was almost always their feudal lord.[2] Nuisances that resulted from millponds were most likely to be raised by the lord, for he ordinarily owned the village mill. And in general, after we begin to get regular records of lawsuits in the king's court, from 1194, it becomes clear that the assize was constantly used by tenants against their lords.[3] But whether the protection of tenant against lord was the specific governing purpose is, in my judgement, more than we can know. Professor Milsom suggests that a free tenant who was disseised by someone other than his lord would hardly have needed the assize, for he could get back in by calling on his lord, as in duty bound, to put him back in. This was true in principle, and no doubt was often true in fact. But there will have been some lords who were too distant, too inefficient, or too insouciant to give help where it was due, others who were in covin with the disseisor, and others yet again who were too weak to make their help effective against a disseisor-adversary who might himself be a greater lord. Where the power of his feudal lord failed him in any of these ways the victim of disseisin by an outsider might have cause to use the assize. But we really have no idea how likely it

[1] 'Introduction', pp. xxxix–xliv, and *Historical Foundations*, pp. 117–19.
[2] Milsom, 'Introduction', pp. xlii–xliii.   [3] Below, pp. 48–50, 96–7.

was that lordly protection would thus fail, still less how large this possibility may have loomed in the thoughts of the inventors of the assize. It depends on one's estimate of how effective the institution of feudal lordship was in twelfth-century society, and on this the views of experts diverge widely.[1] The legislation of Northampton of 1176 assumed, to be sure, that every lord was always in command of his fee so that if ever an heir was refused entry into his ancestor's holdings after his ancestor's death it must be the feudal lord who refused him, and it gave the assize of mort d'ancestor for such cases as an action specifically against the lord.[2] But this one document, though its evidence is unambiguous, cannot be taken as settling a complicated question on which a great deal of other evidence also bears.

The matter is, truth to tell, not much in point for our study of novel disseisin. Nothing about the assize throws any light on the relative importance of feudal lordship in Henry's reign, nor does the assumption that lordship was very powerful help us to understand anything that we know in particular about the assize. If feudal lords were very powerful indeed over their tenants, if they were the usual disseisors against whom tenants needed new protection, the designers of the assize made their work not one whit different on that account, but cast it in the form of an action good against all the world.[3] So we can only say that its object was to give freeholders better protection, from whatever quarter they might be threatened.

[1] See Note B, p. 214.

[2] *Select Charters*, p. 180, quoted in part above, p. 17.

[3] Other arguments that have been brought to bear on this matter have little or no independent force. The charge in novel disseisin that the defendant disseised the plaintiff 'without a judgment' may or may not imply that the defendant is a feudal lord with a court of his own that *could* have given a judgment. The alternative directed in the writ, that if the defendant himself cannot be found then his bailiff should be attached to come to court, proves nothing: the plaintiff's feudal lord would be likely to have a bailiff, but so would any other man of considerable wealth.

In the thirteenth century the law knew two 'assizes of nuisance', one an action before the sheriff for 'petty nuisances' and the other an action in the king's court developed out of the assize of novel disseisin. There is nothing to indicate (as has been suggested) that the petty nuisances were typically offences of neighbour against neighbour in contrast with the nuisances remediable in the king's court as offences of the lord against his free tenant. Most of the petty nuisances were likely to be the work of a landlord: erecting a sheepfold, enlarging his courtyard, building a windmill, and the like: see below, p. 63.

The restriction to freeholders meant that two very different kinds of non-freeholding tenants were left out: serfs on the one hand and gageholders, termors, and feudal guardians on the other. Since we are offered no special explanations by contemporaries, we must simply assume that the principal characteristic distinguishing each of these classes from freeholders was one that impressed the twelfth-century legislators as marking a bound for their purposes. Serfs were unfree; servile holdings did not seem of such dignity as to deserve the protection of the king's court and the king's law. Gageholders and termors were investors of cash: the former held the land as security for a debt, the latter generally as a means of recouping capital sums with which they had accommodated their grantors. So too, the holders of feudal wardships had very often bought them from the lords to whom they fell in, for there was a lively market in these rights; and even unsold in the hands of the lord himself, a wardship was thought of like money, as part of the income from an estate and not as an estate in itself.[1] Freeholders of the twelfth century, on the other hand, did not often come to their estates by purchasing them for money, and even if they did the rights that they bought transcended the purchase price in a way that the rights of these others did not. The gageholder, termor, or feudal guardian was obligated to return the land when he had had his money's worth or when his time for taking his profit was up, while the freeholder had the land as his own, at least for himself if not for his heirs as well.[2] The designers of the assize wanted to protect rights in lands and tenements as such.

The Roman law of the interdict *unde vi* may also have had a bearing here. The interdict could not be used by the *servus* or *colonus*, and in twelfth-century England the position of the serf answered to the standing of *servi* or *coloni* in Rome. But this will

[1] P. & M. ii. 106–24.

[2] This explanation, suggested by Maitland, P. & M. ii. 116–17, seems preferable because it is simplest. Maitland's other hypothesis, P. & M. ii. 114–15, supposes a misinterpretation of Roman learning about *possessio* which we do not encounter under the pen of an English writer before Bracton. Professor Milsom suggests that 'the difficulties may at least diminish' if we understand novel disseisin as an action meant specifically for tenants against their feudal lords, because 'the termor was not in the feudal sense a tenant at all'. 'Introduction', pp. xliii–xliv. This merely restates the problem: why was the termor or gageholder not a feudal tenant like the freeholder? Cf. P. & M. ii. 113.

not explain the exclusion of the gageholder and the other investors, for the Roman *creditor* could have the benefits of the
interdict for land that he held as security.[1] The example of the
interdict may have had a subtler influence. For a given piece
of land at a given time there could be only one *possessor* in
Roman law, only one party protected by the interdict, and the
assize copied the interdict in this respect. So choices had to be
made. A free tenant in demesne holding of the baron of X is
ejected by a stranger claiming to hold of the earl of Y; both
the baron and his tenant have suffered loss but if the law gives
the assize to the baron it will not give it to the tenant; the law
determines to give it to the tenant because he has the more
immediate and more important interests at stake.[2] A serf is
ejected by a stranger claiming the freehold, to the injury both
of the serf and of his lord; if you give the assize to the serf the
lord may not have it; the law decides to give it to the lord, for
he is the worthier as being a free man. So also when a gageholder, termor, or feudal guardian is put out by a stranger: the
debtor, the grantor of the term, the infant ward will have the
assize, for his is the more lasting interest in the land. But again
following the law of the interdict, the assize held that it was a
man's status in the land that told whether he was entitled to
the remedy, and not a question of who his disseisor was. If the
villein, the gageholder, the termor, the guardian cannot have
the assize against strangers it is because they are not such as to
have it; so neither can they have it against the lord, against the
debtor, or against anyone at all.

Behind this concern to protect freehold property rights there
may have lain a deeper purpose. Henry II and his ministers
may have been aiming to exalt the king's authority.[3] They

---

[1] Some medieval legists, however, read the Roman law otherwise: P. & M. ii.
121 n. 2.

[2] In later times the right of the lord to customs and services was regarded as a
distinct tenement in itself, for which he could bring novel disseisin while his
ousted tenant could have the assize to recover the land in demesne. But this seems
to have been a new development in the 1190s: see below, pp. 50–1.

[3] So Stubbs, *Constitutional History* (6th ed.), i. 482, 638, (4th ed.) ii. 110; Adams,
Origin of the English Constitution, pp. 96–105, 127–8; Jenks, *A Short History of English
Law*, pp. 54–5; Joüon des Longrais, 'La portée politique'; S. E. Thorne, 'Livery
of Seisin', p. 358.

Financial profit is not likely to have been a major consideration, as some modern
writers have thought. See the discussion of this matter by Professor van Caenegem,
Royal Writs, pp. 173–6.

opened the king's court to every freeman however humble by
offering him there the protection of the assize. This detracted
from the jurisdiction both of feudal lords and of sheriffs in their
county courts and instead brought the business before the king
himself or before those specially appointed commissioners of
his from headquarters, the justices. It offered men who were
disseised by strangers an alternative to dependence on their
feudal lords: they could choose instead to invoke the king's
justice in the form of the assize. Most of all, it cut off the feudal
lord's power to make his own decisions on his own principles
in dealing with his free tenants. Any tenant whose lord put him
out could sue by the assize and get himself restored to the land
if the lord's act seemed arbitrary to the jurors and justices in the
king's court. But a superior who has no power to make decisions
of his own becomes a superior in name only.[1] The assize brought
it about that the king should be the only true superior for freemen.

All these effects were in fact produced by the assize, and from
what we know of Henry II and his government it is easy to
believe that they planned it that way. But we cannot be sure.
No such purpose was ever acknowledged, no such aim is implied
by any unambiguous evidence. If this was indeed the deeper
object of the assize, still the chosen path toward its fulfilment
lay wholly through the offering of better protection for freehold property, and the better protection of freehold property
remains therefore the principal purpose that is visible to history.

If that was the principal purpose, then we may be able to
account in some detail for the reasoning that went into the
assize and for the form that its provisions took. The problem
that the king and his ministers put to themselves was not, 'How
can we restrain disseisins?' for the decision to restrain disseisins
was only a reflection of a more fundamental goal. Rather they
asked themselves, 'How can the law give better protection to
the rights of freeholders?' They felt that existing law was not
good enough, and from what they did in the assize and in some

---

[1] Professor Milsom is certainly correct in arguing, *Historical Foundations*, p. 119,
that the assize strengthened feudalism by enforcing the rules of feudal law and by
insisting that lords get proper judgments from their feudal courts before taking
action against their free tenants. But the lord and his court were to be deprived of
all discretion, and their authority weakened in that important sense.

of their other reforming legislation we can tell wherein they believed its inadequacies to lie.

In the first place, formal suits for the recovery of land by the action of right were terribly slow. The tenant of the land, against whom the suit was brought, did not have to come into court to answer the claim until he had been summoned repeatedly for successive court days or until he had exhausted a series of essoins which by themselves might drag the proceedings out for more than a year. When he did come he could vouch a warrantor, who had then in his turn to be summoned and who might essoin himself. The warrantor when he came could vouch over again, and so on to the third warrantor. When the demandant had finally driven his suit to a decisive issue there would be further delays before the rituals of trial by battle. 'Law must be slow in order that it may be fair', said Maitland;[1] but Professor van Caenegem is surely right in supposing that this traditional procedure was slow not only for fairness' sake but also because it was hoped to avoid, if possible, bringing suits to decisive issues. Suing at law was not so much a means of enforcing claims through the authority of the courts as of bringing pressure to bear on the opponent. In a long, slow process a compromise would probably be worked out between the parties somewhere along the line.[2] This view of the legal process is common in every age and has in every age a great deal to commend it. But to Henry II compromise and accommodation were not among the very highest values; to him and his counsellors a law that delayed trial and judgment in the hope of seeing a compromise was wrong-headed. In order to give due protection to property rights they wanted to give every freeman a swift and decisive means of enforcing his claims in court.

Secondly, the action of right seemed inadequate because under its rules if a claimant to lands did succeed after all in forcing the issue and bringing his case to the point where it was to be judged decisively for or against him, the resolution of the issue would depend on trial by battle. If one thought of the health of men's bodies and souls, trial by battle was dangerous; if one thought of the interests of justice, it was capricious. Henry II and his counsellors did not like it. In the

[1] P. & M. ii. 51.   [2] *Royal Writs*, pp. 41–6.

Assize of Windsor of 1179 they found a way to replace it in part with trial by jury in the form that came to be called the grand assize. Already in the years around 1160, as they planned the assize of novel disseisin, they were anxious to find a way by which decisions on claims to freehold could be tried by rational proofs rather than by battle.

In the third place, when men avoided the formalities of actions of right and betook themselves instead to the informal procedure of complaining to lord, king, or sheriff about wrongs committed against their property-interests, all was much *too* informal. Nothing required the superior to hold an investigation, and often he did not do so. If he held an investigation, nothing obliged him to call in the person who was accused of wrongdoing, nothing prescribed definitely what means he should use to conduct the inquiry, nothing required him to proceed with dispatch. If the business was carried on in a feudal lord's court, since it was not a judicial proceeding at all in the strict sense there was (apparently) no way of appealing to the king against false judgment, and hence no means of enforcing any uniform rules as among different courts. The designers of the assize wanted to give a standardized and reliable process.

These may have been, then, the first reflections which guided the makers of the assize. Rights in free tenements would be better protected by the law if every freeman could be given a formal judicial procedure that was speedy and decisive and dependent on rational proofs. They decided to devise such a procedure. It should be available, they decided further, only in the king's court. Perhaps they believed that better justice could be done there than in feudal or county courts, perhaps they thought in particular to assure better uniformity of practice by keeping everything under one jurisdiction, perhaps they wanted to build up the jurisdiction of the king as a way of strengthening the royal power.

But if a legal procedure was to be granted for the recovery of free tenements by swift process, through rational means of trial, and always in the king's court, it was wholly impossible to make it available to all demandants for the pursuit of all lands and tenements to which they had good claims. If every freeman should be admitted to sue for all his rights directly before the king or his justices it would derogate from the jurisdiction of feudal lords, who would be offended by this and who were too powerful for the king to offend as a group. If everyone should be allowed to vindicate all his claims through offering rational proofs it would cancel out the recognized right of men who held lands to defend them in the last resort by battle, a valued liberty, as it seemed to conservatives, which guaranteed that a man might hold his lands freely in reliance on himself under God and not subject to the king's will or to the word of such of his neighbours as might happen to be sworn on a jury. Most troublesome of all, perhaps, was the reflection that many kinds of claims to land seemed in fairness and good reason to require delay in their adjudication. It was true in some measure, after all, that law had to be slow if it was to be fair. If a man had for years been in possession of land which he had, let us say, inherited from his father, it would be unjust according to twelfth-century ideas to call him summarily to account without allowing time for negotiation between the parties, for planning a defence, for difficulties of travel, or for delays due to illness. The law had to recognize, furthermore, that many tenants were entitled to have their lands warranted to them by their lords. If land which the tenant's lord was bound to warrant was to be taken from the tenant by judgment and restored to his adversary, then the lord must as a matter of elementary justice be given an opportunity to appear in court and defend the suit. The tenant must be permitted, that is, to vouch his lord, even though this might entail a good deal of delay.

So the inventors of the assize drew once again on the traditions of the canonical learning, the Roman interdict *unde vi*, and the old informal English procedure on complaint, to devise limitations for their new work. An action of the sort that they wanted to give, a formal action, rapid, determinable by rational proofs, and always in the king's court, could be justified and made acceptable if it was given not for the vindication of claims to land in general but only for claims that were founded on the allegation that the defendant had disseised the plaintiff at some recent date. It could be argued in that case that there was no invasion of any other jurisdiction, for the strictly judicial proceeding known to the old law, the action of right, was not founded upon a complaint of a wrong that had been suffered but purely upon the assertion of the demandant's right in the property. If the argument was rejected—and really it was not sound—still the assumption of new jurisdiction by the king's court would appear a limited one, and the more easily tolerable inasmuch as its limits seemed sharply defined. By the same token, the law could reasonably insist on a rational form of proof, namely, trial by jury. The disseisin, as a recent fact and one that was likely to be notorious among the neighbours, must be tried by the verdict of the neighbours so that the alleged disseisor would have no chance in court to disprove by battle what everyone in the countryside perhaps knew by the evidence of his eyes. Where other kinds of claim were raised to land, on facts that might not be at all notorious, there tenants would retain the right to defend their holdings by battle. Above all, an action that was limited to claims based on recent disseisins could be speedy without thereby being unfair. If the plaintiff was required to sue quickly after the disseisin, while the fact remained fresh, then it was not unjust to insist that the defendant for his part come to court without any delay. If the plaintiff was required to sue on the recent and notorious fact of disseisin, then it was not unfair to try his allegation even in the absence of the defendant, for the chance of a miscarriage of justice would be small. But if the defendant himself need not be awaited, the court could, *a fortiori*, proceed without his warrantor. A warrantor could not add anything substantial to the defence of a suit where the claim had to be based on the alleged act of the defendant himself, for against such a claim all possible powers of defence would naturally lie in the defendant alone.

This may be, then, if our conjectures are correct, the route by which Henry II and his counsellors came to the decision that a new proceeding at law should be made available specifically for cases in which the plaintiff alleged that he had recently been disseised by the defendant. It was a limited reform, for it did nothing for demandants of lands whose claims were founded on other sorts of facts. Even within its limits it was bound to operate in an imperfect way. For if the character of the action as swift and as determinable by rational proofs could be established only by restricting the kind of claim on which the plaintiff might rely, it could be maintained only by restricting as well the kind of reply that the defendant might offer. In general, only those defences could be permitted which

(1) could be tried by some rational means known to the king's court, such as the verdict of a jury or examination of witnesses, and did not demand trial by battle, and which (2) could be tried with no more delay than would be required to take the verdict of the jury on which the proceedings ordinarily turned. Thus, the defendant might reply that he did not disseise the plaintiff, and might argue this before the jury and abide its verdict. He could plead that he disseised the plaintiff by lawful judgment, provided that he produced on the spot the suitors of the court that had given the judgment, to settle the matter at once by their witness. He could answer that he disseised the plaintiff but that the plaintiff was his villein, as he could prove by the word of the plaintiff's relatives, men and women of servile status who were here in court and ready to acknowledge their unfree condition. But he must not reply that he had the land from his lord, who should be summoned to another court day to take up the defence as warrantor, for such a plea delayed the proceedings; he must not reply that his ancestor was seised as of right in a previous generation, that the right had descended to him as heir, and therefore his right was better than the plaintiff's, for such a plea required to be tried by battle.[1]

There was this difficulty, however, in restricting what might be said in defence, that to enforce any such restrictions would of course in some cases mean excluding defences that were perfectly well justified. Probably most of the wakeful nights of Henry II's counsellors were spent in thinking out this problem. In the end, they concluded that it would be acceptable to put limits on the defence. Most legitimate defences would be admitted within the rules of the new action. If the defendant really had disseised the plaintiff, and could not show that it was done in execution of the judgment of a court, and could not prove that the plaintiff was his serf, then in most cases the right would in fact lie with the plaintiff and the king's court would be doing quick justice by restoring him. In those few cases where the defendant had a good defence that he would not be allowed to plead, it would be left open to him to sue in the traditional manner, using now as the basis of his claim the material that he had not been allowed to offer in defence in the action on the assize. Roman law knew a similar 'duality of

[1] Above, pp. 19–20.

action', by which a man who lost by judgment in one proceeding might later bring a new suit and recover after all, and in
Roman law it was precisely the interdicts that raised duality of
action, for their judgments left open the possibility of counter-
suit.[1] Novel disseisin could follow the interdict *unde vi* in this as
in so much else. On balance the benefit that would accrue to
the many landowners from having a swift and rationally determinable action in the king's court for recovering tenements of
which they had been wrongfully disseised would far outweigh
the loss that would result for a few landowners through being
forced to establish their right by way of prosecution rather than
in defence.

The limitation of the assize to matters that could in justice
be handled with dispatch and entirely by rational proofs was
described by saying that the assize was concerned only with
seisin. The other legal proceeding that was not so limited, where
there might be successive summonses, many essoins, and trial by
battle, was the action of right. 'Seisin', when it was set thus in
contrast with 'right', meant facts that would support a swift
and rationally determined action at law; 'right' was facts that
would not support a suit of this kind but must be pleaded in a
more dilatory process determinable by the judgment of God.
In practice, 'seisin' amounted to recent and notorious facts,
'right' to older and more obscure facts. The distinction was
purely a matter of degree, and it had reference only to litigation, not to men's substantive rights in the land.

Already in the earliest years of Henry II's reign this contrast
of seisin and right had been pretty well limned out. To Archbishop Theobald of Canterbury, who died in 1161, a 'suit for
seisin' meant a claim to land that could be tried by human
reasonings, while 'right' called for the judgment of God. A certain Peter had brought a 'suit for seisin' in the archbishop's
court, claiming that his parents had been seised of the land that
he now sought to recover until his mother was violently ejected
from it after his father's death. 'His suit for seisin would have
been good if he had had sufficient proof', wrote the archbishop;
but to make out his case he had to show that his parents had
held hereditarily for otherwise no claims of theirs would descend to him, and even after considerable delay 'he produced

[1] Joüon des Longrais, 'La portée politique', pp. 551-2.

neither writings nor witnesses, he had no proof of any kind at hand and could promise none to come' on this point. Judgment was therefore given against him. But the judgment expressly reserved him the option of going on to raise the 'question of right'. Since he had never been in possession of the land himself, any claim that he might put forward must depend upon descent from his parents. He could not show by what the archbishop called 'proof' that they had held hereditarily; if raising the 'question of right' offered him then any hope of success it must be because in a 'question of right' he would be allowed to establish the hereditary character of their tenure by something other than 'proof'. To the archbishop, 'proof' meant reasonable demonstration, as by documents or witnesses, and was required in a 'suit for seisin'; in a 'question of right' something else might take the place of reasonable demonstration, and the something else was surely trial by battle.[1]

For this contrast, however, 'seisin' and 'right' were the most unfortunate terms that could have been chosen. The basic meanings of the two words were 'possession' in the one case, and in the other case what we still sometimes call 'right', sound and justified legal claim. So wherever one man had got possession of land that rightly belonged to another there was presented a second contrast of seisin and right. The usurper had seisin, the true owner had right. This contrast had nothing to do with the other one that we have pointed out but it had to be described in the same terms for there were no other words to use.[2]

That was not even the worst of it. The Roman interdicts were actions concerned with *possessio*, possession, in contradis- tinction to *dominium*, ownership. It was the fact that novel disseisin was modelled on an interdict that led, no doubt, to the unhappy choice of 'seisin' and 'right' to characterize different kinds of proceedings, for these words could be taken as translations or equivalents of the two Roman terms. But in fact they were not equivalent at all. *Possessio* and *dominium* were distinct juridical concepts with no middle ground between them, while seisin and right, when contrasted in the way which now concerns us, were reference-points in a continuum: the more recent and notorious facts, the relatively older and less well-known

[1] For the text of Archbishop Theobald's report of this case, see Avrom Saltman, *Theobald*, p. 390.   [2] P. & M. ii. 31–4.

facts. *Possessio* and *dominium* were categories of substantive law, while the contrast of seisin and right that interests us had to do only with procedure, characterizing the swift and rational proceeding on the one hand, the dilatory proceeding which invoked the judgment of God on the other hand. When the assize of mort d'ancestor appeared Englishmen had little hesitation in deciding that it was, like novel disseisin, an action concerned with seisin, a 'possessory' action—the Roman terminology had at least the merit of providing a convenient adjective. But they were bound to notice that it was not so fully possessory as novel disseisin. The plaintiff could rely on facts a little older, and he had to prove the relatively recondite fact that his ancestor had been seised 'as of fee', hereditarily. Two essoins were allowed, and the defendant might vouch to warranty. For men who understood seisin after the manner of the absolute Roman category of *possessio* it was difficult to account for the relativeness, the shading-off of the possessory quality. Their difficulties came to a head with the invention of the writs of entry, most of which were created in the first half of the thirteenth century, for these actions lay fairly at the mid-point between seisin and right. By the same token, English men of law who understood seisin and right as substantive categories were left with a puzzle when actions of right fell out of use in the late thirteenth century. Right *in property* seemed to have vanished from the law.[1]

All this caused a good deal of intellectual confusion, but it was after all only a minor blemish on Henry II's work in founding the assize. Henry's government set the assize forth as a carefully designed reform with objectives of first-rate importance, aimed to help keep the peace and even more to give better security to the freeholders of England. It enjoyed success from the first, but in later generations showed even more fully the measure of its usefulness and power. It is the foremost example of that high genius in the government of Henry II that knew how to design institutions which would endure, developing and fruitful, to serve distant ages.

---

[1] For these confusions, see P. & M. ii. 72–8; Milsom, *Historical Foundations*, p. 104; Joüon des Longrais, *La Conception anglaise de la saisine*, pp. 63–9.

Recent discussion of the relation of 'right' and 'seisin' in English law is reviewed, with references to the literature, by Milsom, 'Bibliography', pp. lxxxvi–lxxxviii.

II

SUCCESS AND GROWTH:
THE FIRST HUNDRED YEARS

IN the first century of its life, from the 1160s to the 1260s, the assize proved itself an outstanding success. In the course of this time it came to be the most frequently used form of action in the king's court. In the 1190s, the years from which we can first follow the whole work of some parts of the king's court, novel disseisin may already have been more in use there than the action of right. Certainly it was so later in the thirteenth century, as the action of right declined. Mort d'ancestor was the commonest form of action in the 1190s and for some time thereafter, but around the middle of the thirteenth century novel disseisin took first place, and long retained it. The relative frequency of these several forms can best be seen in the records of eyres *ad omnia placita*, whose justices exercised an equal jurisdiction over all kinds of actions. Here are the figures for a few eyres that have been taken by way of sample.[1]

	Novel disseisin	Mort d'ancestor	Actions of right for lands
1198, Herts., Essex, Middx. (surviving rolls)	19	35	13
1202, Bedfordshire	11	37	8
1227, Bedfordshire	58	64	31
1227, Buckinghamshire	89	87	62
1242–3, Somerset	46	38	20
1249, Wiltshire	105	109	31
1256, Northumberland	39	31	8
1269, Northumberland	27	26	1
1279, Northumberland	19	18	2

[1] I have compiled the figures for 1198 (from *Rotuli Curiae Regis* i. 149–219), 1227 (from *Eyres of Beds* iii. 1–206 and *Eyre of Bucks 1227*), and 1242–3 (*Somerset Pleas* i. 133–324). The statistics for the Bedfordshire eyre of 1202 are presented by G. H. Fowler, *Eyres of Beds* i. 137, and those of the Wiltshire eyre of 1249 by M. T. Clanchy, *Wilts Civil Pleas 1249*, p. 29. The figures for the eyres of Northumberland of 1256, 1269, and 1279 are Maitland's, P. & M. ii. 565.

When novel disseisin surpassed mort d'ancestor it had surpassed all other forms as well, as appears from Maitland's table of all the forms of action in the last three of these eyres.[1]

The assize attained this position even though the justices, apparently troubled as mid-century approached by the growing numbers of actions of novel disseisin, tried to encourage settlements out of court. In medieval England men habitually opened lawsuits before undertaking negotiations with the adversary, sometimes even before making requests for satisfaction.[2] They cared little for privacy either in more personal matters or in their business affairs; the courts were close at hand and were traditionally places for announcements and discussion as much as for trial and judgment; their sessions were understood as meetings of the community and their proceedings must have been valuable as social entertainment in a land not equipped with clubs, citizens' committees, and theatres. Hence the many suits that were compromised after genuinely hostile beginnings,[3] hence in general the myriads of cases brought in court.

Against this pattern of custom the king's justices developed, about the 1230s and 1240s, rules for the assize of novel disseisin which attempted to assure that only truly hostile cases that could not be settled elsewhere should be brought before them. They prohibited the defendants from appearing by attorney, a rule first applied in 1227 and consistently enforced thereafter until it was revoked by statute in 1318.[4] The clause of the writ

---

[1] P. & M. ii. 565–7.

[2] Clanchy, *Wilts Civil Pleas 1249*, pp. 27–8. For an example of novel disseisin brought apparently without any previous demand for restitution, see *BNB* no. 781.

[3] For example, *CRR* ii. 93 (1202), 278 (1203), iv. 172–3 (1206), vii. 63, 280 (1214), ix. 261 (1220), xiii. 119 (1227), xiv. 207 (1230); *Eyre of Yorks 1218–19* no. 22. Cf. Bracton, fos. 297, 299b, 313–313b, where he supposes that the tenant sued in Dower may often voluntarily surrender on the first day in court. The matter is acutely discussed by M. T. Clanchy in *Wilts Civil Pleas 1249*, pp. 23–4.

[4] In the records from before 1227 defendants constantly appoint attorneys: e.g. *Lincs Assize Rolls* no. 423 (1202), *Northants Pleas* nos. 840, 870 (1203), *CRR* v. 249 (1207), vii. 58 (1214), *Eyres of Lincs and Worcs* nos. 14, 78, 91, 116 (1219), 930 (1221), *Eyre of Yorks 1218–19* no. 341, *CRR* xii. 963, 1019, 1078, 1095, 1507 (1225), xiii. 129, 305 (1227), 782, 1050 = *BNB* no. 291 (1228), *CRR* xiii. 1552 (1229). These few cases from 1228 and 1229 are the last, except for one anomalous case in *Wilts Civil Pleas 1249* nos. 86 and 504. Already in the eyres of Bedfordshire and Buckinghamshire of 1227 the new rule seems to be enforced, for no defendant appointed an attorney for novel disseisin in those eyres, *Eyres of Beds* iii. 1–206, *Eyre of Bucks 1227*. A case in the Bench in 1228 shows the new rule in practice: the plaintiff appeared by attorney, the defendant by his seneschal, *CRR* xiii. 720. For the

of novel disseisin that directed the sheriff to attach the defendant 'or his bailiff if he himself cannot be found' was always taken to mean that any defendant might appear by his bailiff if he did not come in person, and so it was no question of forcing the defendant to appear personally.[1] A bailiff could plead in defence almost as freely as his principal,[2] but since he had no special appointment for the case he was not allowed to compromise it or give it away by confessing the disseisin;[3] only an attorney could do that. Attorneys were excluded in order to make it more difficult to bring into court assizes where the parties were willing to compromise or the defendant ready to concede. To the same end and at the same time that they excluded attorneys for defendants, that is from 1227, the justices began refusing licences to compromise to those who appeared in person.[4]

legislation of 1318 which again permitted defendants to appoint attorneys see *SR* i. 177.

The plaintiff's right to appear by attorney was always maintained, e.g. *Yorks Assize Rolls* p. 80 (1251), *Somerset Pleas* i. 1422 (1251), *Northumb Assize Rolls* pp. 18, 37 (1256), 217, 218 (1269), C.P. 40/91 m. 291d (1291).

[1] For one who did not want to come himself it was, in fact, easier to have a bailiff represent him, for a bailiff, in contrast with an attorney, needed no formal appointment. In consequence of this rule, anyone at all could come as bailiff for a defendant; he did not have to be in charge of any of the defendant's interests apart from the assize and did not even have to be directed by the defendant to appear for him in the case. Hence Bracton says, fo. 182, that defendants can appear 'by their bailiffs or simply by their friends'. Where several defendants were charged in the same action, one would often speak as bailiff for the others, e.g. K.B. 26/158 m. 18 (1258), *Eyre of Kent* iii. 139 (1313), Y.B. Mich. 9 Ed. II no. 15 (1315). Later on, professional barristers appeared as bailiffs, e.g. J.I. 1/503 m. 13d (1286–9), C.P. 40/131 m. 165 (1300).

[2] Bracton, fo. 212b. For examples of special defences put forth by bailiffs, see *CRR* v. 212 (1208), *Eyres of Lincs and Worcs* nos. 828, 898 (1219), *Somerset Pleas* i. 312 (1225), 1429 (1251), *BNB* no. 754 (1233), J.I. 1/1182 m. 10 (1254), *Casus Placitorum* pp. 86–95 (1276), C.P. 40/17 m. 5, 64d (1276). For later developments restricting the bailiff's power to plead in certain ways, see below, Note E, p. 218.

[3] Bracton, fo. 182: 'cognoscere . . . non possunt disseisinam nec pacisci nec remittere.' But see, to the contrary, cases heard by Bracton in 1253, *Somerset Pleas* i. 1469, 1479.

[4] Before the 1230s final concords were often made in novel disseisin. In addition to the cases cited in n. 3 on p. 44 above, see also, for example, the following cases where formal licence to compromise was given and a chirograph drawn: *Rotuli Curiae Regis* i. 400 (1199), *CRR* iii. 154 (1204), *Lincs Assize Rolls* no. 84 (1202), 1445 (1206), *CRR* v. 157 (1208), vi. 86–7 (1210). But in the eyres of Bedfordshire and Buckinghamshire of 1227 the justices evidently excluded concords in novel disseisin, though they allowed them as freely as before in mort d'ancestor and other forms of action (*Eyres of Beds* iii. 1–206; *Eyre of Bucks 1227*); and after about this time final concords in novel disseisin appear only rarely, though a few examples do occur: *Somerset*

And in the years that followed they developed, although more gradually, the remarkable rule that defendants who appeared in person to confess the disseisin should be sent to prison and obliged to fine for release.¹

In the thirteenth century some men explained all these rules as growing out of a hatred of the violence involved in disseisin. Bracton said that defendants who confessed disseisin were imprisoned because wrongs committed in breach of the peace, like disseisin, naturally called for imprisonment by way of punishment.² He wrote that compromises were ordinarily not permitted in novel disseisin 'because no agreement or compromise should be made about matters that involve the offence of breach of peace, but due judgment should follow'.³ The old printed Register of Writs said that the defendant might not appoint an attorney because novel disseisin was an action, like a 'writ of attachment' or an appeal of felony, in which the defendant

---

Pleas i. 394 p (1238), 567 (1242–3), 1454 (1253), *Northumb Assize Rolls* p. 2 (1256), MS. Y fos. 10–10ᵛ (*c.* 1300), 28 (*c.* 1310).

Less formal compromises, where the terms agreed upon were entered in the court roll but where no chirograph was drawn, were sometimes admitted, e.g. *Wilts Civil Pleas 1249* p. 22 n. 67, and Ralph of Hengham's assize rolls for 1271–89, J.I. 1/1217 and 1/1245, *passim*. The practice is mentioned centuries later in Brooke's New Cases, no. 461 (1554). Bracton apparently refers to it when he says, fo. 215, 'transactio . . . de gratia concedi poterit et pro bono pacis et non de iure'.

¹ In the early period defendants who confessed the disseisin were subject to no penalty other than the amercement that fell on every defeated litigant. See, for example, *PRS* xiv. 72 (1195–6), *CRR* i. 437 (1201), *Pleas 1198–1212* iv. 4166 (1209), *CRR* vii. 62 (1214), *Eyres of Lincs and Worcs* no. 28 (1218–19), *BNB* no. 1806 (1222), *Somerset Pleas* i. 295 (1225), and *CRR* xiii. 1553 (1229). Imprisonment of the defendant who confessed first appears in 1218–19, *Eyres of Lincs and Worcs* no. 413, but this is for its time an isolated example. From 1227 to 1251 practice varied: imprisonment is awarded in *Eyre of Bucks 1227* no. 177, *CRR* xiii. 2276 (1229), K.B. 26/115ᴀ m. 7d (1234), *Somerset Pleas* i. 502 (1242–3), K.B. 27/107 m. 6d (1248). *Wilts Civil Pleas 1249* no. 172, *Yorks Assize Rolls* 51–2, 56, 65, 77 (1251); imprisonment was not awarded in *Eyre of Bucks 1227* nos. 181, 211, 282, *CRR* xiii. 1553 (1229), xiv. 461 (1230), K.B. 26/113 m. 25d (1233), 26/116ᴮ m. 5 (1236), 26/121 m. 30, 34d (1241), *Wilts Civil Pleas 1249* no. 33, *Yorks Assize Rolls* 55, 64, 83, 84 (1251). After 1251 those who confessed were invariably imprisoned: see, for example, K.B. 26/147ᴀ m. 12d (1252), J.I. 1/1178 m. 12, 18, 19, 19d (1253), 1/1179 m. 14, 14d (1254–5), 1/1187 m. 17d (1258), K.B. 26/158 m. 10d, 12d, 13 (1258). In all strictness, the rule was that a defendant should be imprisoned if he was convicted either by his confession or in any other way upon pleadings alone, without a trial: K.B. 27/51 m. 17 (1280), 27/79 m. 27 (1283), Y.B. Pasch. 14 Ed. III no. 35 (1340), 24 Ass. no. 3 (1350).

² fo. 183.

³ fo. 215: 'de iis que presumpta sunt contra pacem domini regis nulla concordia [fieri debet] sive transactio, sed ipsum iudicium.' Cf. fo. 182b.

ought to be imprisoned if he was convicted.[1] But these explanations make little sense. Formally at any rate, no breach of peace
was alleged in novel disseisin. If the defendant was not allowed
to come by attorney, he could always appear by bailiff: there
was never any genuine determination that he should be made
to answer in person for his misdeed, like an accused trespasser or
felon. And disseisin as such did not naturally require imprisonment of the offender, whatever Bracton might say, for that
penalty fell only on the defendant who confessed and not on one
who was convicted. Imprisonment of convicted defendants was
introduced later, by a statute of 1275, and even then it was
applied only to those who were specifically found to have committed disseisin with violence or robbery.[2] But in actions of
trespass, where breach of peace *was* formally alleged and where
the convicted defendant was always 'awarded to prison',
defendants were allowed to appoint attorneys from 1278,[3] while
they had to wait another forty years, until 1318, for the same
privilege in the assize.

Probably permission was given to appoint attorneys in
Trespass because the same statute of 1278 that gave the permission laid down several other rules which it was hoped would
serve by themselves to stem the influx of actions of trespass into
the king's court. In particular, the rule was established that the
damages sued for must amount to at least forty shillings if the
action of trespass was to be brought before the king's justices.
Probably the earlier development of the peculiar rules in novel
disseisin, excluding defendants' attorneys, frowning on compromises, punishing confession more severely than conviction,
was due to the same fear that the royal courts might be swamped
with too much business. They mark the first steps of the centuries-
long process that converted the courts from forums for ordinary
discussion to places of reluctant last resort.[4]

In spite of this, novel disseisin grew to be the most frequent
form of action: a remarkable testimony to its effectiveness. Its
effectiveness is also attested by the fact that countless freeholders
used it to sue for very small pieces of property. It must not have

[1] *Registrum Brevium*, fo. 9.   [2] Below, p. 134.
[3] Statute of Gloucester c. 8, *SR* i. 48.
[4] For other measures taken to limit the numbers of assizes of nuisance in the
king's court, see below, pp. 62–3.

cost much to bring the assize, and the action, once brought, must have been capable of doing justice in detail and with precision, settling the ownership of a particular acre or defining the exact line between two men's holdings. The earliest records we have, from the 1190s and from about 1200, show a suit for three (or perhaps it was six) acres of land, for one-and-a-half rods, for half an acre, for one acre, for 'a balk between their fields which [the defendant] ploughed up', and for the ground occupied by one burial plot.[1] Similar small claims continued to be made,[2] and after about 1240, when the records became more informative in these matters, it becomes clear that small claims were not occasional but frequent.[3]

But the strength of the assize and the good justice that it brought are shown most of all in the fact that it could often vindicate the rights of tenants against their lords and the rights of poor men against the rich and powerful. There are a good many records in which it can be seen that a tenant is recovering against his lord or the lord's steward.[4] In some of these the plain-

---

[1] *PRS* xiv. 243–4 (*tempore* Ric. I), *Northants Pleas* nos. 645, 744, 855, 862 (1203), *CRR* ii. 93 (1202).

[2] For example, *Pleas 1198–1212* iv. 4059 (1209), 4*d.* annual rent; *Eyres of Glos, Warw, Staffs* no. 670 (1221), one-half acre of arable and the headland of a meadow; *BNB* no. 1794 (1222), one acre.

[3] The writ specified the townships in which the tenements lay and told whether the complaint was of nuisance, of disseisin of common rights, or of disseisin of a free tenement. Beyond paraphrasing these terms of the writ the early records made no direct statement of what the tenements were, and it may be that no such statement was made orally in court either: see *Pleas 1198–1212* iv. 4094 (1209). In the 1230s the practice was slowly developed of introducing into the record immediately after the paraphrase of the writ a new clause stating the 'plaint' ('Unde queritur . . .'), where the kinds and quantity of the tenements being sued for were detailed; after about 1240 this was invariably done. This development in the records presumably corresponded to a contemporaneous development in the courtroom procedure, the plaintiff now being required to open the hearing with a statement of his claim which would be for novel disseisin the practical equivalent of the 'narration' familiar in most other forms of action. The earliest example of a recorded 'plaint' is of 1232, *CRR* xiv. 2377 = *BNB* no. 885. Cases in *BNB* from the 1230s sometimes have the plaint and sometimes not. None was recorded in the cases of novel disseisin heard in Somerset in 1238, *Somerset Pleas* i. 112–17, but plaints were always set down in the eyres of Bedfordshire in 1240, of Somerset in 1242–3, and of Yorkshire in 1251 (*Eyres of Beds* ix. 78–143, *Somerset Pleas* i. 142–94, *Yorks Assize Rolls* 43–87); and they are a standard feature in all later rolls.

[4] For example, *PRS* xiv. 40 (1194), *Rotuli Curiae Regis* ii. 58–9, 117 (1199), *CRR* i. 187, 249 (1200), iii. 62 (1203), *Northants Pleas* nos. 782, 786 (1203), *CRR* iii. 161–2 (1204), *Eyre of Yorks 1218–19* no. 46, *Eyres of Lincs and Worcs* no. 946 (1221), *Eyres of Glos, Warw, Staffs* no. 406 (1221), *BNB* no. 1814, 1906, 1908 (1227), 1149 (1235–6), J.I. 1/1182 m. 10 (1254), 1/1245 m. 34 (1280), 62 (1281).

tiff was so clearly a social inferior that the lord could try to defend himself by contending, in vain in these cases, that he was a serf.[1] There occasionally appear other suits where we can perceive that a rank-and-file freeman is winning against one who, whether his lord or not, is at any rate of much higher status. In 1195 one James the Clerk recovered against Geoffrey count of Perche.[2] In 1200 Philip and Emma of Stapelton recovered against the baron Herbert fitz Herbert.[3] In 1221 Welleniet of Barford and his wife recovered against the abbot of Bordesley.[4] There are other examples,[5] but perhaps it is enough to recall the assizes taken at Dunstable in the spring of 1224, where plaintiffs recovered in sixteen cases against Fawkes de Breauté, the most powerful man in that part of England, and where these judgments, far from being acceptable to Fawkes, provoked him to the violent insubordination against the king's government that brought on his ruin.[6] The cases that we can cite prove a great deal, for it is by chance occasion alone that the early records may happen to reveal a tenurial relationship between the parties, and usually by good historical fortune alone that we can ever know their relative social standings. There must be hundreds of other cases where tenants and other small men recovered against great lords. We have for it the witness of the Statute of Merton of 1236. Small freeholders in large manors,

---

[1] *Northants Pleas* no. 663 (1203), *CRR* iii. 140 (1204), *BNB* no. 1411 (1220), Appendix no. 8 (1219), *Eyres of Lincs and Worcs* no. 176 (1218–19), 1057 (1221), *BNB* no. 1918 (1227), J.I. 1/1245 m. 34 (1280). In two cases of 1227 plaintiffs recovered against the lady Roese of Brocton, who contended in defence, not that the plaintiffs were personally of servile status, but that the tenements in question were held of her in villeinage: *Eyre of Bucks 1227* nos. 187, 309.

[2] *PRS* xiv. 120–1.

[3] *Rotuli Curiae Regis* ii. 187.   [4] *Eyres of Glos, Warw, Staffs* no. 670.

[5] Thomas of Sotby *v.* Simon of Kyme, *Lincs Assize Rolls* no. 1456 (1206); Alexander of Menestok *v.* Henry of Bollei, *CRR* ii. 267 (1203), where the defendant was a baron; Sibyl of Calveton *v.* Thomas of Lascelles, *CRR* vi. 331–2 (1212), where Sibyl's damages were one shilling and Thomas's amercement £20; Henry of Burton *v.* William of Valoygnes, *CRR* vi. 335 (1212), where it was doubted whether the plaintiff was free or serf but where the defendant, upon conviction, was amerced 100 marks; Lisius the Hermit *v.* William of Forz count of Aumale, *CRR* xi. 4 (1223); John fitz William *v.* William of Warenne earl of Surrey, *BNB* no. 1243 (1238–9); Richard Reeve and his wife against the Hospitallers, J.I. 1/1245 m. 21 (1279), where the plaintiffs' son said that he was a serf of the Hospitallers; Ralph de la More *v.* Ralph fitz Richard, ibid. m. 55d (1281), where the plaintiff was married to one of the defendant's villeins; Hugh of Chadeleshunt and his wife *v.* the Hospitallers, ibid. m. 79 (1282).

[6] Powicke, *Henry III and the Lord Edward* i. 61–5; *Eyres of Beds* ix. 51–60.

the statute says, have been using the assize against their lords in a way which, while legally correct, is in substance unreasonable. If the lord attempts to bring under the plough or otherwise to 'approve' any part of the wasteland, woods, or pastures of the manor, the freeholders sue for disseisin of their rights of common of pasture in the area, and win their cases even though they have all the pasture that they rightly need left to them in other areas that the lord has not touched. Henceforth, ruled the statute, lords may approve their lands under such circumstances and the assize shall not prevent them.[1]

When tenants recovered against their lords and poor against rich, we must not assume that their victories always represented good justice, for the lowly may sometimes prevail wrongfully against the great. But since opportunity for defeating justice lay mostly with men of high degree, most of these recoveries must have been by good right. That the rights of the weak against the strong were uniformly or even ordinarily made good is of course more than we can say, but at least it is clear that the king's court could often provide justice in such cases and that very many poor freemen had cause to be glad of the assize.

The success of novel disseisin was mostly due to Henry II's good work, the sound general tradition of justice that he established in the king's court, and the speed, simplicity, and rationality which he built into this assize in particular. In Richard I's reign, however, one or two changes were made which may have added a great deal to the assize's popularity.

It may have been in the early years of this reign that the assize became available for the recovery of rents. If rent was withheld by one who ought to pay it, or if he paid it but to the wrong recipient, the man who was rightly entitled to receive it could sue for disseisin. Just when the assize began to be used for this kind of case is not clear. The earliest plea rolls that we have, those of 1194, tell of a suit for rent by the assize, and other cases appear from the years that follow,[2] so we might guess that the assize protected rents from its first foundation. But Glanvill, writing in the late 1180s, says nothing about suits for rent under the assize, and his silence is likely to be significant, for he care-

---

[1] SR i. 2–3.

[2] *Rotuli Curiae Regis* i. 71 (1194), *CRR* i. 123, 408 (1200), *Pleas 1198–1202* ii. 632 (1201), *CRR* iii. 55–6 (1203), 135 (1204), and numerous cases from all later times

fully shows how the basic form of the writ of novel disseisin was varied to fit the special cases that the assize handled, nuisance and disseisin of common of pasture. Probably, then, we are dealing with an innovation of the years 1187–94, and if that is so then it is tempting to assign it to the latter year and to see here another sign of the fertile genius of Hubert Walter.[1]

From later times when the evidence becomes fuller we can see the details of the law. The assize could be used either by a lord to enforce payment of rents owed him from his tenants or by anyone else who was entitled to rent.[2] But the rent must be charged on land or on some other definite tenement: the assize could not be used for 'chamber rents', charged simply on the payer's cash box.[3] Where the rent was withheld and the person entitled to receive it had a right of distraint, he must attempt a distraint before he could consider himself disseised and bring the assize. But if the tenant resisted and prevented him from making the distraint, or if he allowed him to make it and then 'rescued' the impounded cattle or got them released by bringing an action of replevin, that was disseisin enough; and of course

---

[1] Cheney, *Hubert Walter*, discusses the brilliant career of the archbishop-justiciar-chancellor. For his work in secular government see especially Chapter V, 'King's Minister'. He was appointed Chief Justiciar at the end of 1193.

[2] Examples of suits for 'rent service', due to the superior lord, are *CRR* iii. 135 (1204), *Eyres of Glos, Warw, Staffs* no. 1131 (1221), *BNB* no. 1239 (1238–9). 'Rent charge' or 'rent seck', due to someone other than the superior lord, is the subject of the assize in these examples: *CRR* vi. 395 (1212), *Eyres of Glos, Warw, Staffs* no. 602 (1221), *Somerset Pleas* i. 1488 (1254), J.I. 1/1217 m. 7 (1271), K.B. 27/81 m. 17d (1284). Most recorded cases of the thirteenth century do not reveal whether the plaintiff is the feudal lord. But in Edward I's reign the rule developed that a plaintiff who sued for rent 'out of his fee', i.e. rent from lands and tenements of which he was not the feudal lord, must show how the rent originated. Generally he proffered a deed by which the rent was constituted in his favour. After a period of hesitation around 1300, the courts decided to require the plaintiff to show such evidence if the defendant demanded it: C.P. 40/110 m. 239d (1295), 40/133 m. 75 (1300), MS. Y fos. 10–10ᵛ (c. 1300), C.P. 40/135 m. 260 (1301), 40/143 m. 129 (1302), Y.B. Pasch. 5 Ed. II no. 41 (1312), Mich. 7 Ed. II no. 20 (1313), *Eyre of London 1321* pp. 117–21, 229–35, Y.B. Mich. 17 Ed. II p. 509 (1323). The defendant could impose this demand, however, only if he was the tenant of the lands charged, not if he was a rival receiver of the rent: Y.B. 18 Ed. II p. 588 (1325). Later on, early in Edward III's reign, the courts required the show of special title *ex officio*, even if the defendant did not call for it: Y.B. Hil. 2 Ed. III no. 21 = 2 Ass. no. 4 (1328), Y.B. Hil. 3 Ed. III no. 19 (1329), Pasch. 7 Ed. III no. 26 (1333), Trin. 8 Ed. III no. 43 (1334), Mich. 13 Ed. III no. 24 (1339), 22 Ass. no. 68 (1348).

[3] Bracton fos. 180, 180b, *Eyre of Yorks 1218–19* no. 29, J.I. 1/1245 m. 77 (1282), Y.B. 18 Ed. II pp. 586–7 (1325), Pasch. 10 Ed. III no. 10 (1336), Pasch. 14 Ed. III no. 54 (1340).

the withholding of rent was an immediate disseisin where the receiver of the rent had no right of distraint.[1]

A second change in the working of the assize undoubtedly belongs to Richard I's reign, and specifically to the year 1198. In that year it was decided that at novel disseisin damages should be assessed in favour of every successful plaintiff.[2]

In the assize as originally designed the sheriff had been instructed in the writ to see to it that any chattels removed by the disseisor from the tenement were restored and that nothing else was taken away until the assize had been held, so that the plaintiff if he was successful would get back all his moveable goods along with the land. Glanvill also assured his readers that the sheriff would 'arrest' the profits that accrued from the tenement, to restore them too to the successful plaintiff.[3] Now in 1198 the award of damages was introduced, perhaps under the influence of Roman law,[4] as a substitute for this procedure.[5]

---

[1] Bracton fos. 169, 181, 203. The requirement that distraint be attempted is illustrated in these cases: *Eyre of Yorks 1218–19* no. 391, *BNB* nos. 1844, 1861 (1226–7), C.P. 40/17 m. 64d (1276). The requirement did not apply where the suit was against a rival receiver of the rent: *BNB* nos. 338 (1229), 1239 (1238–9). Any move that frustrated the power of distraint—even the invoking of legal process—was a disseisin: K.B. 26/205 m. 26 (1272), K.B. 27/16 m. 67d (1275), 27/129 m. 55d (1291), 27/156 m. 48 (1298), MS. Y fos. 7ᵛ, 10ʳ–10ᵛ, 26ʳ–26ᵛ, 34ᵛ–36ᵛ, 36ʳ (c. 1300). But if the receiver of rent had no right of distraint, the mere withholding was a disseisin in itself: Bracton, fo. 180, J.I. 1/1178 m. 1 d (1251), *Derby Assizes* p. 71 (1269), K.B. 27/81 m. 17d (1284).

In the thirteenth century novel disseisin for 'rent seck'—rent where the receiver had no power of distraint—was very rare, so much so that in 1302 counsel could plead that the assize lay only where there was a right of distraint, C.P. 40/143 m. 16. The argument was overruled, and the availability of the assize for rents seck was confirmed in another case of the same year, C.P. 40/143 m. 129, and afterwards in two cases of 1321, Y.B. 14 Ed. II pp. 409–10, *Eyre of London 1321* pp. 185–8. But some men thought that the assize was extended to protect rents seck not by the common law but by the Statute of Westminster II of 1285, which gave the assize 'de . . . proficuo capiendo . . . in certis locis' (c. 25): *Eyre of London 1321* pp. 185–8, Y.B. 18 Ed. II pp. 586–7 (1325), Pasch. 10 Ed. III no. 10 (1336). I doubt that this was true, for the words of the statute of 1285 do not seem to refer to rents. Gilbert of Thornton, who wrote his treatise shortly after the time of the statute and in whose writing the term 'rent seck' first appears, regarded such rents as freeholds protected by the assize but did not say that the statute had made them so: Lincoln's Inn Hale MS. 135 fo. 60, Harvard Law Library MS. 77 fo. 55ᵛ.

[2] Woodbine, *Yale Law Journal* xxxiii (1923–4), 806–7.

[3] Book XIII c. 38.   [4] Woodbine, op. cit., pp. 811–13.

[5] *Rotuli Curiae Regis* i. 451 (1199), defendant surrenders by licence, and promises to return to the plaintiff 'catalla sua inde capta'; *CRR* i. 411 (1201), damages are equated with 'saisina catallorum'; ii. 120 (1202), instead of an award of damages chattels are to be returned to the plaintiff; iii. 287 (1205), 'consideratum est quod

It must have been a considerable improvement. Although the original writ, which never changed its form, continued to tell the sheriff that he must restore to the tenement the chattels that were seized there and must keep them in peace, these words became a dead letter[1] and the sheriff was saved a good deal of trouble. The accused disseisor, who might after all be acquitted when the case came to trial, was left free to manage the holding without interference while the suit was pending. And for the successful plaintiff the award of damages gave a more complete remedy. He could get the value of the chattels which in the old way the sheriff would have brought back to the tenement,[2] and the value of the profits of the land.[3] But the assessment of damages could also cover much more: chattels consumed or destroyed or placed beyond the sheriff's reach;[4] harm done in the tenements, certainly that done by the disseisor himself and perhaps also any accidental loss suffered while he was in occupation;[5]

catalla restituantur per vicecomitem'. Cf. *CRR* xi. 607 (1223), where at this late date a judgment is given that the successful plaintiff recover the livestock taken with the land.

[1] Bracton fo. 179b.
[2] *CRR* v. 247–8 (1208), *Eyres of Glos, Warw, Staffs* no. 1165 (1221), *CRR* xiv. 249 (1230), 2377 (1232).
  The Statute of Gloucester of 1278 speaks as though damages customarily included only the profits of the land for the time when the disseisor held it, and not the value of chattels found in the tenements: *SR* i. 47. But this is contradicted by the Statute of Westminster I, c. 37 (1275), and by a number of cases from the same period: *Northumb Assize Rolls* pp. 147–8 (1269), K.B. 27/129 m. 56d (1291), 27/150 m. 37 (1297), MS. Y fos. 12ᵛ–13ʳ (1302). In the early fourteenth century the justices became concerned that plaintiffs who recovered damages in novel disseisin in respect of their chattels might sue again in Trespass and get damages a second time for the same goods, and it seems that this led them normally to exclude the value of chattels from the damages assessed at the assize: K.B. 27/162 m. 69 (1300), *Eyre of Kent* iii. 60–4 (1313), Y.B. Hil. 9 Ed. III no. 4 (1335). Still, there was no objection to giving damages for chattels if the record of the assize said explicitly that this was being done, for then the record would serve to bar the plaintiff from any second recovery at Trespass; and from later times there appear a good many records that duly specify damages for chattels. See, for example, J.I. 1/1543 m. 1d, 13, 39 (1431–9).
[3] *Pleas 1198–1202* ii. 632 (1201), *CRR* iii. 135 (1204), v. 258 (1208), *Pleas 1198–1212* iv. 4059 (1209), *Eyre of Yorks 1218–19* no. 108, *CRR* x. 35–6, 142 (1221), *Somerset Pleas* i. 1427 (1251).   [4] *CRR* iii. 287 (1205).
[5] *CRR* iii. 287 (1205) gave damages for destruction of garden, woods, and buildings. Bracton, fo. 187, says that the disseisor is liable for buildings accidentally burned; but the justices in Northumberland in 1269 were not sure: *Northumb Assize Rolls* pp. 147–8.
  If the disseisor had invested in the tenement and furthered husbandry, as by

loss from disruption of his husbandry;[1] and loss that resulted from nuisances or from disseisin of rights of common.[2] Eighty years later the Statute of Gloucester of 1278 also provided that the damages should cover the expenses that the plaintiff incurred in bringing his suit.[3]

In the first part of Henry III's reign a third improvement was introduced, less important than the other two but still worth while. It had always been customary for men who were called away from their homes in the king's service, particularly those who were sent abroad, to be given 'protection' from lawsuits during their absence, so that actions brought against them had to stand over until their return. These protections usually took the form of royal letters close, directed to the justices, instructing them to give the beneficiary 'respite' from pleas of all kinds, including assizes of novel disseisin.[4] But in 1229 the standard form of letter close was changed to provide that the respite given against suits in general should not cover actions of novel disseisin, darrein presentment, or Dower *unde nihil habet*: actions of those types were to proceed regardless of the protection.[5] For some years after that, in the 1230s, it was still possible to obtain postponement even of these privileged cases by purchasing not the usual letter close but a letter patent with the clause *volumus*: 'We wish, furthermore, and command that he and all his demesnes be quit in the meantime of suits to shires and hundreds and of all pleas and plaints except the pleas of the crown.' This special clause had been invented in 1223.[6] But the government

planting a new crop with his own seed, the value of these 'ameliorations' could be set off against the damages, sometimes even to the point of reducing the damages to nothing. See, for example, *Northants Pleas* no. 816 (1203), *BNB* no. 1281 (1239–40).

[1] *CRR* iii. 287 (1205), damages for delaying the plaintiff's planting.

[2] Cases are very frequent in all periods. For an early example, see *Pleas 1198–1202* ii. 85, 93 (1198).

[3] *SR* i. 47.

[4] e.g. *Rotuli Curiae Regis* i. 306–7 (*tempore* Ric. I), 325 (1199), ii. 246 (1200), *CRR* v. 1 (1207), *Somerset Pleas* i. 294 and cf. *Rotuli Litterarum Clausarum* ii. 79 (1225), *CRR* xii. 1022 and cf. *Rotuli Litterarum Clausarum* ii. 64 (1225), *Close Rolls 1227–1231* pp. 146, 157, 190, 198 (Jan.–July 1229).

[5] *Close Rolls 1227–1231* pp. 255 (Oct. 1229), 266 (Nov. 1229), 322, 329–30 (1230), *CRR* xiv. 4 (1230), *Calendar of Patent Rolls 1232–1247* p. 64 (1234). When the king departed on his Breton expedition in 1230 he granted that during his absence his lieutenants in England might appoint justices to deliver gaols and 'to hold assizes of novel disseisin and darrein presentment and to hold other assizes against defendants who have not gone abroad with us'. *Patent Rolls 1225–1232* pp. 340–1.

[6] *Patent Rolls 1216–1225* pp. 386, 407.

could not long maintain one law for letters close and another for letters patent. In 1235 the *volumus*-clause included in one letter patent specified that no respite was to be given in assizes of novel disseisin,[1] and in 1242 the *volumus*-clause was permanently reworded to bring it into line with the rule of letters close: 'We wish, furthermore, that he be quit of suit to shires and hundreds and of all pleas and plaints except novel disseisin, darrein presentment, and Dower *unde nihil habet*.'[2] The list of pleas excepted, against which no protection was to be given, varied somewhat in later times,[3] but always included novel disseisin until 1421, when an act of parliament allowed protection to be granted against the assize.[4]

All these changes were valuable reforms, which as they were introduced must have worked to make the assize more popular than ever. In turn, its growing popularity worked some changes in the assize. Growing popularity accounts, in the first place, for the fact that the period of limitation became longer and longer. The several limitations established from time to time are shown, as far as we know them, in the following table. The first column

	Assize limited to	Limit set	Approximate length of time allowed
1.	May 1175	January 1176	8 months–?
2.	April 1185? February 1187? } July 1188?	in force *c.* 1188	6 months?–2 years?
3.	September 1189	before October 1194	?–8½ years
4.	April 1194	early 1198	4 years–5 years
5.	September 1198	June 1199	8 months–3½ years
6.	March 1201	spring 1202	1–18 years
7.	August 1210	autumn 1218	8–18 years
8.	May 1220	January 1229	9–17 years
9.	May 1230	June 1237	7–46 years
10.	May 1242	June 1276	34–304 years
11.	the past 30 years	1546	30 years[5]

[1] *Calendar of Patent Rolls 1232–1247* pp. 120, 147.

[2] Ibid., p. 276; *Rôles Gascons* i. 78.

[3] Bracton, fo. 339b–340, lists darrein presentment, 'causa dotis', mort d'ancestor 'secundum quosdam', novel disseisin, and all assizes that can be taken by the defendant's default. *Registrum Brevium*, fo. 22b, excepts Dower *unde nihil habet*, *quare impedit*, novel disseisin, darrein presentment, attaints, and pleas summoned before justices itinerant.

[4] 9 Henry V stat. I c. 3. The act was renewed by 4 Henry VI c. 2 (1426) and 8 Henry VI c. 13 (1429); cf. 14 Ed. IV c. 2 (1474–5).   [5] See note C, p. 215.

gives the limit-date itself, the second column the time when that limit was first imposed, and the third column the length of time that was thus allowed for bringing the action while the limit in column one was in force.

The most significant change appears to come in the 1210s, when the existing limitation to March 1201 (no. 6 in the table) was left in force, unchanged, until it represented an allowance of nearly eighteen years. When the date was finally moved up again as shown in no. 7 it was advanced only to 1210, allowing eight years where previous limitations when first imposed had usually left only a year or so. Now it is possible that the lengthening of the limit in the 1210s is a symptom of the unusual political and administrative problems of that decade rather than a sign of any change in men's thinking about the assize. After the spring of 1209 no regular eyres were held for nearly ten years, the Common Bench was in abeyance for most of the same period,[1] civil war troubled the land from 1215 to 1217, and would-be litigants hardly had a fair opportunity to bring their suits. It may have seemed unreasonable to move up the date of limitation under such circumstances. When the land was settled again and the limitation could be advanced, at the end of 1218, the government may have reflected that it would take several years to catch up with all the pleas not pleaded and all the wrongs not righted from the 1210s, and may on this account have made the unprecedented allowance of eight years in setting the new limit at August 1210. But however that may be, a change in attitude toward the assize itself had clearly come about by the 1220s. In this decade of peace and firm government the limit at August 1210 was allowed to stand until 1229 when it was almost eighteen years old, and was then advanced only to May 1220, leaving nine years. Later limitations only accentuated the new policy.

'The action is showing itself to be useful'[2]—surely that is the explanation of the new and longer limits, as Maitland suggested. Men wanted the kind of justice afforded by the assize to be more generally available, to those who waited or delayed in negotiations as well as for those who betook themselves straightway to

---

[1] Doris Stenton, *English Justice*, pp. 101–13; Flower, *Introduction to the Curia Regis Rolls*, pp. 19–20; *Eyres of Lincs and Worcs* pp. xxxvi–xxxvii.

[2] P. & M. ii. 51.

the law. In turn, of course, the relaxing of the limitation contri-
buted to the increase in the number of assizes that were brought.
Around 1200 it must have made a real difference to the relative
numbers of cases that the limitation in novel disseisin was fixed
ordinarily at about one to three years back, while nearly fifty
years were allowed in mort d'ancestor.[1] About 1230, when ten
years or so were allowed in novel disseisin and some forty years
in mort d'ancestor, the difference was less significant, because
most suits in either form would be brought within ten years in
any case.

As long as the limitation in novel disseisin remained very
short the old rule seemed reasonable that a plaintiff by suing
his disseisor alone could recover the tenements out of the hand
of any third party to whom they might have passed since the
disseisin.[2] With longer limitations this became unfair, for the
third party who was holding the land might have come in years
after the disseisin and held in good peace for a long time before
the assize was brought. Hence about 1212, just when the limitation was being allowed to grow longer than it had ever been
before, the classical rule of 'tenant and disseisor' was developed.
If when a plaintiff purchased his writ of novel disseisin the
current tenant of the land was someone other than the original
disseisor, then, ran the new rule, both the disseisor and
the tenant must be joined as co-defendants. Without naming the
disseisor as a defendant the plaintiff could not succeed, for the
assize was an action against disseisin; without naming the tenant
as a defendant the plaintiff could not recover the tenements, for
no tenant might be put out of his holdings by judgment in a suit
to which he was not a party.[3]

---

[1] Flower, *Introduction to the Curia Regis Rolls*, pp. 147–8.   [2] Above, pp. 18–19.

[3] Bracton states the rule, fos. 175b–176b. The requirement that the tenant be
named as a defendant first appears in these cases: *CRR* vi. 324 (1212), vii. 7 (1213),
63 (1214), *Eyres of Glos, Warw, Staffs* no. 404 and cf. nos. 406, 1044 (1221), *BNB*
no. 1972 (1221), 894 (1224).

Bracton observed, basing himself partly on *BNB* no. 617 (1231), that the innocent
tenant who had come to the lands some time after the disseisin should be distinguished from the tenant who, though he had not himself participated in the act of
disseisin, had taken over the lands so soon thereafter, while the offence was still
flagrant, that he must be held to share its guilt (fo. 164, 171, 175b). The innocent
tenant could lose his lands by the assize just as readily as the guilty, but he would
not suffer personal penalties for disseisin. The law continued to observe this distinction: J. I. 1/492 m. 50 (1282), MS. Y fo. 11ᵛ–12ʳ (c. 1300, two cases), B. M.
Egerton MS. 2811 fos. 345ʳ–345ᵛ (1330).

The form of the original writ was never adapted, however, to make any room for a defendant who was named simply because he was tenant and not because he was supposed to be guilty of disseisin. The only way the plaintiff could join the innocent tenant as a co-defendant was to purchase a writ in which he 'complained' that the tenant as well as the actual disseisor had 'wrongfully and without a judgment disseised him'.[1] From this there followed two curious corollaries. In arguing his case the plaintiff must never openly admit that any of the defendants was not guilty of disseisin, for he had formally brought the accusation against them all. And if it turned out in the trial that one or more of the defendants were innocent tenants, even though the plaintiff won his case and recovered his land still he must be amerced for falsely accusing those persons. These two rules were so idiosyncratic that the justices occasionally disregarded them, but on the whole they were maintained.[2] Probably it was felt that they were needed to preserve the logic of the law. The rules that made novel disseisin such an expeditious action—the procedure by default, the exclusion of vouchers to warranty, and the rest—were justified on the ground that the charge was of disseisin, a direct and personal offence for which every one of the defendants must answer directly for himself and at once. If the plaintiff should admit that some of the defendants were no disseisors, he would destroy the basis of this reasoning. So his writ and everything that he said must accuse all the defendants of disseisin; and then if some of them were found innocent of course the plaintiff had to pay the penalty of amercement that fell on everyone who brought any false charge. In another age such sophistry might have been un-

---

[1] See the form of the writ, above, pp. 14–15.

[2] The plaintiff must not admit that any of the defendants is innocent: K.B. 26/191 m. 7d (1270), K.B. 27/81 m. 2 (1284), Y.B. Hil. 8 Ed. III no. 22 (1334), Trin. 11 Ed. III pp. 121–2 (1337), 46 Ass. no. 10 (1372). Exceptions to the rule: *Somerset Pleas* i. 342 (1225), 1427 (1251), K.B. 27/128 m. 19d (1291).

The successful plaintiff is amerced for a 'false plaint' against the innocent tenant in hundreds of records, e.g. *Eyres of Lincs and Worcs* no. 953 (1221), *BNB* nos. 1890 (1227), 617 = *CRR* xiv. 1896 (1231), 1153 (1235–6), K.B. 26/131 m. 20d (1244), *Somerset Pleas* i. 1427 (1251), K.B. 26/181 m. 17d (1267), K.B. 27/16 m. 70 (1275), *Sel. Cases in K.B.* ii. 17 (1290), C.P. 40/139 m. 50 (1301), *Eyre of Kent* iii. 65–73 (1313), Y.B. Mich. 7 Ed. III no. 55 (1333). Exceptions to the rule appear, for example, in *CRR* iv. 201 (1206), *Eyres of Glos, Warw, Staffs* no. 406 (1221), K.B. 26/121 m. 7(2) (1240), 26/185 m. 23 (1268), K.B. 27/81 m. 26d (1284), C.P. 40/139 m. 154 (1301).

acceptable, but thirteenth-century plaintiffs were long-suffering folk.

Provided that the plaintiff named both the tenant and the disseisor as defendants, he could recover on any illegal disseisin committed against him within the lengthening limitation period. It would not stop him even if the disseisor had conveyed the lands to the tenant by means of a final concord in the king's court. Generally speaking, a final concord would set running a short term—a year, as it seems usually to have been, although Henry of Bracton said that only two weeks were allowed—within which any third parties who had adverse claims must assert them or else lose their rights for ever.[1] But in 1224 it was decided that this 'preclusive bar' raised by a final concord should not apply in actions of novel disseisin brought by third parties, and that decision was generally adhered to for the rest of the Middle Ages.[2]

The popularity of the assize explains the lengthening of the limitation-time and the doctrinal consequences which that development brought in its wake. It also accounts for the fact that in the thirteenth century novel disseisin resisted the prevalent tendency toward centralization of the work of the king's court.

In organizing and increasing the business of the king's court as he did, Henry II had arranged that most cases should be heard in their counties before his itinerant justices. A minority, including cases of unusual importance or difficulty, would be brought before the king himself with the justices whom he chose to assist him—the King's Bench of later times—or before the permanent central court at Westminster, the Exchequer, out of which in time developed the Common Bench.[3] This pattern of

---

[1] P. & M. ii. 101–2.

[2] For the decision, see *BNB* no. 1012 = *CRR* xi. 1664 (1224). For later doctrine, see Bracton fo. 437, MS. Y fos. 10ᵛ (*c.* 1300), 35ʳ (1307–8), and Y.B. Hil. 10 Ed. III no. 7 (1336). In 1360 a statute (34 Ed. III c. 16) wholly abolished the preclusive bar against third parties. But in 1290 the King's Bench barred an assize brought by a third party, K.B. 27/125 m. 81, and in a case of 1384 it was assumed that a fine made before the statute would raise a bar against third-party suits, even suits by the assize: Lincoln's Inn Hale MS. 77 fo. 220b. When the preclusive bar was re-established in a different form by legislation of 1483 and 1489 (1 Ric. III c. 7, 4 Henry VII c. 24), it was good against suits by novel disseisin as against all others.

[3] For the origins of the Common Bench (Common Pleas), see Richardson and Sayles, *Governance*, pp. 210–12.

judicature applied to novel disseisin as well as to other kinds of business, as can be seen from the earliest plea rolls of the years around 1200.[1]

During the thirteenth century, business flowed increasingly away from the itinerant justices, out of their sessions in the counties, and into the Common Bench, making that court eventually the ordinary place for civil litigation for the whole kingdom.[2] But as for novel disseisin, the direction of development was just the opposite. Already in King John's reign a strong body of opinion developed which considered it grievous that these actions should *ever* be brought outside their counties before the king or the Common Bench. Thus, when the Common Bench and the eyres of the itinerant justices ceased to be held in 1209, in the case of the general run of civil litigation the Common Bench was missed and King John had to promise in Magna Carta that he would restore this 'fixed place', but in the case of novel disseisin, and of the assizes of mort d'ancestor and darrein presentment, it was only the absence of the eyres enabling these cases to be heard in their counties that was resented. The rebels who wrung Magna Carta from the king insisted on the provision that

Recognitions of novel disseisin, mort d'ancestor, and darrein presentment shall not be taken except in their counties, and in this manner. We or, if we are out of the kingdom, our chief justiciar, will send two justices to each county four times a year. Together with four knights of the county chosen by the county court they shall take the assizes on the day and in the place where the county court is held. If the assizes cannot be taken on the day of the county court, enough of the knights and freeholders who come to the county court shall remain so that those cases may be properly disposed of, whether the business is great or small.[3]

This provision was simply repeated in the Magna Carta of

---

[1] In Trinity term 1194 the court at Westminster presided over by the Chief Justiciar handled three assizes of novel disseisin and received appointments of attorneys in two others: *PRS* xiv. 1–59. In the following Michaelmas term it heard twenty cases, *Rotuli Curiae Regis* i. 1–137. But during that Michaelmas term the justices in eyre heard twenty cases in the county of Wiltshire alone, *PRS* xiv. 65–77, and presumably handled scores of others in the other counties that were being visited about that same time. Assizes were common enough in the central courts, but most of them were brought in eyre.

[2] The development is summarized by Milsom, *Historical Foundations*, pp. 15–22.

[3] cc. 18–19.

1216. The second reissue of the Charter, in 1217, made a good many changes, and all of these were followed in the definitive version of 1225. Only one visit a year was promised for each county, not four, and the regency government, more sophisticated than the rebels of 1215, provided for adjourning difficult cases out of their counties so that they could be resolved by the itinerant justices as they went on to visit neighbouring counties or by the justices of the Common Bench. Assizes of darrein presentment were always to be held in the Bench. But for novel disseisin and for mort d'ancestor the basic rule was kept, that these assizes should be taken only in their counties.[1]

At first the rule does not seem to have been strictly obeyed, for the records of the Bench for the 1220s show a good many assizes of mort d'ancestor and some of novel disseisin, that appear to have begun there, outside their counties.[2] But in general the rule was followed, and by the later thirteenth century it was scrupulously observed.[3]

From the 1220s, then, cases of novel disseisin almost always received their initial hearings in the county. Most of them were ended there as well, without ever being adjourned outside.[4] The hearings might be held in the King's Bench as it visited one

---

[1] Magna Carta 1217 cc. 13–15; Magna Carta 1225 c. 12.

[2] The following cases, for example, were begun in the Bench in apparent violation of Magna Carta: *CRR* viii. 8–9, 36, 39, 178 (1219), 192–3, 258, 334–5 (1220), ix. 190–1 (1220), x. 317–18 (1222), xi. 1825, 1830 (1224), xii. 1022 (1225), xiii. 80 (1227), 388, 720 (1228), xiv. 249, 854 (1230). It is possible that they may have originated before justices of assize or in eyre and been adjourned to the Bench, but there is nothing in their records to indicate this.

In 1230 the justices of the Bench began admitting Middlesex assizes, since the court sat at Westminster in that county and so a hearing in the Bench did not remove those cases from their county; *CRR* xiv. 1024 (1230) is an early example. Later in the century Middlesex assizes were brought in the Bench as a matter of routine, and this was prescribed as regular practice in the *statutum de justiciariis assignatis* of 1293, *SR* i. 112.

[3] K.B. 27/121 m. 37 (1289), *Early Registers of Writs* p. 260, *Registrum Brevium* fo. 198b.

[4] The rule of the later versions of Magna Carta, that difficult cases might be adjourned to other counties or to the Bench, was interpreted to allow the recognition itself to be taken outside the county in such cases: Bracton fo. 105b, and these cases, for example, *Eyres of Lincs and Worcs* nos. 439, 732 (1219), *Eyres of Glos, Warw, Staffs* no. 233 (1221), 1451 (1222), *CRR* xi. 2002 (1224), *Somerset Pleas* i. 294 (1225), *CRR* xii. 1019, 1022, 1145 (1225), 1613 (1226), xiii. 782 (1228), 1855 (1229). Certifications and attaints (for which see below, pp. 74–6) could also be brought in the central courts: Bracton fo. 105b, *CRR* viii. 75 (1219), xii. 1723 (1226), xiii. 1001, 1198 (1228), K.B. 26/146 m. 5 (1252), 26/152 m. 11d (1254).

county after another in its travels,[1] and of course the justices who held general eyres handled these pleas as they had since 1166. Special justices were also sent out from time to time with more limited commissions to take assizes of novel disseisin and mort d'ancestor and perhaps to do some other particular business such as delivering the local gaols. These limited commissions might be given to two regular king's justices, or they might appoint a single regular justice who was instructed to choose local gentlemen to sit with him as his colleagues in each county that he visited.[2] As general eyres became less and less frequent in the thirteenth century these limited commissions came to be the typical means of holding assizes.

But for a time a great deal of work was also done under commissions issued to local gentlemen alone, without any colleagues from Westminster; in the years from 1220 to 1240 most of the assizes that were heard outside general eyres were heard before these amateur justices.[3] It was not very clear whether they possessed the quality of justices holding the king's court. If there was complaint in the Bench about their proceedings they might be summoned as defendants, like the suitors of a feudal or local court that was accused of false judgment, and on one occasion at least some of them may formally have been convicted of false judgment.[4] But any two such justices acting together (as they were always supposed to do) possessed the prerogative characteristic of the king's court, of bearing an incontrovertible record.[5]

Decentralization could be carried just a little further. Under

---

[1] e.g. *Calendar of Patent Rolls 1232–1247* p. 127 (1235). In Edward I's reign, if not before, the Court of the Verge would hear by simple plaint cases of disseisin committed during the king's current stay in the county, C.P. 40/89 m. 131. This was prohibited, however, by the *Articuli super cartas* of 1300, *SR* i. 138.

[2] So the later versions of Magna Carta (above, p. 61 n. 1), had provided, 'mittemus iusticiarios . . . qui *cum militibus comitatuum* capiant in comitatibus assisas'.

[3] *History of Wiltshire* v. 18–20, *Wilts Crown Pleas 1249* pp. 4–5, Bracton fo. 182.

[4] *BNB* no. 530 (1231): the record said: 'ad iudicium de iusticiariis et iuratoribus', and the annotator commented, 'iuratores . . . convicti de periurio et iusticiarii de [falso] iudicio, quia falsum sacramentum et falsum iudicium'. Justices were summoned as defendants in the following cases, for example: *CRR* xi. 1459, 2633 = *BNB* no. 917 (1224), xii. 655 (1225), xiii. 559 (1228), xiv. 207, 211 (1230). Cf. P. & M. ii. 668.

[5] *CRR* xiii. 508 (1228), *BNB* no. 1285 (1239–40). It was a reversible error, when two or more justices were commissioned jointly, for one of them to take the assize alone: K.B. 26/174 m. 7d, 17 (1265).

the 'little writ of novel disseisin' sheriffs could hear and determine actions of nuisance, including charges of interference with
common rights in pasture, estovers, and fishponds.[1] In fact,
from some time early in the thirteenth century certain kinds of
nuisances were left entirely to them, being excluded from the
king's court: these were nuisances created by building a new
house, wall, mill, sheepfold, cowbarn, gate, weir, or oven, by
planting an orchard, by enlarging a courtyard or the garden
surrounding a house, or by other operations of comparable scale.
In particular, if any such works took over a bit of land where
tenants or neighbours had enjoyed common rights, the offence
was to be understood as a nuisance and not as a disseisin of
common, and was to be handled by the sheriff not by the king's
court. Only four kinds of nuisances were heard in assizes before
the king's justices, namely those that resulted from constructing
millponds, raising banks or planting hedges, obstructing rights
of way, and diverting watercourses.[2] These rules figured, no
doubt, as part of the effort to control the rush of business into
the king's court; but from another point of view they represent
a spreading out to local jurisdictions of the justice available
under the assize, which was so much in demand.

In some outlying parts of the kingdom the sheriffs were
further allowed, perhaps from about the middle of the thirteenth
century, to hold actions of novel disseisin of all types, for lands
and other tenements as well as for nuisances. Like assizes of
novel disseisin held in borough courts,[3] these actions before the
sheriff were called 'pleas of fresh force'. Even in a county as
remote as Northumberland the assize could thus be made
available quickly and cheaply.[4]

In 1236 the Statute of Merton entrusted to the sheriffs a new
jurisdiction over 'redisseisin'.[5] If a man recovered freehold by
judgment in the king's court and was later unlawfully disseised

---

[1] Bracton fo. 233, 'Fet Asaver' p. 105, *Early Registers of Writs* pp. 32, 85, 261, *BNB*
no. 469 = *CRR* xiv. 854 (1230).

[2] See Note D, p. 216.

[3] P. & M. i. 644.

[4] See Morris, *The Early English County Court* p. 120. The sheriff's pleas of fresh
force in Northumberland had been arrented in the Exchequer in the time of Henry
of Bath and William Heyrun: *Calendar of Inquisitions Miscellaneous* i. 380–1. William
Heyrun was sheriff of the county from 1246 to 1258, *Lists and Indexes* ix. 97.

[5] *SR* i. 2. The details of procedure were worked out after the announcement of
policy in the statute itself.

of the same tenements by the same adversary, a writ from Chancery would direct the sheriff to take the coroners and some other good knights of the county and go in person to the tenements. There, without even troubling to summon or attach the defendant, he should hold an inquest, calling as jurors both recognitors of the original action and others. If the inquest bore out the charge, the plaintiff should again be restored to the holdings and the defendant gaoled until he ransomed himself at the king's pleasure. Before 1236 cases of this sort had been handled in the Common Bench upon writs of *Quare intrusit*.[1] But to disseise a man after he had recovered against you by judgment of the king's court showed contempt of the king as well as of the law. A quicker remedy should be available to the offended party and a heavier penalty should be laid against the offender, and hence the new action of redisseisin. It continued permanently in use and kept all its original stringency.[2]

Henry of Bracton's careful account[3] together with the thousands of cases recorded in the plea rolls show in detail how the assize worked in and about the first half of the thirteenth century. The plaintiff began by going to Chancery and purchasing his original writ. If the disseisin had been committed during a general eyre in the county, the justices in eyre could

---

[1] e.g. *CRR* xiii. 2241 and 2704, 2242, xiv. 235. Cf. *CRR* xiv. 1677 = *BNB* no. 583.

[2] Bracton fo. 236b, Statute of Westminster II (1285) cc. 8, 26. The Statute of Marlborough of 1267 provided that men held in prison for redisseisin must make fine 'with the king' and be released 'by his special command' and not otherwise. *Registrum Brevium* fo. 222b–223 shows that later on the sheriff was sometimes directed to fix the fine in individual cases, but FNB 422–3 says that fine must be made in the King's Bench. Actions of redisseisin had to be heard by the sheriff in person, in the presence of two coroners, at the tenements in question and not elsewhere (since there had been no 'view'), and by a majority at least of the surviving recognitors in the original action: K.B. 27/156 m. 30–31 (1298), 27/160 m. 7d (1299), 27/163 m. 53 (1301). Even so, the proceedings could be very rapid. In 1297 one plaintiff obtained his original writ on 5 May and recovered by judgment of the sheriff on 22 May, K.B. 27/156 m. 30–1. In 1300 a writ was issued at Dumfries on 16 July and the sheriff held the consequent inquest in Hertfordshire, on 5 Sept., K.B. 27/163 m. 53. A writ of 20 Nov. 1428 brought an inquest, with recovery for the plaintiff, on 3 Mar. 1429, K.B. 27/714 m. 80. If the defendant disseised the plaintiff yet again, after he recovered in Redisseisin, the sheriff should seize and hold land of the defendant's up to the value of the tenements he had taken, K.B. 26/200B m. 5 (1270). In the fourteenth century the action of redisseisin did not lie if the tenements had been granted over to an innocent party since the commission of the offence, Y.B. Hil. 13 Ed. III no. 12 (1339).

[3] fos. 161–237b.

issue the original writ themselves, saving the offended party a trip to Chancery.[1] Having secured his writ, the plaintiff then found security for prosecuting. This took the form of two pledges, men who offered themselves to be subject to amercement along with the plaintiff if the plaintiff did not follow through with his prosecution of the case. It was necessary for Bracton to observe that the pledges should not be penalized if the plaintiff fought the case to the end but lost, for there the prosecution was complete even though unsuccessful.[2] The pledges were generally nominated before the sheriff, who reported their names to the court. As in other kinds of actions, plaintiffs who were poor were excused finding security for prosecution and allowed to proceed upon merely giving their promise—the *affidavit*—to see the case through. As soon as the pledges or *affidavit* had been given, the sheriff instructed his bailiff to empanel the recognitors.

This was done with some formality. The plaintiff and defendant were invited to be present if they wished and they might offer challenges for cause against proposed jurors; in a preliminary way, the veniremen were 'tried and elected'.[3] Those thus chosen might be just twelve in number; but because some veniremen might essoin themselves on the day in court and because further challenges before the justices might remove some, more than twelve were often named—occasionally as

[1] Bracton fo. 236b. This practice is constantly attested from 1202 to 1329, e.g. *Northants Pleas* no. 422, 592 (1202), *Eyre of Yorks 1218–19* no. 188, 413, *BNB* no. 1837 (1227), *Somerset Pleas* i. 607 (1242–3), *Eyre of Kent* i. 158 (1313), *Eyre of London 1321* i, pp. lxxxvii, xcviii, John Rylands Library Latin MS. 180 fo. 2ᵛ (1329). On rare occasions the justices may even have proceeded without a writ: *Procedure w/o Writ*, p. xcviii. Strictly speaking, the procedure without a writ from the Chancery was available for any disseisin done 'within the summons', that is, after the proclamation that the eyre was to be held in the county.

[2] fos. 179–179b, 185b. Cf. C.P. 40/105 m. 8d, a case of 1294.

[3] Bracton fo. 179b. In a case of 1204 the veniremen are described as 'elected before the sheriff', *CRR* iii. 247. The procedure of election is described in detail in a case of 1219, *Eyres of Lincs and Worcs* no. 365, and cf. *CRR* xiv. 1511 (1231). By the mid fourteenth century practice had changed, for a statute of 1368 specified only that the sheriff must let the parties know who the veniremen were, if they asked for this information: 42 Ed. III c. 11, *SR* i. 390–1.

It must have been natural to have the bailiff of the hundred in which the disputed tenements lay hold the election, for some at least of the recognitors had, as appears from later evidence, to come from that hundred: Y.B. Trin. 10 Ed. III no. 3 (1336), Mich. 13 Ed. III no. 54 (1339), B.M. Add. MS. 34783 fo. 20 (1376), Lincoln's Inn Hale MS. 77 fo. 221 (1384), Y.B. Mich. 48 Ed. III no. 17 (1374).

many as twenty-four.[1] Those who were empanelled were
assigned their day in court and sent in the meantime to make a
view, as the writ prescribed: in the presence of the defendant or
his bailiff if he wished to be there, the plaintiff should point out
to the prospective jurors the lands from which he claimed to
have been wrongfully ejected, the nuisance which had been
raised against him and his own freehold tenements which were
thereby troubled, or the lands where he had been shut out of
his rights of common and his freehold tenements to which the
right belonged. This 'viewing' must not be overlooked; the
majority at least of all those who were eventually to be sworn
of the assize must be there.[2]

While all this was going on the sheriff, ordinarily acting
through one of his bailiffs, would attach either the defendant or,
if he could not find him, his bailiff. The attachment was the
counterpart of the plaintiff's giving pledges to prosecute: the
defendant or his bailiff was required to furnish two pledges that
he would appear in court on the day assigned for the case, and
if he did not come he and his pledges would each be amerced.
If the sheriff could not find anyone to attach, he reported that
fact to the justices.[3]

On the day set for appearance in court the plaintiff could

---

[1] Bracton, fo. 179b, speaks of the election of twelve veniremen only, and so the
matter was commonly handled: e.g. *Pleas 1198–1202* i. 3514, *Rotuli Curiae Regis* i.
416 (1199), *CRR* vi. 192 (1212), vii. 26 (1213). In a case of 1200, fifteen veniremen
were called, *Rotuli Curiae Regis* ii. 241–2; in two cases of 1206, twenty and nineteen,
CRR iv. 90, 162; in a case of 1278, fourteen, K.B. 27/45 m. 6. Larger panels seem
to have been required in later times. In 1322 Justice Spigurnel told a sheriff that
he should always empanel twenty-four men, Y.B. Trin. 15 Ed. II p. 467, and the
same instructions were given a century later, in 1428, by Justices Babington and
Fulthorpe to the sheriff of Yorkshire, J.I. 1/1542 m. 1.

[2] Bracton fos. 179b–182. Assizes were postponed if it was discovered that the
recognitors had not made a view, e.g. *Rotuli Curiae Regis* i. 35–6 (1194), *CRR* iii.
279 (1205), *BNB* no. 1192 (1236–7), *Somerset Pleas* i. 1468 (c. 1253). The plaintiff
pointed out the tenements, as appears in *CRR* iv. 156 (1206). From Bracton fo.
179b, *Yorks Assize Rolls* pp. 82 (1251), 123–5 (1260), and J.I. 1/1182 m. 9d (1255–
6) it appears that not all the recognitors needed to have made a view but only a
majority of them. The view never became a fiction: Y.B. Pasch. 24 Ed. III nos.
16, 37 (1350), Mich. 15 Henry VII no. 8 (1499).

[3] Bracton fo. 182. If the defendant or his bailiff was attached and did not come,
he and his pledges were in mercy even though someone else might appear to speak
for the defence: *Pleas 1198–1212* iv. 4288, 4295 (1209), *Eyres of Lincs and Worcs* nos.
73, 74, 172 (1219), K.B. 27/20A m. 20 (1276), *Sel. Cases in K.B.* iii. 15 (1287). The
defendant or his bailiff might be distrained to force him to furnish pledges if he
would not do it willingly, *CRR* v. 248 (1208).

essoin himself if he wished and the case would be continued.[1]
Since plaintiffs normally wanted their suits to proceed as fast
as possible, this was not very often done. If the plaintiff defaulted, he lost his case immediately.[2] But as in the original
constitution of the assize, the defendant on his side was allowed
to create no delay. He was not entitled to the usual two weeks'
advance notice of the proceedings against him.[3] If he did not
appear and no one came as his bailiff, the case would proceed
by default, and this regardless of whether the sheriff had succeeded in making an attachment.[4] It was common for the assize
to be taken by default. But the recognitors, if not the defendant,
could cause unwanted postponements by essoining themselves
or by defaulting. If so many of them did this that it proved
impossible on the first day to swear the required number of
acceptable jurors who had duly made the view in advance, the
case had to be put off.[5] The court would nevertheless proceed on
that day as far as it could go without calling for a verdict from
the assize.[6]

Now it might seem that what it could do without calling for
a verdict would amount to very little and that in ordinary cases
the justices had nothing to do but 'take the assize'—hold the
trial and receive the verdict—as soon as the jurors could be
brought in and sworn. The original writ warned that the jurors
should be prepared to render their verdict when they first came

[1] Bracton fo. 340b.   [2] Bracton fo. 182–182b.
[3] Bracton fo. 366. But by 1382 this rule was changed and the attachment had
to be made a fortnight before the court day: Lincoln's Inn Hale MS. 77 fo. 185b
(1382), J.I. 1/1542 m. 1 (1428).
[4] Bracton fo. 183–183b, *Rotuli Curiae Regis* ii. 167 (1181–1200), *Pleas 1198–1212*
iv. 4051 (1209), K.B. 26/158 m. 18 (1258), 26/189 m. 17 (1269). But the proceedings of the assize could be quashed if it was afterwards shown that the sheriff failed
to attach the defendant or his bailiff when he might have done so: *CRR* i. 456
(1201), 'Annals of Dunstable' *sub anno 1289*, K.B. 27/138 m. 44d (1293), Y.B. Trin.
19 Ed. III no. 52 (1345).
[5] Twelve jurors was the normal but not invariable number. Bracton, fos. 179b,
255b, says that the assize must never consist of less than seven, but that more than
twelve may sometimes be sworn for good reason. Cases appear in which the assize
was taken by seven (*CRR* ix. 265–6 (1220)), eight (*Northants Pleas* no. 865 (1203),
Eyres of Glos, Warw, Staffs no. 177 (1221)), eleven (K.B. 27/98 m. 10d (1286)), and
thirteen (*CRR* xiii. 2153 (1229)). Certifications (for which see below, pp. 74–6) can
be found taken by eight (K.B. 26/131 m. 20d (1244), 26/167 m. 17d (1260)), and
by ten (*CRR* xiii. 1986 (1229)).
[6] Bracton fos. 184b–185, *Rotuli Curiae Regis* ii. 19–20 (1199), *CRR* ii. 254 (1203),
v. 130 (1208).

into court, and a great many records of individual cases read as
though that was just what they did, without any forensic pre-
liminaries. Arguments and evidences that the parties wanted
to present to the jurors could be shown them before the court
day, perhaps when the veniremen were elected by the sheriff's
bailiff, or when they held the view in the presence of the parties,
or as the parties approached them informally and individually
—a procedure that was both lawful and very commonly practised.[1]

In fact, however, the justices did not usually take the assize
directly the case came up. From the 1230s if not before, they
first called upon the plaintiff to state his 'plaint', repeating the
charge of disseisin that he made in the writ and specifying
the kinds and quantity of tenements which had been taken from
him, or the nuisance that troubled him.[2] And from long before
the 1230s, even the first surviving plea rolls of the 1190s show
that before the assize was taken the defendant or his bailiff
would be invited to say whatever he might wish to say in defence.
In some cases they had nothing to say, if they were satisfied that
they had told the jurors beforehand all that they had to tell
them and were content now to abide the verdict in the principal
matter. But on other occasions a more or less elaborate defence
might be put up and discussion would ensue among the parties
and the justices. And even if the defendant offered nothing, even
if no one appeared for the defence, Henry of Bracton advised
his fellow justices that they should not rush to take the assize but
should inquire *ex officio* what rights each of the parties claimed
in the land and what was the real issue between them.[3]

In the preliminary discussion the defendant might choose to
enter some 'dilatory exceptions', the 'pleas in abatement' of a
later age, technical objections not to the plaintiff's basic claim
but to the way in which he was bringing his suit on this occasion:
that the present justices had no jurisdiction to try this case, that
the plaintiff was under sentence of excommunication, that the

---

[1] Bracton fos. 179b–180, 224, J.I. 1/1182 m. 10 (1254?), Y.B. Hil 12 Ed. II no.
31 (1319), 1 Henry VI no. 5 (1422–3), Stat. 6 Henry VI c. 2 (*SR* ii. 233, *anno* 1427).
But the parties were forbidden to approach the jurors after they had withdrawn
to their room to consider their verdict: Bracton fo. 185b, *Northants Pleas* no. 448
(1202), 744 (1203), *CRR* vi. 380–1 (1212), *Eyres of Lincs and Worcs* no. 946 (1221),
Sel. Cases in K.B. vii. 39 (1391).

[2] Above, p. 48 n. 3.   [3] fos. 183b–184b, 185b–186b.

plaintiff was a married woman whose husband was not suing with her as the law required, that the writ named wrongly the township in which the tenements lay, and so forth. If any such exception succeeded the plaintiff's suit was quashed, though he was left free to sue again in due form and under the proper circumstances.[1]

Whether he pleaded any dilatory exceptions or not, the defendant could proceed to the principal matter and offer evidences, arguments, and proofs to demonstrate that he had not committed an illegal disseisin.

If he had evidence that he had not already shown to the jurors, he could show it now. He might say, for instance, that he was no disseisor because the plaintiff had given him the land, and might proffer the plaintiff's deed of gift in evidence. A deed of gift from a third party would have the same effect, for one who entered by a feoffment was, on the face of it at any rate, not a disseisor. Without anything tangible to put before their eyes, other kinds of facts that would tend to show his innocence could simply be suggested to the jurors: that the defendant's father had died seised as of fee and that he had straightway taken over the holding as rightful heir; that his tenant had died seised without an heir and that he had immediately entered as the superior lord to claim his escheat; that he had exchanged lands with the plaintiff; that the lands belonged to the plaintiff but that he was under age and that the defendant had therefore taken them to hold as feudal guardian; and the like. All these 'evidences' tended simply to deny that there had been any disseisin.[2]

[1] Bracton fos. 187b–190, 203, 211, 289b. Some early examples appear in *Rotuli Curiae Regis* ii. 218 (1200), excommunication; *CRR* iii. 147 (1204), excommunication; *CRR* i. 434 (1200), iii. 345 (1205), married women suing without their husbands.

[2] That the parties could show evidence in court appears from these cases: *BNB* no. 825 (1233), J.I. 1/1182 m. 7 (1255), K.B. 26/186 m. 31 (1268), C.P. 40/3 m. 4, 40/4 m. 2 (1273), K.B. 27/127 m. 58d (1291), MS. Y fo. 10ᵛ (*c.* 1300). From Bracton, fo. 185b, it appears that evidence was presented before the jurors were sworn, so that 'evidence to the assize' was not properly distinct from 'pleading' before the court. Around 1300 the custom grew—gradually, I think—of postponing the evidence to the assize until after the swearing-in of the jurors, making its presentation a part of the trial and thus clearly separate from pleading. Presentation of evidence seems to be a part of the trial in a case of 1291, Sutherland, 'Peytevin *v.* la Lynde', pp. 543–6, and this was regarded as normal in *Eyre of London 1321* p. 232 and Y.B. Mich. 13 Ed. III no. 54 (1339).

If the discussion was left at that, the court could proceed to take the assize. The jurors had heard the defence now, so what was their finding on the 'points of the writ': had the defendant wrongfully and without a judgment disseised the plaintiff of his free tenement since the limitation-date, or had he not? The parties were given a new opportunity to object for cause to any of the individuals summoned as jurors,[1] those who were accepted were sworn, and the question was put to them. They retired to a private room to deliberate, and returned with their verdict.[2]

But in many cases the discussion would run more to argument than simply to evidence. The defendant might admit at least tacitly that he had disseised the plaintiff, but might argue in one way or another that he was within his rights. The plaintiff was his villein, he would say. Or, he himself held a term by grant from the plaintiff, his term had not yet expired, the plaintiff put him out and he moved back in 'as well he might'. Or, the plaintiff was his stepfather, the wife-and-mother died leaving a heritage of lands, the stepfather continued to hold the lands after her death claiming by right of courtesy where in truth he was not entitled to courtesy for no children had been born of his marriage, and therefore the defendant came and put him out and took the heritage that was rightfully his own. Or, after the Statute of Merton of 1236, in a case of disseisin of common of pasture: the defendant was feudal lord and the plaintiff his tenant, the lord 'approved' some of the common land and so— admittedly—disseised the plaintiff of his rights of common there, but the plaintiff still had adequate common in other parts of the manor and therefore according to the statute was not entitled to any remedy at law.

When a case was argued in this style, the resulting discussion generally came down to some special point. Was the plaintiff a serf? Had the defendant's term expired or not when the plaintiff put him out? Were no children born of the plaintiff's marriage,

---

[1] Bracton fo. 185. Early illustrations appear in *Rotuli Curiae Regis* i. 387–8 (1199), ii. 241–2 (1200), *CRR* ii. 122 (1202). If a challenge to a juror rested on matter of fact that was disputed—a charge, for instance, that one of the veniremen was unfree and therefore ineligible—it would be settled summarily and without prejudice by an informal verdict of the other veniremen, or of some few of them chosen for this purpose. Bracton alludes briefly to this procedure, fo. 190b, and it is fully described in Y.B. Mich. 8 Ed. III no. 35 (1334).

[2] *Eyres of Lincs and Worcs* no. 946 (1221), *Sel. Cases in K.B.* ii. 41 (1288), MS. Y fo. 7ᵛ (1308).

so that he was not entitled to courtesy? Under the Statute of Merton, had the lord in fact left sufficient common for the plaintiff? Very occasionally the point might be one of law, which would require no trial but rather a ruling by the court.[1] Much more commonly, and as in the hypothetical examples just given, the point was such as to call for trial by jury. In that case the justices would sometimes summon a special panel to make up the jury and would sometimes use the recognitors who had come for the assize, not as an 'assize' to speak to the points of the writ but as a 'jury' in the strict technical sense, to try the special issue.[2]

Finally, the defence might offer not only evidences or arguments but, in addition to these, some alternative kind of proof in place of the verdict of twelve sworn men. The plaintiff had given the lands to him, the defendant might say, and he had to show for it not an ordinary deed of feoffment of which the jurors might be judges to prove or disprove the transaction by their verdict, but a part of a chirograph made in the king's court which was proof in itself, for the gift had been by final concord in the king's court. Or, the defendant had recovered the lands by judgment in court, and could prove it by the record of the court: either in the king's court whose record lay in the written enrolments and in the memory of the justices, or in a county or feudal court whose record consisted in the witness of some of its suitors. Or, the defendant had entered into the land under a direct order from the king, as he could prove by showing the king's writ or by the witness of the sheriff. Or, the plaintiff could

---

[1] e.g. *BNB* no. 291 (1228), K.B. 26/151 m. 41 (1254).

[2] In particular, if issue was joined on the genuineness of a deed that had been shown in court, the witnesses named in the deed would be called and associated with the jurors in reaching a verdict: Bracton fo. 214, *Northants Pleas* no. 638 (1203), *BNB* no. 1891 (1227), 825 (1233), K.B. 26/189 m. 12d (1269), K.B. 27/135 m. 31d (1293), Y.B. 3 Ed. II no. 30 (1310). Cf. K.B. 26/171 m. 42 (1261), J.I. 1/1178 m. 16, 18 (1250–3), 1/1182 m. 7 (1255).

In Bracton's time the most vital difference between an 'assize' and a 'jury' was that the process of attaint (below, p. 74) was available to review the verdict of the former but not of the latter: Bracton fos. 289b–290, P. & M. ii. 541, 623. In theory the parties had voluntarily agreed to abide by the verdict of the jury, so neither of them could afterwards call it in question. The distinction was abolished by the Statute of Westminster I, c. 38 (1275), making it possible to attaint a jury as well as an assize.

Some special issues were tried not by any form of jury but by other means, such as compurgation (Note A, p. 214), or a bishop's certificate (Bracton fo. 216b).

have no action for he was the defendant's serf and the defendant was ready to prove it, not this time by the verdict of a jury but by witness of the customarily required number of the plaintiff's relatives who were ready to testify that they were unfree. Later, by the middle of the thirteenth century, defendants sometimes pleaded that the plaintiff could have no action because he had released to the defendant all his rights in the land, and put forth in proof the deed of release, which was proof in itself because it was a dispositive document and not merely evidentiary like a deed of feoffment.

When this kind of defence was put up, trial might take the form of simple examination of the alternative proof offered by the defendant, or might be diverted into some other form by the plaintiff's reply. If the defendant pleaded recovery by judgment in court, the plaintiff could answer that the person against whom the recovery was awarded was not in seisin of the land at any time during the course of that lawsuit, so that the judgment had no legal force. That would be an issue for trial by jury. If the defendant pleaded a release, the plaintiff might reply that it was a forgery. Such an issue would be tried by a jury together with the witnesses named in the document. And so for a great variety of other cases. As with the defence by argument, the case was likely to be taken far away from the original points of the writ of novel disseisin.

In the generations that followed Bracton, in Edward I's reign and after, lawyers made valiant efforts to classify these different kinds of defences and draw clear lines of division among them. In particular, they came to distinguish sharply between 'evidence to the assize' which would be followed by a verdict on the points of the writ and, on the other hand, defences by way of argument or with offer of special proof, which they joined together as 'pleas in bar of the assize'. A great forest of learning eventually grew up around these categories. But through most of the thirteenth century the distinctions among the types of defences remained indefinite and the men of the law may have been well advised to leave them so. It was not always easy to say what was evidence and what was argument; a defence that began with an offer of special proof might end in argument. And the inherent difficulties were increased by the way in which the justices often handled trial by jury.

If the assize was taken on the points of the writ, a conscientious justice of the mid thirteenth century would not accept a merely general verdict, 'Yes, he disseised him as charged', or 'No, he did not'. The justices would question the jurors in detail about the evidences shown by the parties. 'Did the plaintiff not enfeoff the defendant, then? Was there no feoffment at all, or do you find that the deed was good but that no livery of seisin was made?' Or, 'Is the defendant entitled, then, to hold the land as feudal guardian, and is that why you find that he committed no disseisin? Is it clear that the land is held by military service, so that the feudal lord is the rightful guardian?' In whatever ways the case seemed to require, the justices coached the jurors through the details to the general verdict and accepted the general verdict only when they were satisfied about the facts and reasonings on which it was based.[1]

In practice it was often difficult to distinguish this procedure from what went on in the trial of special issues that arose out of arguments advanced by the parties, when the special issues were tried by the jurors of the assize. For when special issues were joined—or special proofs taken, apart from trial by jury—the law never fully made up its mind, either in the thirteenth century or any time after, whether the action of novel disseisin could be decided on these matters alone. Sometimes it was reasoned that in pleading to a special issue or invoking special proof the parties had in effect agreed on the one side and the other to stake everything on that one point, accepting a 'split

[1] This 'coaching' and 'drawing out' of recognitors by the justices is alluded to by Bracton, fos. 288b, 289, 290b, and illustrated in the following records, for example: Eyres of Glos, Warw, Staffs no. 177 (1221), K.B. 26/152 m. 11d (1254), J.I. 1/1178 m. 18 (1250), Northumb Assize Rolls p. 21 (1256), J.I. 1/1179 m. 27d (1260), K.B. 26/174 m. 9d (1265), 26/204 m. 29d (1270), C.P. 40/3 m. 28d (1273), K.B. 27/43 m. 14 (1279). The practice continued in the fourteenth century: Y.B. Pasch. 5 Ed. II no. 17 (1312), Mich. 7 Ed. III no. 9 = 7 Ass. no. 10 (1333), Trin. 16 Ed. III no. 66 (1342).

Since the justices were ready to help, they sometimes insisted that the jurors come finally to a general verdict, for which they would share responsibility with the justices, and refused to receive purely special verdicts which recited the facts and left judgment to the justices' discretion. The practice is evident in K.B. 27/37 m. 32 (reciting a case of 1258–60) and in K.B. 26/182 m. 21–1 and 2 (1268). It was condemned by the Statute of Westminster II c. 30 (1285). Special verdicts were never entirely excluded, for they appear from time to time right through the thirteenth century, e.g. Pleas 1198–1212 iii. 1002 (1204), J.I. 1/1178 m. 5d (1250–2), K.B. 27/11 m. 31 (1275), J.I. 1/492 m. 16d (1281–2).

game', a 'jeopardy' as Bracton called it.[1] But at other times it was thought that, if the plaintiff won on the special matter, still his basic complaint was of disseisin and the court must therefore continue and try that charge by taking the assize on the points of the writ.[2] If a special issue was found for the plaintiff and the assize then went on to render a general verdict on the points of the writ, the process would not be much different from the coaching of the assize toward its general verdict, when the assize was taken on the points of the writ after a display of evidences.[3]

In every case where the victory fell to the plaintiff, even if he won on a 'jeopardy', the assize was called on to assess his damages, unless he waived damages. Judgment could then follow, generally without any delay, and the sheriff would restore the plaintiff to seisin in the presence and 'by view of' the jurors: they would point out exactly what properties they had awarded the plaintiff. The sheriff was entitled to receive an ox, or its equivalent in money, from the disseisor.[4]

After it was over there were two different procedures by which the party who lost could have the case reviewed. He could sue an action of attaint, which brought together a jury of twenty-four to confirm or to upset the verdict of the assize. If they upset it then the judgment that had followed from the original verdict was reversed.[5] Much more common than attaint, and apparently older, was a loosely structured process called certification. Here simple judicial writs, issued by the court that was to make the review, brought in the justices of assize with the record of their proceedings, the adversary, and,

---

[1] fos. 212b, 214.   [2] See Note E, p. 217.

[3] The ambiguity appears, for instance, in these cases: K.B. 26/116A m. 10 (1236), 26/120 m. 28 (1239), K.B. 27/18 m. 15 (1275), 27/47 m. 32 (1278–9).

[4] Bracton fos. 161b, 187; K.B. 27/5 m. 16d (1273). The money equivalent is variously stated as 5s. or 5s. 4d. The Statute of Westminster II c. 25 (1285) indicates that in some cases the sheriff had been collecting an ox both from the disseisor and from the successful plaintiff, and rules that thenceforth he is not to consider himself entitled to have one from the plaintiff.

[5] The earliest surviving evidence of procedure by attaint is from 1202, *CRR* ii. 97–8, and cf. *Pleas 1198–1212* iii. 909 (1204), *CRR* iii. 134–5 (1204), 332–3 (1205). Bracton's account of it appears in fos. 288b–296. Writs of attaint were expensive: 20s. for attaint of an assize of nuisance, *Eyre of Yorks 1218–19* nos. 404, 411, 5 marks for attaint of an assize concerning common of pasture, *Somerset Pleas* i. 487 (1242–3), 1 mark for attaint of an assize concerning one-half rod of arable and some pasture rights, *Yorks Assize Rolls* pp. 91–2 (1260).

generally, the jurors of the assize.[1] Sometimes certification was used to clarify an unsatisfactory record or to supplement a special verdict whose story raised further questions.[2] But usually it brought about a general re-examination of the case. The parties could put forth new arguments and show new evidences —documents, perhaps, which they had not had at hand during the original hearing.[3] The court would review the law and procedure applied by the justices of assize and would re-examine the assize itself as to the basis of its verdict, a business which might result in a reversal of the verdict under new and different coaching, and consequently bring a reversal of judgment.[4] Certification seems already to be in use in the first surviving plea rolls of 1194[5] and may go back to the earliest years of the assize itself.

Later on, in the 1280s, the formal procedure by writ of error became available,[6] and from about that time certification became much less wide-ranging. Eventually it was confined to cases where the justices wanted more information before proceeding to judgment on a special verdict,[7] where there had been delay between the verdict and the judgment for the plaintiff so that the damages had to be assessed anew as of the

---

[1] Bracton fos. 288b–296. The justices of assize were summoned to 'certify', or more commonly to 'make a record': *CRR* xi. 1459, 2633 = *BNB* no. 917 (1224), xii. 655 (1225), xiii. 508 (1228), K.B. 26/130 m. 17 (1243). The writ of certification proper, to bring the jurors and the adversary, appears in *Registrum Brevium* fo. 200.

[2] Bracton fos. 289, 293b; *Northants Pleas* no. 508 (1202), *Eyres of Lincs and Worcs* nos. 123, 514 (1219), *CRR* xiii. 2005 (1229), *BNB* no. 1281 (1239–40).

[3] *CRR* xii. 1674 (1226), *Somerset Pleas* i. 1514 (1255). Generally speaking, no delay would be granted for the production of documents that ought to be in the defendant's possession: Bracton fos. 205b, MS. Y fos. 37^v–40^r (*c.* 1300). If, for example, a release was pleaded in bar, it had to be shown in court when it was pleaded: J.I. 1/492 m. 67 (1281–4), C.P. 40/98 m. 59 (1293), MS. Y fo. 10^r–10^v (*c.* 1300), Y.B. 19 Ed. II pp. 658–9 (1326), Mich. 13 Ed. III no. 50 (1339).

[4] *Early Registers of Writs* p. 87; *CRR* iii. 97–8 (1204), viii. 75 (1219), xiv. 207 (1230), *BNB* nos. 530 (1231), 1209, 1212 (1236–7), K.B. 27/37 m. 32 (1258–60), *Yorks Assize Rolls* pp. 130–1 (1260), K.B. 27/11 m. 31 (1275).

[5] *Rotuli Curiae Regis* i. 83 (1194) seems to be a certification brought by one who believed that he could get the verdict reversed by showing further documents. Other early cases appear in *Rotuli Curiae Regis* i. 338 (1199), *Northants Pleas* no. 508 (1202), *CRR* iii. 97–8 (1204).

[6] The earliest cases I have seen in which novel disseisin is reviewed by proceedings in error are K.B. 27/79 m. 27 (1283), *Calendar of Documents relating to Ireland 1285–1292* pp. 198, 230, 231, no. 525 (1288), and K.B. 27/81 m. 19, 27/125 m. 48d, 27/126 m. 66 (1290).

[7] e.g. Sutherland, 'Peytevin *v.* la Lynde', p. 544.

time judgment was given,[1] or where the defendant who had lost at the assize wanted to plead special proofs which he had been prevented from pleading in the original hearing.[2]

[1] e.g. K.B. 26/160 m. 1d (1258), 26/167 m. 2d (1260), K.B. 27/20A m. 20 (1276), MS. Y fo. 17 (1305).
[2] Statute of Westminster II c. 25 (1285), MS. Y fo. 26ᵛ (c. 1310), Y.B. Hil. 14 Ed. III no. 42 (1340).

III

DISSEISINS LAWFUL AND UNLAWFUL

THE assize was never intended to restrain all disseisins of freehold. There were circumstances in which one man was entitled to go to another's free tenement, put him out of the land or the house or whatever it was, and take the property. For a justice holding assizes it was the most important branch of substantive learning in the law to know which disseisins were lawful and which were unlawful. At one extreme was the case of the mere ruffian who, without having or claiming any right, threw out a free tenant who had been in long and peaceable occupation of his own land. There was no question but that the assize should correct such an offence. At the other extreme was the case of the demandant who had won a recovery of land by due and lawful judgment in the king's court and who now brought the sheriff with him to execute judgment, disseise the occupant, and turn the land over to him. The tenant who was disseised in this way obviously should not be allowed to recover by the assize. Between these extremes was an immense spectrum of possible cases that were less clear and easy—where a woman's heir put out her widower, where a lord took over tenements because the services were in arrears, where the grantee of lands broke promises he had made to the grantor and the grantor took the lands back, and so forth in nearly endless series. Through this spectrum the law had somehow to draw a line that would mark off the lawful disseisins from the unlawful.[1] The unlawful ones were characterized in the writ of novel disseisin as those done 'wrongfully and without a judgment', but these few and general words were only a hint of the law that was needed.

Disseisin was legal if it was done by an officer in execution of

---

[1] In later times the word 'disseisin' was applied to illegal disseisins alone. 'Entry and ouster' became the term for disseisin as such, and lawful disseisin was called 'entry congeable'. Littleton, *Tenures*, iii. 3. In this chapter I shall use the older terminology.

a judgment given in court. This was true not only when judgment had been given in the king's court but also when it had been given in the county or feudal court: the sheriff or his bailiff acting for the king's court or the county, the lord or his bailiff acting for the feudal court, could disseise a free tenant if judgment had been duly given beforehand. If the disseised tenant brought an assize in consequence his action could be barred by the record of the earlier judgment.[1] Such a defence was usually good even if the former tenant, dispossessed now and suing by the assize, wanted to argue that the judgment against him had been legally wrong ('false'), erroneous, obtained by deceit, or based on perjury. If it could be clearly and quickly established—say, from the statements of the parties themselves —that a judgment had been bad, then its execution might sometimes be regarded as an unlawful disseisin and be corrected by the assize. But the justices considered that actions of novel disseisin were not an ideal occasion for reviewing judgments given in earlier lawsuits and were reluctant to proceed except where the injustice was very evident. Only occasionally did they upset the judgments of county or feudal courts, and they never corrected those of the king's court itself.[2] If a tenant who lost his lands as a result of a suit against him wanted to get the judgment reversed on a writ of deceit, writ of false judgment, writ of error, certification, or attaint, all these ways were available for different kinds of circumstances and he should take one of them. Until he did so, and prosecuted, and succeeded, the judgment that stood against him was generally enforceable and he could not ordinarily complain that its execution amounted to an unjust disseisin. The assize would do him no good.

Of course, judgment in court was no justification for disseisin if no judgment had in fact been given. The record of the king's

[1] Above, p. 19, and Note A, p. 214.

[2] Bracton fos. 165b, 205b, 367–367b. Execution of a wrongful judgment seems to have been regarded as an illegal disseisin correctable by the assize in *CRR* i. 434 (1201), iii. 136–7 (1204). Execution was treated as lawful until the judgment should be reversed in *CRR* iii. 66 (1203), C.P. 40/58 m. 11d (1285); and when the judgment had been in the king's court this rule was applied in every case that I have seen, e.g. K.B. 26/161 m. 8 (1259), *Procedure w/o Writ* pp. 141–2 (1260), Y.B. Trin. 18 Ed. III no. 17 (1344). The lawbooks of Edward I's time seem to reject even Bracton's mild doctrine and to hold that judgments wrongly given can never be corrected at novel disseisin: Ralph of Hengham, 'Summa Parva', p. 64; *Fleta* iv. 15. 3; *Britton* ii. 19. 1.

court was not allowed to be disputed: if the king or his justices 'recorded' that judgment had been given thus and so, one might contend that the judgment ought not to have been given, but the fact itself, that it *was* given, was legally beyond question. County and feudal courts enjoyed no such prerogative. The records of suits heard in these jurisdictions consisted in the word of several members of the court, commonly four, who had been present at the proceedings. When they came and recorded a judgment that would bar the assize of novel disseisin the plaintiff could, if he liked, roundly deny that the judgment to which they were testifying had been given. In that case trial by battle was theoretically in order, between the plaintiff and the record-bearers, but we lack any notice of battles actually being held.[1] The king's justices sometimes allowed the plaintiff to defeat the record by compurgation.[2]

But even when a judgment was given, and given according to good law, it was still possible that its execution might amount to an illegal disseisin. It would be so, in the first place, if the court that gave the judgment had no jurisdiction. If an ecclesiastical court should be so rash as to give judgment in a plea concerning lay landholdings, when execution followed it would be an actionable disseisin.[3] So also if a court gave judgment after forcing a tenant to answer for his freehold without the king's writ. When the question of jurisdiction arose, there was no need for the case to be especially clear. An action of novel disseisin was the proper occasion for deciding whether a court had exceeded its jurisdiction, however difficult the decision might sometimes be. At any rate in the later thirteenth century, even the king's justices could be corrected in this way if they went beyond the terms of their commissions.[4]

In the second place, it was illegal to put into execution a judgment for freehold lands and tenements that had been won

---

[1] Note A, p. 214, at the end.

[2] Note A, p. 214. But for trial of the record of the county by its officers' testimony alone see Bracton fos. 330–330b.

[3] Bracton fos. 175, 496b, 411; *Eyres of Lincs and Worcs* no. 1290 (1221). An ecclesiastical court could lawfully give and execute judgment concerning a benefice and the lands and tenements attached to it: *Sel. Cases in K.B.* ii. 72, *Rotuli Parliamentorum* i. 96 (1293).

[4] K.B. 27/125 m. 6d (1290). A case of 1270 seems to show the contrary, but it had such powerful political implications that it may not be good evidence of the ordinary course of the law: Clifford *v.* Breuse, K.B. 26/200B m. 5.

against someone other than the true tenant: as if John should sue Henry for Roger's lands and win his case and get execution.[1] Here again, the case would be handled at novel disseisin however difficult it might be; it had to be handled there, for Roger had been no party to the suit between John and Henry and therefore could not sue directly to reverse or annul that judgment.

These rules sat lightly upon the king's justices. Their judgments were never reversed through actions of novel disseisin, their records could not be disputed at all, and, acting as they did under clearly drawn commissions, they were not likely to exceed their jurisdiction.[2] Except in rare cases, disseisins done pursuant to their judgments would be illegal only where they themselves had been deceived by a demandant who had brought his suit against someone other than the true tenant. But the rules must have worked powerfully to destroy the business of county and feudal courts in litigation about lands and tenements. Men were in any case flocking to the king's court to avail themselves of the assizes and to get their final concords put on record. And even a conservative litigant, whose own inclination would be to pursue his claims by an action of right in the county or before his feudal lord, might have to question the value of the judgment that he could get there. If he sued and recovered and got execution, his adversary might bring novel disseisin against him. If the judgment had been faulty it might, sometimes, be corrected at the assize. In any case, to defend himself at the assize he would probably have to go to the trouble of bringing in the record of his judgment, not a convenient written docu-

---

[1] See these cases, for example: *Rotuli Curiae Regis* i. 369–70, 422 (1199), *Lincs Assize Rolls* no. 249 (1202), *Northants Pleas* no. 817, 838 (1203), *CRR* iv. 306 (1206), *Eyre of Yorks 1218–19* no. 58, *Eyres of Lincs and Worcs* no. 1277 (1221), *BNB* no. 1793 (1222), Y.B. 32 & 33 Ed. I p. 518 (1303–5), Pasch. 12 Ed. II no. 45 (1319), Hil. 19 Ed. III no. 18 (1345). One refinement was necessary. If lands passed from one tenant to another while a lawsuit for them was pending, and if the demandant later won the lawsuit, he was entitled to execution against the new tenant even though that person had not been named in his action. It was enough if he had brought his case against the man who was really tenant on the day when he began to sue. Bracton fo. 171, *CRR* i. 418 (1201), *Procedure w/o Writ* pp. 141–2 (1260), Y.B. Trin. 18 Ed. III no. 33 (1344).

Further learning about the 'judgment that does not bind' appears in Ralph of Hengham, 'Summa Parva', p. 64, *Fleta* iv. 14. 1, and *Britton* ii. 11. 12, 20, 19. 1.

[2] But see Bracton fos. 411–411b on various faults that may void the authority of royal justices.

ment as from the king's court but several men representing the county or feudal court, who would have to be summoned. Once they were there, their testimony might be disputed and tried—perhaps by compurgation—and rejected. Or it might be found that the judgment was invalid because the court had exceeded its jurisdiction, a danger particularly for the feudal courts.[1] In any of these cases, conviction of disseisin and loss of the tenement and a charge for damages would follow in consequence. Contemplating all these possibilities, many intending litigants must have decided that it would be best to bring their suits in the king's court.

If this was done in a case where the jurisdiction properly belonged to a feudal court, the lord could appear and claim the case and the king's justices would surrender jurisdiction. But the reclaiming of cases could not do as much to restore the business of feudal courts as the attraction of pleas into the king's court did to ruin it: at best it could offset to some extent the tendency to go to the king's court. A better remedy was written into Magna Carta, which provided that writs of right for hearing in the king's court—writs of *Precipe*, as they were called—were not even to be issued from the Chancery in cases where jurisdiction might belong to a feudal lord.[2] But the growth of the writs of entry in Henry III's reign robbed this rule of most of its effect. For special cases of one sort and another, the appropriate writ of entry provided an alternative to suit by an action of right, and these writs were developed in such profusion that the alternative came almost always to be available to the intending litigant

---

[1] In the early thirteenth century they were occasionally guilty of giving judgment unlawfully without the king's writ: *CRR* i. 186 (1200), *Northants Pleas* no. 782 (1203), and perhaps *CRR* iii. 62 (1203); an isolated example appears much later, C.P. 40/100 m. 132 (1293). In *CRR* v. 265–6 (1208) the feudal court proceeded illegally, when the tenant wished to put himself on the king's grand assize. Sometimes it was held that a feudal court exceeded its jurisdiction whenever it gave judgment against a tenant who did not willingly admit that he held of the lord of the court, even if his denial was unwarrantable. Glanvill, Book XII chapter 8, implies such a doctrine, and it is illustrated in *CRR* iii. 98 (1204) and K.B. 27/136 m. 35 (1293). But at other times it was held that the feudal court was entitled to proceed if the tenant in fact held of the lord, even though he denied it: *Rotuli Curiae Regis* i. 48, 62–3 (1194), ii. 22–3 (1199). Cf. K.B. 26/113 m. 20d (1233), 26/135 m. 8d and 26/136 m. 10d (1249), 26/171 m. 16d (1261), actions of replevin in which issue was joined whether the plaintiff held of the avowant.

[2] Magna Carta 1215, c. 34. This provision was repeated without change in all the reissues of the Charter.

whatever his particular circumstances. Where it was available, he usually chose it. Writs of entry gave speedier process and guaranteed a rational form of trial, excluding trial by battle, and, perhaps most important of all, the actions held under them were always in the king's court.

So when in the course of the thirteenth century the business of county and feudal courts in judging claims to freehold declined almost to the vanishing point, and their work passed over to the king's court, the assize of novel disseisin was responsible for this more than any other single institution. Along with the assize of mort d'ancestor, the grand assize, and the actions of cosinage, ael, and entry, it was one of those new forms that attracted plaintiffs into the king's court: indeed, in the long run it was the most important of them all. But unlike the others it was more than just a counter-attraction. It directly reduced the value of the judgments that demandants could get in feudal or county courts by raising the lively possibility that execution of those judgments might be treated as an unlawful disseisin.

Lords retained jurisdiction over the customs and services owed them by their free tenants. If the feudal superior found that his tenant was failing to live up to his obligations—as, for example, by refusing to render homage and fealty after entering into his inheritance, or by missing his day for the payment of rent—he could use his own power to compel the tenant to answer for it in his own court, and could himself enforce the court's judgment. But although every lord undoubtedly had this authority, the lord could never claim thereby any right to disseise his free tenant. Failure on the tenant's part to render customs and services never entailed forfeiture of his holding, however long and however contumaciously it might be continued. This rather strange rule was firmly established and was as old as anything that we know in detail about the common law.[1] When at length it was abrogated by statutes of 1278 and 1285,[2] the new legislation gave the lord no authority in himself or in his court to disseise the neglectful tenant, but only allowed him, after the services were two years in arrears, to sue in the king's court to recover the land in demesne.

---

[1] *CRR* i. 320–1 (1200), *Eyre of Yorks 1218–19* no. 46, *Wilts Civil Pleas 1249* no. 52, MS. Y fo. 35^r (1302–9).

[2] Statute of Gloucester c. 4 (1278) and Statute of Westminster II c. 2 (1285).

The lord's jurisdiction over customs and services empowered him not to disseise but to distrain.[1] Without waiting to seek the judgment of any court, even his own,[2] he could distrain a delinquent tenant by his chattels. If the tenant had villeins holding of him, the lord must start by impounding their livestock. During the ploughing season he should take the beasts of the plough only if there were no other animals that would suffice for distraint; and the same rule applied in all seasons to sheep. If the villeins had no livestock, or not enough to provide an effective distraint, the lord could 'arrest' the produce of their land, such as grain or hay, forbidding anyone to consume or remove or otherwise convert it to use. Goods in buildings could be arrested only if there were not enough to be found out of doors. Unlike livestock, arrested goods must not be taken away to the pound.[2]

If the lord could not find enough chattels on the villeins' holdings, or if there were no villein holdings, he could pass on to distrain by chattels in his tenant's demesne, observing the same rules of precedence as in the villein tenements. If the demesne did not suffice, or if there was none, he could, always keeping the same order of precedence, take chattels on the holdings of free subtenants.[3]

If all distraint by chattels proved ineffective, the lord could distrain 'by the fee', putting his tenant out and taking the lands 'into his hand', that is, under his own control.[4] But he must not do this unless he had first attempted distraint by chattels,[5] and even if he had duly distrained by chattels beforehand still he must not take the land without getting a prior judgment from

---

[1] Bracton fos. 217–217b is the chief authority for what follows.

[2] *BNB* no. 1207 (1235–6).   [3] Bracton fo. 22.

[4] Bracton says, fo. 365b, that when a tenant is distrained by his lands for default in the king's court he is not put out of the tenement. The distraint was hardly more than a summons and a warning. But it seems that when the lord distrained by the fee he ejected the tenant. Bracton speaks of the lord 'restoring possession' of the land when the tenant 'returns' and offers satisfaction, fos. 205b, 217b–218, cf. *BNB* no. 1767 (1227). In a case of 1199 the clerk allowed himself to use 'dissaisivit' and 'cepit in manum pro defectu servicii' as equivalent terms, *Rotuli Curiae Regis* ii. 58, 117, and from the year 1200 we hear that after his lord distrained him by his fee a certain tenant ejected the lord, *CRR* i. 320–1. In 1249 a lord pleaded in novel disseisin that he was justified in disseising his tenant for he was entitled to distrain by the tenement for failure of service, *Wilts Civil Pleas 1249* no. 473.

[5] *CRR* iii. 133, 133–4 (1204).

his own court to authorize this measure: he might not do it simply on his own motion.[1]

In making any kind of distraint, by chattels or by the fee, the lord must always conduct himself as one who was holding the property of another. Inasmuch as he was holding it in lawful distraint he could prevent the tenant from using or enjoying it, but because it was the tenant's property that he had the lord for his part must not use or enjoy it either. The lord could impound cows but not milk them, arrest produce but not sell it, take the land into his hand but not work it or appropriate any of its profits.[2] The only legitimate purpose of distraint for customs and services was to compel the tenant to render them by his own hand, not to give the lord a way of compensating himself for the default. If the tenant came after being distrained and offered satisfaction the lord must immediately release the distraint, even if the tenant had suffered him to hold it for a long time before giving in.[3] If the tenant wished to dispute his obligation for particular customs and services for which the lord had distrained him, the lord must similarly release the distraint as soon as the tenant provided pledges to appear, in the lord's court or elsewhere, to abide judgment in the matter.[4] The lord must not give or sell tenements that he had taken in distraint.[5] While he had them they remained the tenant's free holding and not the lord's: if the lord should be ejected, by the tenant or by anyone else, he could not recover by novel disseisin.[6] Distraint by the fee involved putting the tenant off his holding but it was, for all that, not a disseisin.

If a lord overstepped any of the bounds of lawful distraint, his tenant could call him to order by bringing an action of replevin or of novel disseisin. Replevin, which was usually heard in the county court, was the proper resort where the lord had

---

[1] *Rotuli Curiae Regis* ii. 58, 117 (1199), *Eyre of Yorks 1218–19* no. 46, *Eyres of Lincs and Worcs* no. 946 (1221), *BNB* no. 1149 (1235–6), J.I. 1/1182 m. 10 (c. 1254).

[2] *Eyres of Glos, Warw, Staffs* no. 406 (1221), *BNB* no. 270 = *CRR* xiii. 388 (1228), *BNB* no. 348 (1229).

[3] Bracton fos. 218, 262. The tenant must make up all the payments that he had missed and all other services and duties that he had not rendered; or must offer sufficient pledges to do this.

[4] *Britton* i. 28. 6, and these cases: *PRS* xiv. 134 (1195), *Rotuli Curiae Regis* i. 366 (1199), *CRR* iii. 133–4, 161–2 (1204), *Eyres of Lincs and Worcs* no. 991 (1221), *BNB* nos. 1767 (1227), 270 = *CRR* xiii. 388 (1228).

[5] Bracton fo. 218.   [6] *CRR* i. 320–1 (1200).

taken chattels and then refused to release them when the tenant offered pledges for satisfaction or for appearance in court.[1] Novel disseisin could be brought for violation of the proper precedence in taking chattels,[2] for carrying off and impounding goods that ought only to have been arrested on the land,[3] and, according to Henry of Bracton, for any violation at all of the rules governing distraint, even in the cases where remedy could also be obtained by Replevin;[4] but certainly it was available, and in fact regularly used, whenever the lord offended against any of the canons that governed distraint by the fee. If all the law's limits were not carefully observed, distraint by the fee became an illegal disseisin.[5]

Under these circumstances distraint by the fee fell out of use in the course of the thirteenth century. It was a troublesome business. Before he could legally attempt it the lord had to gather his feudal court into session (and meetings of feudal courts were becoming less and less a matter of routine) and get its judgment against the tenant. If the tenant brought novel disseisin in consequence of the distraint the lord would probably have to produce members of the court to testify to the judgment.[6] The record that they bore might be disputed.[7] If it was successfully disputed the lord would be convicted of disseisin, as he would also be convicted if it was found that he had broken any of the other rules, as by appropriating profits of the land or failing to return the tenements promptly when satisfaction was offered. Against all this, distraint by the fee did not offer any

---

[1] Issue was taken on the alleged refusal to release the distress in these cases: K.B. 26/113 m. 20d (1233), 26/132 m. 10 (1244), 26/135 m. 8d and 26/136 m. 10d (1249), *Northumb Assize Rolls* pp. 43–4 (1256). Later on that part of the charge in Replevin came to be a fiction, and the action served to try in the county or the king's court the question which in earlier times would have been handled in the lord's court, whether the lord was justified in levying distress in the first place, that is, whether the services that he claimed were indeed due from the tenant. Milsom in *Novae Narrationes*, pp. cciii–cciv. In those latter days, if the lord refused to release the distress when he ought to have done so, the sheriff dealt with his offence by direct executive measures: Plucknett, *Legislation*, pp. 59–60.

[2] J.I. 1/1245 m. 34 (1280).

[3] *BNB* no. 1207 (1236–7). Cases frequently appear in which a defendant is convicted of disseisin because he carried off the produce of the plaintiff's land, e.g. *Northants Pleas* no. 448 (1202). Without revealing it explicitly, some of these may represent an unlawful impounding of goods that ought only to have been arrested by way of distraint. [4] fos. 205b, 217–18.

[5] See the cases cited above, p. 83 nn. 5, p. 84 n. 1, 2, 4.

[6] Above, p. 20 n. 1. [7] Above, p. 79.

proportionate advantages. The lord had in any case to attempt distraint by chattels first. If he impounded all the livestock the tenant would hardly be able to work his land, and if he arrested all the produce as it came in the tenant could draw no profits. After that, a further taking of the fee itself would mean only that the tenant was totally prevented from doing any work and that he was put out of his home if his home was in the holding. This was not enough further advantage to make distraint by the fee worth while. By Edward I's reign it was, to all seeming, wholly obsolete as a means of enforcing customs and services.

It survived and grew, however, and was freed from some of the entangling restrictions, when it was used for certain other purposes. In the first place, it could be used to put a stop to 'waste'. If a tenant for life used his possession of lands to wring profit from them in a way that would detract from their ability to produce revenue in future years, he was committing waste: as if he should cut and sell every bit of timber on the land, or should so squeeze and oppress the serfs that they abandoned their holdings and fled. In that case, the lord or anyone else who had a legitimate interest could take the holding into his hand by way of distraint, putting the life tenant out to prevent him from continuing the offence. No previous judgment of a feudal court was necessary. As usual, the distrainor must take no profit for himself, and he must stand ready to return the property as soon as the life tenant offered satisfaction for the past and security for good conduct in the future. The same law applied to the guardian of a minor. If the guardian committed waste his ward or his ward's friends could enter to impede him.[1]

In the second place, during the years from about 1250 to about 1300 feudal lords successfully asserted a new authority to take into their hands the holdings of their free tenants if the tenants attempted to alienate the holdings in ways that prejudiced the lord's rights. During these decades they won legal recognition of their right to do this, and to do it without seeking any previous judgment either of the king's court or of their own.

The problem that led to this development is famous in legal history.[2] By the end of the twelfth century free tenants had gained,

---

[1] Bracton fos. 169, 217, 315. The case of a minor ousting his guardian is illustrated in J.I. 1/503 m. 12 (1287).

[2] P. & M. i. 329–49; Bean, *Decline of English Feudalism*, pp. 40–103.

as it seems, a very full right to give or sell their holdings as they pleased without need of the lord's consent. As the law conceived the matter, the lord's interests could not be harmed. He was entitled to customs and services and if these were not duly rendered his remedy lay in distraint; since he could distrain against any tenant of his fee whomsoever, mediate or immediate, it was nothing to him who his tenant was. But the law could hold this view only by permitting itself a generous disregard of every-day facts, for free alienation actually entailed a good deal of loss to the superior lords. An honest, provident, and wealthy tenant who had long stood on friendly terms with his lord might sell his holding to a peevish and penniless dodger, with provision that this new purchaser should hold of the lord. He foisted off on his lord, 'by way of substitution', one from whom it would be more difficult to get regular performance of customs and services. Or a tenant might sell half of his land for the purchaser to hold of the lord, and leave the lord thereby with two tenants severally responsible for fractions of the customs and services for which the lord had formerly to look to one man only.

It was worse when the tenant granted his holding, in whole or in part, for the purchaser to hold of him, the grantor, as intermediate lord: when the grant was 'by way of subinfeudation'. In that case the grantor remained the sole tenant of the lord paramount, responsible to him for all the services, but the mere fact that he had given away part of his holding made him less wealthy and therefore, potentially at least, less able to fulfil his obligations; particularly if he had given the land to be held of himself free of services or for nominal services only. More important, the lord paramount lost nearly the whole value of the casual 'incidents' of lordship in respect of the subinfeudated property. If the purchaser should die without an heir, or commit felony, the consequent escheat would go to the grantor as the immediate lord. If the grantor should die without an heir or commit felony the lord paramount would get an escheat for himself, but it would consist only in the mesne lordship over the purchaser's holding. The value of the mesne lordship was bound to be less than that of the land itself and might be nothing at all. The lord paramount would get the land in demesne by way of escheat only if the grantor and the purchaser should both die without heirs or commit felony, and this was rather unlikely.

What was true of escheats was also true of the incidents of ward-ship and marriage. The lord paramount would be entitled to hold the land in demesne by way of wardship, and to give the land in demesne in marriage with an heir, only if both the grantor and the purchaser should leave minor heirs whose minorities overlapped, and then only for as long as both heirs, and not only one of them, remained under age.

The damage to the lord was greatest of all when his tenant gave his lands to a religious foundation. The lord's feudal incidents—relief, wardship, marriage, and escheat—were all occasioned by the death, felony, or outlawry of his tenant. A church never died, never committed felony, never was outlawed, and the incidents were lost to the lord completely and hope-lessly.

Notwithstanding all these painful truths, the king's courts observed and enforced the rule that free tenants might alienate their holdings whether their lords liked it or not. The first glimmerings of a reaction against this appeared when Magna Carta was reissued for the second time, in 1217. The regency government wrote into the Charter a provision that 'no free man may henceforth give or sell to another so much of his land that he cannot from [the income of] the remainder adequately perform the service that he owes to the lord'. In 1225 this section was included in the definitive version of Magna Carta.[1] It purported to deal, however, with only part of the problem, it laid down no procedure for its own enforcement, and there is little evidence that it was enforced. Only one case has come to light, a case of 1238 in which it appeared that a tenant had given to a church his entire holding, amounting to a whole knight's fee, to be held of him for 6d. a year. The lord para-mount seized the land and the king's court upheld his right to do so.[2] It was a particularly flagrant violation. But no other cases have been found and there is some reason to think that this one was unique.[3] For the rest, we have from the first half

---

[1] Magna Carta 1217, c. 39; 1225, c. 32; Select Charters pp. 343, 350.

[2] BNB no. 1248.

[3] In Bracton's time some men thought that the provision in Magna Carta applied only to gifts to religious foundations: Bracton fos. 168b, 169b. That there should be doubt about such an important point thirty years or so after the definitive version of Magna Carta suggests that the Charter's provision had seen very little use. There is no warrant at all in the language of the Charter for limiting this provision to

of the thirteenth century only an ordinance of 1228 which prohibited the king's immediate tenants from giving any of their lands to churches,[1] and which seems to have been enforced.[2]

Pressure of opinion continued, however, to mount. Evidently the growth of commerce made sales of lands more frequent as time went on and thereby aggravated the losses that lords suffered on account of unrestricted alienation. In his treatise written in the 1250s the conservative Henry of Bracton still affirmed the old law of free alienation, but he was at great pains to justify it;[3] 'the very earnestness of his argument shows that he had to combat a strong feeling'.[4] Just as he was writing, in fact, the reaction set in powerfully and serious restrictions began to be placed on the old freedom.

The king had always been called upon from time to time to confirm subjects' gifts of lands, for his ratification was valuable in a number of ways. But from 1242 on there appear some royal licences and confirmations which look as though they were intended to secure to tenants-in-chief a permission to alienate which they needed from the king as their feudal lord.[5] In 1254 the itinerant justices were instructed to inquire about lands of the king's demesne that had been bought and sold.[6] Then, in 1256, a new law was openly proclaimed. An ordinance informed the sheriffs that because alienations of land by tenants-in-chief caused the king loss of wardships and escheats and left his tenants less able to perform their services, no tenant-in-chief might thenceforth give or sell his land, either in whole or in part, without royal licence. If anyone should do so the sheriff was to take the land into the king's hand and hold it until further order.[7] These provisions became a permanent law for tenants-in-chief and an important part of the king's prerogative.

In 1258 the barons of the kingdom petitioned that all grants of land into 'mortmain'—to religious foundations or other

---

grants to churches; the opinion that it should be so limited looks, therefore, like an inference from the case of 1238. Probably there were no other cases to help interpret the law.

[1] *Close Rolls 1227–1231*, p. 88.
[2] Bean, *Decline of English Feudalism*, pp. 58–62.   [3] fos. 45b–46b.
[4] P. & M. i. 332.   [5] Bean, op. cit., p. 69.
[6] *Rotuli Hundredorum* i. Introduction and p. 20.
[7] *Close Rolls 1254–1256*, p. 429. For the most recent discussion, with references to earlier literature, see Bean, op. cit., pp. 66–79.

corporate bodies—should be forbidden unless the grantor's lord
had given his consent, and this was enacted the next year in
the Provisions of Westminster.[1] The Statute of Marlborough of
1267, which re-enacted after the civil war most of the Provisions
of Westminster, left out this particular section, but in the late
1270s Edward I's government spoke of it as though it was still
in force and stated, indeed, that it had been included in the
Statute of Marlborough.[2]

In effect it had been in force, and so, since the 1250s, had been
other restraints on alienations by the tenants of mesne lords. In
1249 a lay tenant gave his holding to the priory of Sherborne
and the representatives of the feudal lord, incensed at this grant
into mortmain, came a few days later and put the monks out.
The prior brought the assize, but on the finding of these facts
the king's court would not award him his recovery: judgment
was suspended.[3] From 1255 we hear that when a certain tenant
tried to make a grant by way of subinfeudation his lord interfered ('contentionem apposuit') and that his intervention was
effective: the purchaser had to agree to hold directly of the lord
and may have been driven to accept other important conditions
as well.[4] In 1256 the court of the abbot of Ramsey informed
Ralph Punchard, one of the free tenants, that 'he cannot give
up his homage and holding and cannot put another in his place
to do homage and perform his other duties to the abbot, without
the abbot's consent'.[5] In 1258 or shortly before the lord Ralph
of Tichmarsh prevented his tenant Sibyl of Pitford from giving
her holding to William Delisle by telling Delisle's servant, who
had come to receive livery of seisin, that he must get out. The
servant left, to Sibyl's intense anger, for she sued her lord for
disseisin. The case was compromised.[6] In the county of Chester,

---

[1] Select Charters, pp. 375, 393.

[2] Calendar of Close Rolls 1272–1279, pp. 500–1 (1278); Statute of Mortmain, SR i.
51 (1279). See Bean, op. cit., pp. 51–2.

[3] Wilts Civil Pleas 1249 no. 74. Cf. two other cases from the years just following,
where lords sued by the assize pleaded in defence their right to put out would-be
purchasers in their fees who were obnoxious to them, whether the purchasers were
laymen or ecclesiastics: Yorks Assize Rolls pp. 68–9 (1251), J.I. 1/1179 m. 8d (1253).
In each of these cases the plaintiff won, but the lords' defences may have been
acceptable in principle.   [4] J.I. 1/1182 m. 4.

[5] Court Rolls of the Abbey of Ramsey and of the Honor of Clare, p. 34. I am grateful to
Dr. John Beckerman for drawing my attention to this document.

[6] J.I. 1/1179 m. 22.

which enjoyed palatine liberties, a law was laid down in 1260 that if a free tenant enfeoffed a stranger without his lord's permission the lord could expel the feoffee.[1] This is exactly what was done in 1262, without any ordinance and not in Cheshire but in Middlesex, by the lord William of Say. When his bailiffs found that one of the free tenants had sold his holding they came immediately after seisin had been delivered and ejected the purchasers. The purchasers had to come to terms with the lord before he would let them back in, and it took them more than three weeks to arrange this.[2]

How far these new powers of lords developed and how fully the law came to recognize them is revealed in a case of 1269. In Henton, Hampshire, a free tenant of the lady Gillian d'Aubeney attempted to give his holding—a house and twenty-four acres of arable—to one Henry of Huntingfield. As soon as the feoffor delivered seisin to Huntingfield, the lady Gillian came and put Huntingfield out. He sued her for disseisin, but it was decided in the King's Bench that on these facts he could not recover.[3] The pleadings seem to show that the lady was not very confident of the law on which she relied. As she presented her side of the story, she had entered and taken over the holding as soon as she got wind of her tenant's agreement to enfeoff Huntingfield and before Huntingfield had received any livery of seisin at all; so that whatever disseisin she might have committed it was not against him, for he had never had seisin. Furthermore, she said, she had been given to understand that Huntingfield intended, if he ever got the land, to regrant it to a church, the most objectionable kind of transaction for the superior lord and forbidden, unless the lord's permission was obtained, by the Provisions of 1259. But she need not have troubled to colour her case so heavily, for the court was more favourable to her than she knew. The assize assured the justices that seisin had been delivered to Huntingfield and that he was the one whom Gillian ejected. They said nothing about any intended further grant to a church. Even so, the decision was in the lady's favour.

In the same session and the same court Henry of Huntingfield had to make terms with another chief lady of the county of Hampshire, Isabel of Merlay, before she allowed him to accept

---

[1] Plucknett, *Legislation*, pp. 108–9.
[2] K.B. 26/222 m. 7.
[3] K.B. 26/189 m. 12.

a feoffment of land in her fee in Westbrook.[1] From the next two
decades, the 1270s and 1280s, there are other cases that seem
to confirm the lord's lawful power to eject a purchaser in his fee.[2]

When he seized a holding under these circumstances the
lord had actually to keep the purchaser out, or eject him if he
was already there. It was not enough if he took 'simple seisin'
and left the purchaser in occupation.[3] Even so, the lord's power
was to distrain by the fee and not to disseise. Bracton, who would
allow the lord to interfere if his tenant held on the explicit
condition *ne fiat donacio*, said that the lord must return the lands
to the original tenant unless he was willing to pay their full
value.[4] Even the king claimed under the ordinance of 1256 no
right to take the lands for himself,[5] and as for private lords we
hear of their returning the land to the purchasers after they
made terms,[6] or protesting, when suit was brought in the king's
court, that in preventing the purchaser from having seisin they
were claiming no more than lordship and that the seisin of the
original tenant had never been taken from him.[7] In one case the
lord claimed to hold the tenements in demesne, for himself, but
only because his original tenant had released them to him after
he had seized them to prevent the alienation.[8] Otherwise, if the
lord attempted to treat the holding as forfeit his entry was an

[1] K.B. 26/189 m. 12.
[2] It was pleaded in defence, but unsuccessfully as it turned out, in K.B. 27/41
m. 48d (1278), J.I. 1/492 m. 16 (*c.* 1282), and 1/503 m. 34d (1289). In none of
these cases is the principle itself rejected; the last of them strongly suggests that the
court accepted it. So does a judgment given in the King's Bench in 1280 that a
feoffment made just a few hours before the grantor's death was good since the lord
'did not in any way impede [the feoffee's] seisin while [the grantor] still lived', J.I.
1/1245 m. 32d. The lord's power to intervene was again pleaded in J.I. 1/492 m.
49 (*c.* 1282), where the suit ended in compromise, and in C.P. 40/110 m. 207 (1295),
where no judgment was given. In 1279 an assize reported in its verdict that when
a tenant enfeoffed his son, 'the bailiffs of the chief lord of that fee would not allow
it', so that the son 'had no free tenement', J.I. 1/1245 m. 4. Other records recite
incidentally that would-be purchasers of lands had to make terms, and sometimes
onerous terms, with their grantors' lords: J.I. 1/1217 m. 8 (1271), 1/503 m. 9d
(1287), Y.B. 21 & 22 Ed. I p. 272 (1293), 559 (1294), C.P. 40/108 m. 113 (1295).
[3] In 1289 the lord John of Neville failed in his attempt to obstruct a feoffment
on account of this rule, J.I. 1/503 m. 34d.
[4] fos. 48–48b.
[5] Bean, op. cit., pp. 67, 74.
[6] J.I. 1/1182 m. 7 (1255), K.B. 26/222 m. 7 (1262), J.I. 1/503 m. 9d (1287),
Y.B. 21 & 22 Ed. I p. 272 (1293), 559 (1294), C.P. 40/132 m. 156 (1300).
[7] *Wilts Civil Pleas 1249* no. 74, K.B. 26/189 m. 12 (1269), J.I. 1/740 m. 10 (1292).
[8] C.P. 40/110 m. 207 (1295).

illegal disseisin and either the original tenant or his grantee could recover by the assize.[1]

The development of this new law put lords in a much more powerful position. But probably they were not quite comfortable with it. Some of the king's justices seem to have kept to the old ways, ignoring the new law and punishing lords who ousted purchasers. Henry of Bracton was opposed to the whole development; a generation later Gilbert of Thornton repeated Bracton's doctrine while Ralph of Hengham, though he recognized the new law, would nevertheless limit it rather strictly.[2] In the King's Bench in 1286 a lord was convicted on the simple finding that he had disseised his tenant's feoffee immediately after the feoffment.[3] But even where the new law was observed, it demanded a good deal of the lord who would use it. It was conceived of in these terms, that the lord could stop a feoffment by seizing the tenements so as to prevent the grantee from ever gaining seisin, or at any rate peaceable seisin.[4] But under a rule so conceived the lord had to act very fast, for it did not take long for a purchaser to acquire a good seisin. Gillian d'Aubeney, in 1269, pleaded that she took the land before the purchaser ever came into it, and Huntingfield replied that he was seised for five weeks under the feoffment before Gillian interfered; the time allowed the lord was evidently assumed to lie somewhere between these extremes. In its verdict the assize carefully specified that Huntingfield received seisin about noon on a Tuesday and that Gillian ejected him early in the morning on the following Thursday, and the King's Bench considered that this was not too long a delay.

Similarly, records of 1249 and 1251 tell that the lord 'forbade [the purchaser] to enter his fee' or that he took the land 'before

---

[1] J.I. 1/1217 m. 9 (c. 1271), where the lord comported himself as owner by granting the tenements, after he seized them, to his own son; J.I. 1/503 m. 34d (1289), where he put himself in seisin by forcing the villein sub-tenants to attorn to him and taking their fealties.

[2] Bracton fos. 45b–46b; Harvard Law Library MS. 77 fo. 23b; Ralph of Hengham, 'Summa Parva', p. 61.

[3] K.B. 27/98 m. 14. Another case, K.B. 27/125 m. 78 (1290), may also be in point here.

[4] In 1290 it was ruled that a lord had no right to seize the holding after the purchaser had 'good and peaceable seisin', K.B. 27/125 m. 78. The statute of *Quia emptores* had been made but had not yet come into force when this case was heard.

[the purchaser] had any seisin thereof'.[1] In 1295 Gilbert of Clare's counsel pleaded that his lord had 'seized the tenements before [the purchaser] could have any seisin'.[2] The same sort of language appears in other cases.[3] In 1262, when his tenant delivered seisin to purchasers early in the morning, the lord's bailiffs came and ousted them about three hours later.[4] A case of 1253 shows that it was an illegal disseisin to put the grantee out after six months;[5] in 1295 the justices were unsure whether it was permissible for Earl Gilbert of Clare's bailiffs to enter upon a purchaser after thirteen weeks;[6] and from two records of the 1280s it appears that even three weeks' delay was too much.[7] The legislation in Cheshire in 1260 may have been relatively generous when it allowed the lord forty days to eject a purchaser in his fee. Eternal vigilance was the price of the new lordly authority.[8]

In view of the uncertainty and difficulty of the new law, lords must have welcomed the Statute of Mortmain of 1279. In clear terms the statute ruled that if a tenant granted his lands into mortmain the immediate superior lord should be allowed a whole year to enter and oust the purchasers; and when he did so he could hold the land in demesne as forfeit on account of the wrongful alienation. Since this was royal legislation, the king assumed the right to dispense from it, so that if a tenant granted his lands to a church after negotiating with the king for a licence

---

[1] *Wilts Civil Pleas 1249* no. 74, *Yorks Assize Rolls* pp. 68–9.

[2] C.P. 40/110 m. 207.

[3] J.I. 1/1217 m. 20 (1273): the lord pleaded that when his tenant alienated to a monastery he entered 'freshly, so that the abbot never had seisin'; the abbot replied that he was seised for five days before the lord ejected him; the jurors found that the abbot was seised for one day and a few hours more but that he took no esplees and received no fealties from the subtenants. J.I. 1/503 m. 34d (1289): the lord entered 'before [the purchasers] had full and peaceable seisin'. K.B. 27/125 m. 78 (1290); '[the lord] impeded [the purchaser] so that he was never in seisin'. J.I. 1/740 m. 10 (1292): 'he impeded him from taking seisin.' K.B. 26/222 m. 7 (1262): 'as soon as [the grantor] put [the purchasers] in seisin . . . the chief lord of the fee ejected them . . . so that they were never in seisin as of their free tenement.' K.B. 27/41 m. 48d (1278): '[the lord] impeded [the purchaser] from entering the tenements.'

[4] K.B. 26/222 m. 7.   [5] J.I. 1/1179 m. 8d.

[6] C.P. 40/110 m. 207.   [7] J.I. 1/492 m. 16 (1282), 1/503 m. 34d (1289).

[8] When contemporary lawbooks make such cryptic remarks as 'six weeks' possession is good' (*Casus Placitorum*, p. 36 no. 95; cf. *Brevia Placitata*, p. 197), they are probably referring to this short but badly defined period allowed for the lord to intervene after a feoffment by his tenant.

then his lord had no right to prevent him at all. There was protest against this, and in 1292 the king agreed not to give licences unless the consent of the immediate superior lord had been obtained.[1]

The statute *Quia emptores* of 1290 was more of a compromise. Under the newly developed law of the preceding decades lords had been allowed to intervene in order to obstruct any sort of feoffment that was unacceptable to them. But where grants among laymen were in question, it was in practice the gift by way of subinfeudation that was most likely to rouse their opposition; a feoffment by way of substitution, though it too might entail some loss for the lord, was generally much less objectionable. Now in 1290 the statute *Quia emptores* gave every free tenant the right to alienate his holdings, either in whole or in part, by way of substitution, and took away from the lord any right to obstruct him. But on the other hand, the statute ruled, grants in fee simple by way of subinfeudation were to cease altogether. Whenever a gift was made in fee simple, regardless of what language the grantor might use in his deed the feoffee was to hold directly of the grantor's lord and not of the grantor himself.

In long retrospect, *Quia emptores* was a great piece of legislation, since it succeeded in laying down a clear rule on a fundamental matter of the law of property in a way that stood unchanged for many centuries. But in its own day it probably appeared as a hasty attempt to impose an overly simple solution on very complicated conflicts of interest. The Easter parliament of 1290, in which it was made, had been a heady affair. It began as a festival, with the marriage of the king's daughter Joan to Earl Gilbert of Clare; next it saw an important conflict between the government and a party of magnates over the law of franchises, where the king had to give way; the making of *Quia emptores* itself coincided with a second royal wedding in which the king gave his daughter Margaret to John of Brabant; a few days later all the Jews were expelled from England.[2] When they got home and had time for sober reflection many of those who

---

[1] Bean, op. cit., pp. 54–7. Lords claimed forfeitures under the statute in the following cases, for example: J.I. 1/503 m. 31 (1289), C.P. 40/87 m. 25d (1291), K.B. 27/150 m. 8 (1297), Y.B. Hil. 6 Ed. II no. 34 (1313), Pasch. 15 Ed. III no. 20 (1338).

[2] Powicke, *Thirteenth Century*, pp. 512–13.

made and consented to the statute may have repented. Certainly its full acceptance was long delayed. The statute read as though the king's tenants-in-chief were to have the same full freedom as others to alienate their holdings by way of substitution, for it gave that right to 'every free man'. If such had been the intent, it was soon changed, for the king continued to require that his tenants-in-chief obtain his consent. It was only in 1327 that the royal consent became automatic and even then the feoffor had to pay the king a 'reasonable fine'.[1] Meanwhile, private lords may have reflected that the abolition of subinfeudation in grants of fee simple was far from solving all their problems. Subinfeudation continued when the grant was in fee tail, and even a gift by way of substitution could complicate the enforcement of customs and services and, if it was made to joint tenants, might cheat the lord of his feudal incidents for a long time.[2] After the statute lords continued to seize lands that were alienated by their free tenants without their consent, and their right to do so continued to be recognized.[3] They did not finally give up this power until a quarter-century later, when in the parliament of 1315 they agreed 'that henceforth [lords] would neither demand nor take any fine from free men to enter lands and tenements which are of their fees, provided always that by such feoffments they were not deprived of their services nor their services lost'.[4] Even in 1412 it was still said that in Cheshire, Durham, and the honour of Gloucester the lord was entitled to a fine from every purchaser of tenements in his fee.[5]

Altogether, the right of a lord to disseise his free tenants was very restricted. As long as feudal courts met, if such a court gave due judgment within its jurisdiction in favour of a demandant

---

[1] Bean, op. cit., pp. 81–6, 97–103.   [2] Ibid., pp. 86–9.

[3] For a case of 1300, see C.P. 40/132 m. 156. In 1292 a lord ejected a purchaser in his fee on the ground that he had entered by a gift made by way of subinfeudation, contrary to the statute of *Quia emptores*. The statute would appear to make his entry unnecessary, for it voided the terms of such grants in so far as they provided for the feoffee to hold of the feoffor; but the court upheld the lord's right to prevent the purchaser from taking seisin. J.I. 1/740 m. 10.

[4] *Rotuli Parliamentorum* i. 298. For the enforcement of fines of this type, see *Economic History Review* ii. 306, which shows a manorial steward, early in the fourteenth century, distraining purchasers of free tenements to pay fines at the lord's will. Dr. John Beckerman was kind enough to draw my attention to this document.

[5] Kiralfy, *Source Book*, pp. 74–82 (1412).

in an action of right, then the lord could disseise the tenant to execute judgment. After 1279 the lord had a statutory right to disseise churches that received lands granted in mortmain by his tenants, and to keep the lands for himself. But otherwise the furthest limit of his powers was to 'distrain by the fee' under certain circumstances: by judgment of his court if the services were not duly rendered, a practice that presently died out; on his own motion if his life tenant committed waste or, in the half-century from about 1250 to about 1300, if he wished to prevent gifts or sales by any of his free tenants. If the lord went beyond his rights he was likely to find himself sued by the assize and convicted of an illegal disseisin.

The fact that the assize served to enforce such strict limits on the lord's power lends support to Professor Milsom's hypothesis that the basic purpose of the assize when it was first founded was to protect tenants against their lords.[1] Certainly there was a striking contrast between the jealous circumscription of the lord's power to disseise and the large freedom to disseise that the law conceded to one who could show a superior right to hold the land in demesne. If someone who was out of possession had a better title, if he was the true and rightful owner of the land, the law generally allowed him to disseise the sitting tenant and take what was his own.

This needs to be demonstrated with care, for Henry of Bracton, interpreted in modern times by F. W. Maitland, has taught us to believe the contrary.[2] Suppose, Bracton says, that a free man holds a piece of land with perfect unblemished right. Suppose that a mere lawless stranger, with no right and no colour of right, comes and ejects him and occupies the land. The owner may defend himself against being ejected, and if he is ejected nevertheless he may within four days take any opportunity to move back in, putting his adversary out in turn. But after only four days if he has not yet made his move he loses his right of self-help. The law will no longer allow him to disseise the usurping stranger. After only four days if he wants his land back he must go to court and get a judgment and be restored by an officer of the court acting in execution of the judgment. If he should disregard this prohibition and return to his land after

---

[1] Above, pp. 30-1.
[2] Maitland, 'Beatitude of Seisin', pp. 24-39, 286-99, with references to Bracton.

(let us say) a week or two and eject the adversary, he would lay himself open to an action at law: the adversary, even though he had no right at all to the land, could sue by novel disseisin, charging that the owner had ejected him, as the writ said, 'wrongfully and without a judgment'. Here, Bracton explains, the word 'wrongfully' *means* 'without a judgment'. The owner would not be allowed to argue in defence that he acted rightfully because the land was his. He acted without judgment of a court and therefore he acted wrongfully. He should be convicted of illegal disseisin and amerced; the opponent should be put back in seisin of the land. Later the owner could sue at law, as he ought to have done in the first place, and recover his property.

Under some circumstances, Bracton indicates, more than four days may be allowed. If the owner was out of the county when his land was taken from him he would be allowed reasonable time to learn of the trouble and to make the journey. If he was outside the kingdom, yet more time would be allowed. And so for various special circumstances. But the basic rule was, four days. Once upon a time, Bracton says, fifteen days were given; but now only four.[1] It amounted, as Maitland observed, to a surprisingly tight limitation of the owner's right of self-help.

The fact is, however, that the thirteenth-century courts knew no such doctrine, and did not restrain an owner's rights of self-help in any way even nearly so strict. In months of searching I have not found a single record where the four-day rule was applied, where anyone supposed that it might be applied, or where it was even mentioned. The records yield, on the contrary, a great many cases that demonstrate the law's general permissiveness. Let us examine some of them.

(1) 1203. Roger gave lands to Agnes and later gave the same lands to Brice. In receiving livery of seisin, Brice expelled Agnes. Agnes disseised Brice in turn and he brought the assize. Ruled, that he may not recover. The court did not inquire how long Agnes had waited before she disseised him.[2]

(2) 1221. Nicholas disseised Robert and Ralph, and Robert and Ralph disseised Nicholas within a week after. Nicholas may not recover by the assize.[3]

---

[1] fo. 163.   [2] *CRR* iii. 67.
[3] *Eyres of Glos, Warw, Staffs* no. 293.

(3) 1227. Roger had two acres of land. Nicholas 'intruded himself' into them and handed them over to his brother Benedict. Some months passed: Nicholas and Benedict joined in planting the land and Benedict took the harvest. Then Roger ejected Benedict and Benedict brought the assize; but he could not recover because he 'had nothing except by intrusion'.[1]

(4) 1227. A man took land under a lease for a term of years. After his term expired he held on by force, and died seised, and his widow held the land as dower. Ruled, that the lessor may lawfully disseise the widow.[2]

(5) 1243. Rosamund ejected her brother Richard, who was under age, from his lands. He disseised her in turn and she brought the assize. Ruled, that she may not recover, since she entered by disseisin. The court was apparently not interested in how long she might have held before Richard put her out.[3]

(6) 1250. Robert sold his land to Walter and later sold the same land to Richard. Richard ejected Walter. Six months later, Walter returned and disseised Richard, who brought the assize. Ruled, that he may not recover. The presiding justice was Henry of Bracton.[4]

(7) 1255. A defendant, charged with disseising Maud of Burton, pleaded that he was within his rights in doing it because she had come to the land by disseising him, without any good cause, a week earlier. The assize found that Maud had wrongfully disseised him and that he had 'straightway' re-ejected her. He was acquitted. In this case, too, Bracton was the presiding justice.[5]

(8) 1258. In the course of a complicated dispute about lands that had been mortgaged to secure a debt, John ejected Henry and held the land for about a week until Henry came back and disseised John in turn. John brought the assize but could not recover on these facts. Judgment was postponed, apparently because of the tangled difficulty of the underlying quarrel about the mortgage, and the record shows no conclusion.[6]

(9) 1275. About 1262 Richard sued Hugh for lands which Hugh did not hold, and recovered and had the judgment executed. Walter, who really held the tenements, was put out

---

[1] *BNB* no. 1904. [2] *Eyre of Bucks 1227* no. 242.
[3] K.B. 26/125 m. 13, 21. [4] J.I. 1/1178 m. 6.
[5] *Somerset Pleas* i. 1514. [6] J.I. 1/1187 m. 6d.

by execution, and this was, of course, an illegal disseisin.[1] Some
while later, perhaps in 1266, Walter reoccupied the property,
ejecting Richard. Richard brought the assize in 1275 and these
facts appeared. Ruled, that Richard may not recover.[2]

(10) 1276. Simon died leaving Agnes as his true heir. But
Maud pretended to the heritage, and entered the tenements
along with Agnes, and threw Agnes out and held for two weeks.
Then Agnes returned and ejected Maud. Ruled on these facts,
that Maud may not recover by the assize.[3]

There are other cases too,[4] but perhaps these are enough. The
four-day rule is a myth. It remains true, on the other hand, that
if the owner of land left a usurper in undisturbed occupation for
a considerable time, neglecting his right, then the courts would
indeed forbid him to take his land back by disseisin and, if he
did so, would convict him at the assize and restore the holding
to his opponent. Bracton says so in very clear language,[5] and
this time the records bear him out. In 1192 Abbot Samson of
St. Edmunds warned his monks, who were attempting to re-
claim properties that had been usurped against them, that
because of the assize it was not lawful, even if the monks could
show a superior right, to disseise men of free tenements that they
had held 'for many years'.[6] In 1210 a litigant argued in court
that if a lessee of land holds over after the expiration of his lease
and claims the freehold, and if the true owner allows this state
of affairs to continue 'for a long time' without doing anything
to oppose it, then the owner loses his right to disseise the lessee;[7]
and in a case of 1275 there appears a judgment based on that
principle.[8] In 1223 several freeholders were disseised of rights
of common of pasture when the owner of the soil ploughed and
planted it. They waited until the crop sprang up and then
claimed their common rights by putting their animals in to
graze on the shoots. It was ruled that this was illegal.[9] In 1260

---

[1] Above, pp. 79–80.   [2] K.B. 27/37 m. 32.   [3] Sel. Cases in K.B. i. 27–9.

[4] CRR v. 250–1 (1208), Eyres of Glos, Warw, Staffs nos. 508, 1060 (1221), 1461
(1222), K.B. 26/131 m. 7d (1243), K.B. 27/20A m. 20 (1276), 27/98 m. 10d (1288).

[5] See especially fos. 205, 209b, 210.

[6] Chronicle of Jocelin of Brakelond, p. 78.   [7] CRR vi. 76–7.

[8] K.B. 27/18 m. 15. The lessee had held over for eight or nine years, claiming
the freehold by a fraudulent feoffment that he had arranged while his lease was
running.

[9] CRR xi. 614. The law looked with disfavour on any disseisin that involved
destruction of crops; cf. Casus Placitorum, p. lxxxiii, no. 74.

it was likewise ruled, in a case involving the rights of Robert Bruce, John Balliol, and Henry of Hastings, that if one of several parceners appropriates to his exclusive use a portion of the common heritage, and if the other parceners allow him to continue without disturbance for about five months, they may not thereafter interfere with his seisin.[1] In 1281 it was judged that where a tenant had allowed his neighbour to put up a bank that constituted a nuisance, and allowed the bank to stand undisturbed for a whole year, he might not thereafter throw it down on his own authority, not even when it had been presented as a nuisance in the manor court.[2] In a similar case of 1284, the justices were uncertain whether one or two weeks' delay was too long, and reserved judgment.[3]

There was no strict definition of how long the wrongful occupier must hold in order to qualify for protection against disseisin, and apparently no attempt, outside of Bracton's treatise, to find a strict definition. When the court records wish to assure us that the true owner was within his rights in disseising a usurper they say that he acted 'quickly',[4] 'freshly',[5] 'straight-way',[6] or (by far the favourite phrase) 'as soon as he learned of it'.[7] One tenant who was unlawfully put out of his land 'did not consider himself disseised, but took the land back', and the law approved his conduct under that description.[8]

Bracton, too, uses just such indefinite language in most of the passages of his treatise where he touches upon this matter.[9] Only in a few places does he mention his specific four-day rule[10] and only once does he state it directly.[11] But when he first approaches

----

[1] K.B. 26/164 m. 13.

[2] J.I. 1/1245 m. 61d.   [3] Ibid., m. 95d.

[4] 'cito post', *Eyres of Glos, Warw, Staffs* no. 232 (1221).

[5] 'recenter', K.B. 26/147B m. 23d (1252).

[6] 'statim', B.M. Add. Charter 5153 (1276).

[7] 'Quando invenit', *Pleas 1198–1202* ii. 870 (1202); 'quamcito hoc perceperunt', K.B. 26/127 m. 16d (1243); 'hoc percipiens', K.B. 27/94 m. 15d (1285); 'hoc perpendens', K.B. 27/114 m. 5d (1288). In this last case the usurper had actually stayed in the tenements for 102 days before the rightful owner disseised him.

[8] *BNB* no. 1801 (1222).

[9] The true owner must disseise the usurper 'recenter', fos. 51b, 52, 195b, 209b, 212b, 'statim' and 'incontinenti', fos. 31, 52, 168, 196, 205, 'sine aliquo intervallo, flagrante disseisina', fos. 162b–163, 'flagrante facto', fo. 231b, 'statim et recenter flagrante maleficio', fo. 233; he may not eject him 'post longum intervallum', fos. 196, 210, 234, or when he has had 'longa et pacifica seisina', fo. 31.

[10] fos. 6b–7, 23, 218b, and 262.   [11] fos. 163–163b.

that one direct discussion of it he begins by saying, 'Tempus . . . non definitur',[1] and when a few lines further on he comes to state the rule it first appears in the extraordinary form, 'fiat in crastino, tertio die, vel quarto, *vel ulterius cum debita continuatione,* quod fieri debuit primo die'. Where extra time must be allowed for a disseisee who is absent to learn of the wrong he has suffered and come to the scene, 'in veniendo computande sunt rationabiles diete'; when this has been allowed him—'allocatis ei dilationibus rationabilibus'—he should eject the disseisor, Bracton says, within four days after 'vel ulterius ex causa'. It is not until nearly the end of this key passage that he expresses the four-day rule without qualification.

It makes good sense to interpret what is vague in the light of what is precise, and Maitland is therefore correct when he says that the thoughtful reader who works his way through all of Bracton's long book on novel disseisin will conclude that this principal passage where Bracton states the four-day rule should be regarded 'as governing all that is said in other parts of the book'.[2] But when we find that the rule was never used in litigation but that many cases were decided without reference to it, and when we consider how hesitantly and ambiguously Bracton puts it on the one occasion when he explains it directly, then surely his statement of it loses its power to govern the other passages in his treatise, surely his many less definite phrases must be taken after all as expressing the true state of the law.

Maitland thought that Bracton might have found his four-day rule in a venerable legal tradition, and collected several examples of three- and four-day limitations used for various purposes in older medieval law both English and Continental.[3] But none of them can be shown to be connected with Bracton's doctrine and in fact they probably have nothing to do with it; Bracton was not much interested in legal antiquities, and in any case he suggested that his four-day rule was new.[4] I think that we had better take it as a product of his private speculation. There was a rule actually used in the courts that no one could consider himself disseised, and bring the assize for it and recover, unless he had been in firm possession of the tenements to begin

---

[1] Cf. fos. 51b–52: 'Quam longa esse debeat non definitur a iure sed ex iusta discretione.'   [2] 'Beatitude of Seisin', pp. 33–4, 39 n.
[3] Ibid., pp. 31–2.   [4] Above, p. 98.

with: he must have been 'seised and disseised'. Where his seisin
was gained in the face of opposition, as by ejecting an adverse
claimant, it had to be continued for a few days in order to
establish its reality. Even with the best title in the world he
would not enjoy the protection of the assize until then. I have
no specific evidence of it, but the minimum time the law required may have been four days; if there was a definite limit it
was certainly not much more or less than that, and if the limit
was indefinite it was of about that order of length.[1] From the
rule, 'No disseisor is protected by the assize unless he has been
in for four days, however good his title', Bracton reasoned to a
corollary, 'Every disseisor is protected by the assize if he has
been in for four days, however bad his title.' The corollary did
not in fact follow, either in good logic or in English law, but it
was attractive. If accepted it would classify every disseisor as
protected by the assize or not protected on the basis of a single
and clear criterion, whether he had stayed in control for four
days or not, and would free the law of all the complexities and
ambiguities that actually governed the decisions of the courts
in these matters. Bracton liked the idea enough to write it into
his treatise, though only very diffidently, and once ensconced
there it was repeated by law-writers for a long time after.[2]
But no one, not even Henry of Bracton, ever assigned it such
authority as to use it in ruling, as a justice, on a case before him.

The four-day rule was no part of the law. The rule that the
courts really used was that the owner could disseise a usurper
provided that he acted without undue delay. They never defined
exactly what constituted waiting too long, and perhaps they
were wise not to attempt to do so, for the varied circumstances
that might bear on a judgment of the matter in individual cases
would soon make light of any fixed definition. We may surely
believe Bracton that the justices would consider whether the

[1] Below, p. 148.

[2] *Fleta* iv. 2, *Mirror of Justice* p. 156 no. 4, and the gloss on Bracton cited by
Maitland, 'Beatitude of Seisin', p. 30. *Britton* ii. 13. 3, states the law that was
actually applied, namely, that there was no definite limit but that the owner must
act without delay; but in one manuscript this passage is altered to provide a five-
day limit. The repetition by these writers in the reigns of the first two Edwards of
the doctrine of a four- or five-day limit, far from confirming that it was a genuine
rule of law, only tends the more to show that it was a fancy, for as Maitland
recognized ('Beatitude of Seisin', p. 30) it is clear that no such law was enforced
in those later days.

owner was in the region when his rights were interfered with, and how long it took him to learn of the trouble.[1] A man who was ill or in prison might receive similar allowance,[2] and a minor would be allowed all the remaining years of his minority and a reasonable time after he came of age.[3] Some recorded cases suggest that the time allowed may have depended in part on whether the usurper pretended from the first some good colour of right for himself. If he did, the owner might seem to give countenance to his claim by any delay to act against him, and might therefore be the sooner debarred from disseising his opponent.[4] If this was so, Bracton is presumably guiding us well when he says, now and again in his treatise, that an undue delay is one which implies negligence of his right or consent to his adversary's claim on the part of the true owner.[5] Maitland, who believed that the four-day rule was firm law, took Bracton's talk about negligence and consent as an attempt to rationalize the rule.[6] It is more likely to represent the main principle of the law.

Besides this large and loosely defined rule, the law knew a few lesser restraints upon the owner's right to disseise. If he once opened a lawsuit for recovery of his land, he lost the right to put himself back in on his own, even if no considerable time had elapsed. By opening suit he recognized that his enemy was in

---

[1] The law is illustrated in *CRR* v. 250–1 (1208). Bracton, fo. 45b, says that where the owner is out of the realm and therefore presumably ignorant of the interference with his rights it will require a delay of ten years or so to give the usurper any legal protection; and again, fo. 282, 'time does not run against the absent'.

[2] Bracton fo. 279, *CRR* iii. 308–9 (1205).

[3] *BNB* no. 1820 (1227), K.B. 26/116B m. 3d (1236), K.B. 27/125 m. 77d (1290), Y.B. Hil. 6 Ed. II nos. 35, 36 (1313), *Eyre of Kent* ii. 181–3, iii. 87 ff., 145–6 (1313).

[4] *CRR* vi. 76–7 (1210), K.B. 26/125 m. 21 (1243), K.B. 27/18 m. 15 (1275), J.I. 1/503 m. 16d (1288).

[5] 'Acquiritur possessio et liberum tenementum ex tempore . . . per patientiam et negligentiam veri domini', fo. 52; 'quod si per longum tempus expectaverit, videbitur per hoc iniuriam dissimulasse . . . Oportebit [tamen] distinguere locorum distantiam et tempora et diligentiam vel negligentiam disseisiti . . . Si autem verus possessor negligens fuerit post disseisinam et negligens impetrator, patiens et dissimulans iniuriam . . . non succurritur ei nisi per assisam', fos. 163–163b; 'patientia . . . longa trahitur ad consensum, et negligentia sive dissimulatio abolent iniuriam', fo. 209b. Cf. fos. 31, 48, 51, 195b–196, 253, 267b, 282, 313. If the dispossessed owner makes from the beginning continual and determined attempts to oust his adversary, no negligence can be imputed to him, and therefore no time runs against him; if he should finally be successful in disseising his opponent, it is legal even though 'a long time' may have passed: fo. 39.

[6] 'Beatitude of Seisin', pp. 38, 296.

seisin and that he was powerless to do anything about it, and he invoked the aid of the king's court. If he afterwards resorted to self-help he would be upsetting a state of affairs that he had acknowledged to exist and would be showing contempt of the king's jurisdiction.[1]

Again, an owner might lose his right to disseise because his opponent died in occupation of the holding and his claim to it, such as it was, passed on to his heir. The owner might have been entitled to eject the original adversary, but he could not lawfully prevent the heir from taking seisin and could not afterwards put him out without a judgment.[2] So too if the usurper gave or sold the lands to a third party. If the owner entered and disseised the purchaser hard upon the livery of seisin, well and good: the feoffment was frustrated and the owner was within his rights. But like a feudal lord who wanted to prevent a feoffment by his tenant, the owner in this case had to act very fast or he would lose his right to put the feoffee out.[3] These two rules led a fleeting existence in the thirteenth century, for cases to which they might have applied were usually swallowed up in the larger rule that disseisin must be prompt if it was to be lawful. The opponent would not often die and leave the property to an heir, would not often manage a valid feoffment to a third person, unless the owner had delayed long in asserting his rights. But there is enough material to show their existence for the later part of the century if not for the earlier, and in the fourteenth century they came into clear focus for reasons which we shall examine in the next chapter.[4]

Generally speaking, the law allowed disseisin, under these common conditions and restrictions, in every sort of case where a usurper was holding tenements against the true owner,

---

[1] Bracton fos. 163–163b, 226–226b, 234b, *CRR* v. 44 (1207), *Eyres of Glos, Warw, Staffs* nos. 405, 412, 598 (1221), *BNB* nos. 530 (1231), 1170 (1235–6), *Sel. Cases in K.B.* i. 10–12 (1274), ii. 98 (1292), J.I. 1/503 m. 16d (1286–9), Y.B. 20 & 21 Ed. I p. 52 (1292). The doctrine was abandoned in the early fourteenth century, Y.B. Mich. 11 Ed. II no. 26 (1317), Pasch. 15 Ed. II pp. 465–6 (1322).

[2] *Eyre of Bucks 1227* nos. 309, 405, K.B. 26/113 m. 20d (1233), K.B. 27/11 m. 25 (1275), J.I. 1/1245 m. 12d, 14 (1279), K.B. 27/57 m. 40 (1280), J.I. 1/1245 m. 91 (1283), 1/503 m. 2d (1286). A case to the contrary comes from 1221, *BNB* no. 1976.

[3] J.I. 1/1182 m. 7d (1256), K.B. 26/158 m. 10d (1258), 26/186 m. 18 (1268), 26/191 m. 10 (1270), 26/200B m. 11 (1270), Y.B. 20 & 21 Ed. I, p. 415 (1292).

[4] Below, p. 160.

whatever the particular circumstances. If the owner had himself been illegally disseised, he could oust his adversary in turn, as most of the cases already cited go to show. So too if trouble arose not from disseisin but from an interference with proper succession. When a free tenant died in seisin of his lands, the person next entitled could of course go and take possession: the heir if the last tenant had held in fee, the feudal lord as claiming his escheat if the tenant had held in fee and there were no heirs, the 'reversioner' or 'remainderman', as they later came to be called, after the death of particular tenants such as those who held for life. If the new owner came to assume possession and found that someone else had got there first and occupied the tenements and was holding them against him, he could disseise the interloper, provided as always that he acted with reasonable dispatch.

Bracton reported that some people thought there was a special rule which assigned the heir or reversioner a fixed period of one year to disseise an interloper with the law's blessing,[1] and the law-writers of the generation that followed Bracton continued the search for some special and certain allowance in these cases, though they came up with the most varied results.[2] For his own part Bracton only said that an heir or reversioner might disseise the usurper who had forestalled him 'straightway and freshly . . . before he has long and peaceable seisin . . . by virtue of the passage of time, which suffices in place of a title', and before the opponent has had 'time sufficient to give title . . . on account of the negligence or compliance or powerlessness of the owners'— just the same conditions as for the lawful ouster of 'intruders or disseisors'.[3] The records show that this is correct, and cases of this type provide, in fact, excellent illustrations of the general law in all its fluidity and indefiniteness.

(1) 1206. After her husband died, a widow held on in his lands for eighteen months and was then ejected, apparently by one who claimed as heir or reversioner. The court was inclined to think that she could recover by the assize only if she could show that the lands were rightly hers.[4]

[1] fo. 161.
[2] *Britton* ii. 12. 1 and cf. ii. 11. 5. Ralph of Hengham, 'Summa Parva', pp. 60–1. *Fleta* iv. 7. 2. 'Judicium Essoniorum' p. 135. Thornton, Harvard Law Library MS. 77 fo. 47ᵛ.   [3] fos. 253, 206. Cf. fos. 64–64b, 168, 169b, 216–216b.
[4] *Lincs Assize Rolls* no. 1425.

(2) 1225. Roger died seised as of fee. Henry intruded upon the vacant holding. The true heir 'then came . . . and ejected him'. Ruled, that the heir was within his rights. The record does not trouble to tell how long the heir delayed.[1]

(3) 1232. A man died seised of land, survived by the son of his first marriage and by his second wife. The widow entered upon those of his lands which at the time of her marriage had been designated as her eventual dower. She held for four months and one week. Then she was ejected by her stepson, who claimed that the lands were his heritage from his mother. Ruled, regardless of the merits of the rival claims to title, that this disseisin was illegal.[2]

(4) 1250. John enfeoffed William of land and died four days later. William held for three weeks; then John's heir came and disseised him. Henry of Bracton, who heard the case, ruled that his three weeks' seisin was not sufficient of itself to get William a recovery by the assize; he had to prove that the feoffment had been complete, effective, and valid.[3]

(5) 1268. After the death of a burgess of Southampton, several persons occupied his holdings in the borough, claiming as coheirs. They held for one month. Then Richard and Simon claimed that the heritage belonged to them and disseised the others. Ruled in the King's Bench, that this disseisin was unlawful. The judgment may have been influenced by special customs of the borough.[4]

(6) 1278. Robert died seised of lands in fee. A group of three brothers, claiming to be coheirs, entered his lands and held for seven weeks. Then William, who said that he alone was the true heir, disseised them. Ruled, that regardless of who was the right heir this disseisin was illegal.[5]

(7) 1278–9. A life tenant died. His heir entered the lands and held on for ten weeks; then the true reversioner disseised him. Justices Rochester and Saddington ruled that the disseisin was illegal but their judgment was reversed in the King's Bench.[6]

(8) 1291. When John died Roger occupied his lands, claiming under an old adverse title. He stayed in for 'half a year' until

[1] *Somerset Pleas* i. 334.   [2] *CRR* xiv. 2377 = *BNB* no. 885.
[3] J.I. 1/1178 m. 18.   [4] K.B. 26/186 m. 30.
[5] K.B. 27/35 m. 18 d.   [6] K.B. 27/47 m. 32–3.

the heir ejected him. The court of Common Pleas was unsure whether this disseisin was unlawful.[1]

Many other cases go to the same effect,[2] and there are yet others that illustrate in this connection the extra allowance of time, sometimes amounting to years, made in favour of owners who lay under disability, such as minors or those who were absent from the kingdom.[3]

In cases of disputed succession there were, however, a few additional rules that operated to restrain disseisins, especially in the early part of the thirteenth century. If a holding was left vacant by the death of a tenant the feudal lord had the right, or rather the duty, of occupying it in order to hold it for the person next entitled. Since he ought not to surrender it to any-one other than the person entitled, he could continue his control until the true heir, reversioner, or remainderman came and satisfied him as to his right. This meant that no one who came to claim land after the death of a free tenant had any right at all to disseise the feudal lord, if it was the feudal lord whom he found in occupation. The new owner must persuade the lord to admit him or, if the lord would not be persuaded, must sue at law.[4]

From this it was held to follow, in the earlier part of the century, that just as he could not disseise the lord so the person truly entitled could not disseise anyone who had come in through the lord's acknowledgement of his right. The owner was allowed to oust only the false rival pretender who had put himself in without that authority.[5] After about mid century, however, this distinction disappeared, and in Edward I's reign those who came in 'by the lord' were in no different case from those who entered

---

[1] Sutherland, 'Peytevin *v.* la Lynde', pp. 543–5.

[2] *Northants Pleas* nos. 777, 903 (1203), *CRR* vii. 63 (1214), xiii. 1197–8 (1228), K.B. 26/181 m. 17 (1267), K.B. 27/24 m. 23d (1276), 27/94 m. 16 (1285), J.I. 1/503 m. 35 (1289), C.P. 40/92 m. 188d (1292), 40/101 m. 21 (1293), 40/110 m. 258 (1295).

[3] *Sel. Cases in K.B.* i. 10–12 (1274), J.I. 1/503 m. 2d (1286), C.P. 40/60 m. 87d (1285), 40/127 m. 26 (1299).

[4] Bracton fos. 213, 218, 253b, 267b–268. The last of these passages needs to be emended: it should read: 'Si autem seisina vacua non fuerit cum capitalis dominus extiterit in seisina, sine voluntate ipsius *neuter* se ponat in seisinam.'

A case of 1219, *Eyre of Yorks 1218–19* no. 28, shows that this rule did not apply if the lord had entered claiming an escheat to which he was not entitled.

[5] Bracton fos. 253–253b, 314–314b; *BNB* no. 1792 (1222), K.B. 26/120 m. 28 (1239), 26/124 m. 22d (1242).

on their own. The true owner could disseise any of these if he
acted promptly.[1]

As for the lord himself, his right to take control of the tenements and hold them for the new owner applied only when he
found them vacant. He had no right to eject anyone for this
purpose, not even the most blatant usurper.[2] He was allowed to
disseise an interloper only when he was entitled to have the land
for himself as his escheat. Even then, the older law may have
required that he proceed by judgment of his feudal court. In
1199 a lord was convicted of disseisin because he ejected an
interloper without a judgment based on the king's writ,[3] and in
1202 the justices ruled that when a married woman died without an heir and her husband stayed on in her lands the lord
must not on his own authority put the husband out in order to
claim the escheat.[4] But if this requirement had ever been strictly
enforced, it was left behind later on with the decline of the
feudal courts. Bracton said that the lord who came to take his
escheat could disseise any intruder whom he found there, provided that he acted without delay: he need seek no judgment,
of his own court or of any other.[5] His doctrine is confirmed by
one case of as early as 1214 and by several others of mid century
and after.[6] Only if he received fealty from the usurper, accepted
services for the tenement from him, or let him hold on for some
time was the lord prevented from disseising him without a
judgment.[7]

Apart from illegal disseisins and from interferences with proper
succession on the death of a tenant, the orderly maintenance

[1] The old rule was doubted and judgment suspended in 1260, J.I. 1/1179 m. 27d.
Two later cases show that it had lost its force, K.B. 26/189 m. 12 (1269), K.B. 27/47
m. 32–3 (1278–9).

[2] Bracton fos. 218, 253, 418, Provisions of Westminster c. 16 (1259), Statute of
Marlborough c. 16 (1267); *Northants Pleas* no. 782 (1203), *Eyres of Lincs and Worcs*
no. 256 (1219).   [3] *Rotuli Curiae Regis* i. 447–8.

[4] *Eyres of Beds* i. 63. In contrast with the lord claiming his escheat, the woman's
heir, if she had an heir, could oust her widower when he came to claim his heritage:
CRR iii. 66 (1203), vi. 333–4 (1212), *Eyre of Yorks 1218–19* no. 22, *BNB* no. 917 =
CRR xi. 2633 (1224). Of course, no one was entitled to put the widower out,
neither the lord nor the heir, if the widower had a right of courtesy.

[5] fos. 218, 253.

[6] *CRR* vii. 136–7 (1214), *Somerset Pleas* i. 577 (1242–3), K.B. 26/181 m. 20d
(1267), *Derby Assizes* pp. 43–4 (1272), C.P. 40/90 m. 61 (1291).

[7] C.P. 40/143 m. 166 (1302). In the late thirteenth century such a judgment
would usually be not in the feudal court but in the king's court, upon a writ of
escheat brought by the lord: *Britton* ii. 6. 2.

of men's rights was often upset by that peculiar offspring of the medieval common law, the tortious feoffment. Tortious feoffments arose when land was given away by a grantor who was in lawful occupation but who had no right to make the gift. A serf, a guardian, or a bailiff, for example, might give to a stranger freehold rights in the lands that he enjoyed or administered, though he himself had no freehold. A husband managing his wife's holdings while the marriage lasted, or a widow holding her dower for life, might sell the land outright, in fee. A minor, who ought not to dismember his estate while under age, might give away some of his property. And so in a good many other cases.

Those who made tortious feoffments had no right to give as they did, for someone was always injured: the freeholder whose bailiff sold the land that he was supposed to administer, the reversioner who discovered that his life tenant had given the land away forever, the minor who injured himself by his own grant, and so forth. But the feoffments, although they were wrongful, were none the less real, for in the medieval law—and this was its peculiarity—a feoffment of land was a matter of fact, not of right, and as a matter of fact the grantors could carry through the gifts for they were in control of the tenements. The law could not treat these feoffments as void, as though they had not occurred.[1] Instead, it had to provide ways for the injured parties to undo them.

The law gave a series of writs of entry by which the victims of various kinds of tortious feoffments could bring actions in court to recover the lands.[2] But it had also to decide whether the aggrieved party should be allowed a direct remedy without resort to legal proceedings. Should he be permitted to disseise the grantee?

---

[1] In contrast, dispositive writings could accomplish only what they could accomplish lawfully, and any tortious effects that they purported to carry were simply void. Thus if a life tenant made a feoffment in fee it was effective even though tortious, and the reversioner would have to sue to defeat it after the life tenant's death. But if the life tenant gave to another for his own (the grantor's) lifetime, as he might lawfully do, and then released to him in fee, the release was wholly void, as being a dispositive writing that purported a tortious effect. When the life tenant died the reversioner could enter and take possession of the tenements just as though the release had never been made.

[2] P. & M. ii 54 n., 68. A rare writ of entry *sine assensu viri* appears in *Wilts Civil Pleas 1249* no. 464.

Until late in the thirteenth century there were some justices who evidently believed that the answer in every case was No. Probably they reasoned that even if he had nothing else in his favour, everyone who received land by a tortious feoffment had at least come in under colour of good title, namely by the feoffment itself from one who was in peaceable occupation, and that that alone should entitle him to hold until he was removed by process of law. Their opinion shows itself in judgments as late as 1280.[1] But another view, probably always the commoner and certainly the one that prevailed in the end, distinguished among different kinds of tortious feoffments. In principle, it seems to have been thought by those who held this opinion, the injured party was entitled to disseise the grantee simply because the grantee was holding the lands against him wrongfully. So the grantee might be put out where he had come in by the feoffment of a minor, a madman, a married woman acting without her husband, a bailiff, a guardian, a serf, a tenant-at-will, and perhaps a termor.[2] But on the other hand, the law must prohibit the injured party from ejecting the grantee in several other kinds of cases where for special reasons it had to insist that he

---

[1] *BNB* no. 1203 (1236–7), *Somerset Pleas* iv. 62–3, 207–8, 223–5 (1280). Bracton, who held very different views about tortious feoffments, seems embarrassed by this first case, but glides over it without any real effort to explain it away, fo. 31b.

[2] Bracton was an extreme advocate of this view, fos. 13b, 26b, 31–31b, 39, 40b, 43, 52, 58, 165b, 184–184b. It is attested in these early cases, *CRR* v. 250–1 (1208), vi. 81–2 (1210), 305–6 (1212), *Eyres of Lincs and Worcs* no. 935 (1221), *Eyre of Bucks 1227* no. 187, *BNB* no. 1899 (1227), *CRR* xiv. 460, 862 = *BNB* nos. 429, 471 (1230), and in very many cases from Edward I's reign and after, e.g. C.P. 40/138 m. 20 (1301), Y.B. Mich. 4 Ed. II no. 36 (1310), *Eyre of Kent* ii. 181–3 (1313). It is also implied by the doctrine, commonly held by mid century and finally growing into firm law, that a tortious feoffment constituted an illegal disseisin when it was made by a grantor who had no freehold—such as a serf or guardian or bailiff—or who had no right to dispose of his freehold—a minor, a madman, or a married woman acting alone: below, pp. 146–7. For if it was an illegal disseisin, obviously the injured party was entitled to put himself back in by prompt action.

Where the person injured by a tortious feoffment was entitled to disseise the grantee he must, like any other lawful disseisor, act without delay. In some men's opinion this rule may have worked to prohibit disseisin of the grantee who came in under a feoffment by a termor. If the feoffment was made well before the term expired, it might be reasoned that the injured party had no right to act until the term was over and that it was too late for him to act then against the grantee who had by that time been in long and peaceable occupation. *Eyres of Lincs and Worcs* no. 38 (1218) seems to express such a view. But Bracton held that a tortious feoffment by a termor was a disseisin, so that the injured party could take immediate action, fo. 161b, and this rule was enacted by the Statute of Westminster II c. 25: below, p. 146.

await the death of the man who made the feoffment before
seeking any recovery.

It was, for instance, wrong for a man to sell lands that belonged
to his wife. But if he did so, the lady must not oppose the transaction as long as she remained his wife, for the law would not
allow a married woman to act against her husband. Only after
the marriage-bond was dissolved could she move to regain her
lands, and this ordinarily meant waiting until his death. But
precisely because the maker of the tortious feoffment was then
dead, the law would not let her put herself back into the tenements on her own: she had to seek her remedy by suing in
court.[1] We may reasonably guess that the same rule applied, as
it certainly did in later times, where an abbot alienated the
lands of his house without the assent of the monks. They could
not oppose their abbot; only the abbot's successor could seek
remedy, after the abbot's day, and the successor had to seek it
through the courts and not by self-help.[2] After the establishment
of entails by the statute *De donis conditionalibus* of 1285 the rule
applied to alienations by tenants in fee tail. Such alienations
were tortious, but the right to interfere belonged in the first
place to the heir in tail. Since a living man had no heir, no one
could be given a right to interfere until after the death of the
tenant who had alienated, and then it was too late to allow any
disseisin without a previous court judgment.[3]

The rule that there might be no self-help after the death of

---

[1] The writ of entry *cui in vita* was provided for her case. The rule that she might
not oust the feoffee is illustrated in *Rotuli Curiae Regis* i. 189 (1198–9), *CRR* v. 130
(1208), *London Eyre of 1244* no. 247, MS. Y fo. 15ʳ (1306).

It might happen that a right to recover the tenements accrued before the husband
died: to the woman herself, if the marriage was dissolved by divorce, or to her heir
if she died before her husband and he was not entitled to courtesy. Perhaps it would
have been held, as it might be held in the case of a grant by a termor (see previous
note), that the substantial delay between the making of the tortious feoffment and
the accrual of the right to remedy had left the grantee in seisin so long that he could
not be put out without process of law. But I have never seen a case that would bear
on the matter. If the divorced woman or the woman's heir wished to sue, the writs
of entry *cui ante divorcium* and *sur cui in vita* were available for their respective cases.

[2] Littleton, *Tenures*, c. 9. Bracton gives the appropriate writ of entry, fos. 323,
346b–347.

[3] J.I. 1/503 m. 8 (1287), MS. Y fo. 14ʳ (1305). But the rule may have been in
doubt for a while after 1285. In a case of about 1300 the court held that if a tenant
in tail granted over in fee then the reversioner was entitled to disseise the feoffee
'pur salver [son] estat', MS. Y fos. 6ʳ–6ᵛ; and the same rule is applied to a deathbed
gift by a tenant in tail in Y.B. Pasch. 4 Ed. II no. 19 (1311).

the grantor rested on sound policy. Honest and valid feoffments made by true owners would often disappoint the donors' expectant heirs, who as soon as they became actual heirs upon the death of the donors were likely to try to put the grantees out—particularly if their ancestors had made the gifts when at death's door. So purchasers needed special protection after the death of their grantors, and the law judged that it could best provide this by prohibiting all self-help against purchasers whose grantors had died, whatever the circumstances. Besides, it had to be considered that heirs in tail, remaindermen, reversioners, and others who were wronged by the sort of tortious feoffment that could not be undone in the grantor's lifetime might often turn out, once the grantors were dead, to be the grantors' heirs general. As heirs general they might be bound to warrant their ancestors' grants, and if they were bound to warrant them then they could not claim the tenements for themselves. But the question of an obligation to warrant could not be decided through self-help and in consequent assizes of novel disseisin, so self-help was best excluded in all these cases.[1]

Two categories of tortious feoffments were thus distinguished, those in which the injured party could disseise the purchaser at once, and those in which he had to await the death of the grantor to seek redress and was therefore forbidden to disseise the grantee at all. Late in the century tortious feoffments by life tenants were moved out of the second category, where self-help was prohibited, and into the first, where it was permitted. In the traditional law, the reversioner whose life tenant made a tortious feoffment had to wait until the life tenant died before he could have a remedy. Only then could he use the writ that was designed to serve his case, the writ of entry later called *ad communem legem*.[2] Obliged so to delay before seeking redress, he could have no redress by self-help.[3] But the case was changed

---

[1] The rule that one might not disseise the grantee after the death of the grantor was independent of the rule that the lawful disseisor must act quickly; it applied even if the grantor's death followed very soon upon the feoffment. See J.I. 1/1179 m. 8 (1253), K.B. 27/24 m. 23d (1276), J.I. 1/503 m. 18 (1288), and J.I. 1/1245 m. 32d (1280) as cited above, p. 29 n. 2.

[2] Bracton fo. 31; *Early Registers of Writs* CC 208, R 804, R 846, *Registrum Brevium* fos. 234–5, Milsom in *Novae Narrationes*, p. cxxxvii.

[3] Bracton thought otherwise, fos. 31, 40b, 52, 58. But there is very little evidence in the records to support his doctrine: *CRR* xiv. 207 (1230) and *Somerset Pleas* i. 394g (1238) are the only cases I have seen that give it any colour at all.

by the Statute of Gloucester of 1278, which provided that where
a widow alienated her dower lands in fee the reversioner could
sue at once, without waiting for her death, by a new writ of
entry designed especially for him to use during her lifetime. The
relief thus given him was soon extended to all reversioners after
life estates, whether the life estate had arisen by way of dower
or in some other way.[1] But if the reversioner now had a right
to an immediate remedy, then there was no longer any reason
to deny him a right of self-help: he should be entitled to disseise
the man who had come in by the tortious feoffment and take the
tenements for himself. Just so did the justice William Herle, in
1321, reason out the consequences of the Statute of Gloucester.[2]
The implication had probably been seen as early as 1284,[3]
and it was certainly seen a few years later by Gilbert of Thornton.[4] Its full acceptance in practice was delayed for a few years
by confusion with the other rule that the superior lord of a
fee might interfere to obstruct a feoffment that damaged his
interests. In the 1280s and 1290s reversioners who entered and
disseised their life tenants' feoffees sometimes claimed only to
prevent the objectionable alienation and stood ready, as good
lords, to return the tenements to the original life tenant.[5] But
that branch of the law withered after the Statute of *Quia emptores*
of 1290. From 1298 cases begin to appear where the reversioner
claimed a right to enter and take a total forfeiture, and where
this right was upheld by the courts. In the fourteenth century

---

[1] *SR* i. 48; Milsom in *Novae Narrationes*, pp. cxxxviii–cxl. These new rules were
anticipated by a judgment given in 1276, C.P. 40/17 m. 88.

[2] *Eyre of London 1321* pp. 278–80. According to another opinion reflected in this
report, the reversioner's right of entry was by common law and was therefore older
than the Statute of Gloucester. The same two views were expressed in 22 Ass. no. 37
(1348).

[3] The King's Bench ruled in that year that where a life tenant wrongfully
alienated in fee, 'sic statim per statutum Glouc' accresceret ius illis qui habuerunt
feodum . . . et sic [feoffato] nihil accresceret per feoffamentum suum ex quo per hoc
ius ad alios transferretur in quorum exhereditacionem factum fuit feoffamentum
illud.' J.I. 1/1245 m. 99.

[4] Casting loose from Bracton's guidance, Thornton wrote: 'Si [tenentes ad vitam]
donacionem fecerint ad exheredacionem dominorum quibus terra reversura est,
huiusmodi feoffati statim eiciantur per veros dominos, nec recuperabunt seisinam
suam, secundum aliquos, quia forisfecerunt liberum tenementum suum per aliena-
cionem.' Harvard Law Library MS. 77, fo. 19.

[5] This view of the matter is alluded to by Thornton in the passage quoted in the
previous note, and is illustrated in J.I. 1/1245 m. 95d (1284) and K.B. 27/125 m. 77
(1290).

and forever after the law clearly recognized that he had this power.[1] For a time the old rule continued in force that the reversioner's right to disseise the grantee ceased with the death of the life tenant who had made the grant, but that restriction was dropped in 1348.[2]

When a feoffor gave lands and tenements to someone upon condition, if the condition was not fulfilled the feoffor could disseise the feoffee, or any successor of his in title,[3] provided that he acted promptly.[4] A father might give lands to his intended son-in-law on condition that the young man marry his daughter. If the intended bridegroom married someone else, the girl's father could put him out and take the property back.[5] If a lord wanted to make an immediate grant of land to be held of himself but feared the prejudice that he would suffer through the king's rights of primer seisin and prerogative wardship if it should turn out that his new tenant held other tenements in chief of the king, he might specify in his gift that if he should discover within a certain time that the feoffee held anything of the king in chief then he, the lord, should be entitled to re-enter and oust him. Such a condition was enforceable as stated.[6] If a lord took control of vacant lands after the death of his tenant

---

[1] MS. Y fo. 31^r–31^v (1298), K.B. 27/153 m. 28 (1298), Y.B. 33–5 Ed. I p. 569 (1307), Mich. 6 Ed. II no. 66 (1312), *Eyre of Kent* iii. 60–4 (1313). For the later law, which is fully attested from the early fourteenth century, see Littleton, *Tenures*, paragraph 415; Blackstone, *Commentaries*, ii. 18. 2. 3, and Simpson, *Introduction to the History of the Land Law*, p. 113. A tenant in tail after possibility of issue extinct was treated for these purposes as a life tenant; if he granted over in fee the reversioner could enter: Y.B. Mich. 13 Ed. II pp. 394–5 (1319), B.M. Egerton MS. 2811 fo. 251^r (1329–30), 43 Ass. no. 24 (1369).

[2] *Lincs Assize Rolls* no. 1312 (1206), *CRR* ix. 190–1 (1220), J.I. 1/1179 m. 8 (1253), 1/503 m. 18 (1288), K.B. 27/131 m. 53 (1292), Y.B. Pasch. 5 Ed. II no. 8 (1312), Trin. 6–7 Ed. II no. 15 (1313), Hil. 11 Ed. II nos. 2, 10 (1318), Mich. 15 Ed. II pp. 451–2 (1321), B.M. Egerton MS. 2811 fos. 251^r–252^v (1329–30), 9 Ass. no. 15 (1335), Y.B. Pasch. 17 Ed. III no. 25 (1343), 17 Ass. no. 27 (1343), Y.B. Mich. 18 Ed. III no. 16 (1344). From all these years the only contrary case I have found is K.B. 27/24 m. 23 d (1276); but in 1348 the law was changed, and thereafter the reversioner's right of entry was just as good after the life tenant's death as before: 22 Ass. no. 37 (1348), 43 Ass. no. 24 (1369), 43 Ass. no. 45 (1369), *London Possessory Assizes* no. 196 (1399), 243 (1429), 244 (1432).

[3] *BNB* no. 1200 (1236–7), J.I. 1/1245 m. 28 (1279).

[4] Bracton applies his four-day rule to cases of this sort, fo. 23. But I have seen only one case in which a man lost his right to disseise for breach of condition because he waited too long, and in that case he had waited three years, J.I. 1/1187 m. 18d (1258).

[5] Bracton fos. 22b–23, 166; *BNB* no. 1965 (1221).

[6] *Somerset Pleas* i. 1516 (1255).

and was then faced with a claim to the heritage on the part of one about whose right he could not be sure—say, a claim by a younger son of the decedent whose older brother had gone overseas and no one knew whether the older brother was dead or alive—the lord could admit the pretender to the heritage 'saving better right'. If the person with better right later appeared, the lord might join in disseising the tenant whose right was less good in order to admit the true heir.[1] An elderly man might give his lands to someone, perhaps his son, on condition that the feoffee provide him food, lodging, and other reasonable maintenance for the rest of his life. If the feoffee did not live up to his obligations the donor could lawfully disseise him. A borrower of money might enfeoff the lender with lands by way of security, on condition that if the debt was duly paid then the debtor could re-enter and hold the lands as his own. If the debt was paid on time but the creditor held on, the erstwhile debtor could disseise him.[2]

Almost any sort of condition could be laid down: that the feoffee warrant the donor lands that he gave him in exchange;[3] that the feoffee, being a life tenant by the terms of the gift, must not attempt to grant the lands over in fee;[4] that the feoffee and his successors, parsons of a parish, should allow the donor to have his own chaplain, whom they should admit at his presentation;[5] that the feoffee must not abuse the tenements, mistreat the sub-tenants, or fail to render due services.[6] In general, Bracton says that only those conditions are invalid that are impossible of fulfilment: 'I give you this provided that you touch the sky with your finger';[7] for the rest, 'what the parties agree on must always be kept, though contrary to what the law would provide, if it is not to the prejudice of others. A donor may always make any provision he wishes about the thing given, for it is entirely his.'[8] The only condition that I have found actually invalidated by a court was in a case of 1289, where an uncle had

---

[1] Bracton fos. 252b, 272b, 277b; *Sel. Cases in K.B.* iii. 15 (1294).

[2] J.I. 1/492 m. 62 (1282).   [3] *Lincs Assize Rolls* no. 162 (1202).

[4] J.I. 1/1187 m. 18d (1258).   [5] *BNB* no. 1200 (1236–7).

[6] *Eyres of Lincs and Worcs* nos. 218, 763 (1218–19), *Somerset Pleas* i. 1279 (1244), *Casus Placitorum* pp. 86–95 (1276), K.B. 27/153 m. 28 (1298). Cf. J.I. 1/1245 m. 41d (1280), where the court upheld the right of one who had made a feoffment by way of substitution to enter upon breach of the condition that the feoffee should pay him an annual rent.

[7] fo. 19.   [8] fo. 18; and cf. fo. 33.

given his lands to his nephew on condition that if the uncle should be cleared of certain charges of trespass pending against him then he could take the tenements back.[1]

On this large freedom Bracton would impose some very strict requirements of form. Conditions must be stated in writing, he says, and in the deed of grant itself, and in a clause which begins with the word 'si' 'if', and ends by explicitly reserving a right of re-entry. An oral statement is not good enough, and neither is a written statement in a collateral document. If the clause specifying the condition begins with 'ut', 'so that'—'Do tali tantam terram *ut* inveniat mihi necessaria'—or with 'quia', 'because'—'Do tibi hanc rem *quia* mihi bene servies'—there can result no right of disseisin. Nor can any right of disseisin be raised without express words.[2] But all this seems to be an imagining of doctrine. Bracton himself ignores elsewhere his distinction between 'si' and 'ut'.[3] When sitting as a justice he was, like his successors in generations after, ready to recognize conditions laid down orally.[4] From the decisions of other justices it appears that a condition might be set out in a collateral deed of covenant.[5] Neither was it necessary, except perhaps where re-entry was provided for failure of service, to state specifically that the grantor should have a right to oust the feoffee; it was enough if it was implied.[6]

The only restriction that the law in fact imposed was that whatever conditions were laid down must be laid down in connection with a grant of the tenements, either by feoffment

---

[1] J.I. 1/503 m. 34d.   [2] fos. 18–19b.

[3] fos. 22b–23, 166, 48–48b. In the last of these passages, for example, he says that the donor may enter the tenements if the grant provided 'ne fiat donatio vel venditio nisi tantum donatori vel eius heredi'. 'ne' is of course the equivalent of 'ut' in a negative statement.

[4] *Somerset Pleas* i. 1516 (1255), J.I. 1/1182 m. 7d (1255), Y.B. 30 & 31 Ed. I p. 211 (1302), Pasch. 21 Ed. III no. 2 (1347). Cf. *Fleta* iv. 16. 8, *Britton* ii. 5. 4, 12. 6, Thornton, Harvard Law Library MS. 77 fo. 57.

[5] J.I. 1/492 m. 62 (1282), K.B. 27/153 m. 28 (1298), MS. Y fo. 16ᵛ (*c.* 1305). But counsel argued to the contrary in K.B. 27/131 m. 42 (1292).

[6] *Lincs Assize Rolls* no. 162 (1202), *BNB* no. 1965 (1221), 1200 (1236–7), J.I. 1/492 m. 62 (1282), 8 Ass. no. 34 (1334), Y.B. Hil. 9 Ed. III no. 17 (1335), Pasch. 18 Ed. III no. 27 (1344), 21 Ass. no. 28 (1347). But about 1310 it was held that a grant made 'pur trover sustenaunce' was not sufficient to support a right of entry if the grantee failed to maintain the feoffor, MS. Y fo. 28ʳ. Where a right to disseise the feoffee was reserved for failure of service to the grantor as lord, express provision was required, since this was directly contrary to the common-law rule: *Somerset Pleas* i. 1279 (1244).

or by release. If one who was already owner bound himself by covenant to suffer disseisin under such-and-such conditions, the arrangement was void.[1] Perhaps this also implies the rule that was certainly observed in later times, that a right to disseise for breach of condition could be reserved only in favour of a grantor or his heir, and not for any third party.[2]

The right of the true owner to disseise anyone who was holding the tenements against him was, then, very extensive. The generally permissive attitude of the law did nothing to make the English scene any quieter. A man who was entitled to make a disseisin might call upon the sheriff to assist him, and the sheriff might lend his aid if the cause was good, though like the principal he acted at his peril.[3] If the sheriff joined in with his forces, the disseisin would no doubt wear the aspect of an official proceeding, and to that extent would appear a peaceable business. But the principal was under no obligation to invoke the sheriff's help, and most men who went about it to make lawful disseisins did not do so. They carried out the disseisins by themselves, and as a substitute for force under the command of a royal official they took along their own forces: their lords, friends, relatives, retainers, and hirelings, all making up a gang or an army, whichever one cares to call it, of whatever size seemed to be needed for the job.

It was perfectly legal to use these private forces. In 1258 a disseisor came 'with a great company' and took over a manor; the jury which later reviewed the affair said that he had not broken the peace in any way.[4] In 1276 a woman was ejected from her house in London, which she held of the abbot of St. Albans. She went to the abbot and told him of her troubles, and he sent back with her 'certain men' who threw her enemy out and restored her to possession. The adversary sued for this, but it was judged that she had done no wrong.[5] It seems, indeed, to have been more common than not to bring a large and threatening band of supporters to help carry out a disseisin. Bracton said

---

[1] *Yorks Assize Rolls* pp. 95–6 (1260), K.B. 27/159 m. 35 (1299), Y.B. Hil. 4 Ed. II no. 43 (1311).

[2] Simpson, *Introduction to the History of the Land Law*, p. 96.

[3] Bracton fos. 164–164b. He says, however, that some people doubted whether the sheriff ought to take any hand even in a lawful disseisin unless he was specifically ordered by higher authority.

[4] J.I. 1/1187 m. 8.   [5] B.M. Add. Charter 5153 m. 18d.

that the man who was wrongfully put out of his lands could 'call on the aid of his friends' in order to disseise his opponent,[1] and one hears elsewhere of the apparently routine assembling of large groups. In 1287 a minor whose guardian was wasting the tenements brought a 'crowd' of his friends with him to put a stop to it;[2] in 1295 Sibyl of Gurnay brought a 'posse' to help her take back lands from which she had earlier been ejected;[3] and some such proceedings must lie behind many of the hundreds of novel disseisin cases that were brought against large numbers of co-defendants for lands that were claimed by one of the defendants alone.[4]

The right to disseise an adversary involved the right to use violence. When Jocelin Ledecombe died in the 1220s the succession to his house and lands was disputed between Ralph Ledecombe and Robert Hachard. Ralph got to the property first and moved into the house. Nearly two weeks later Robert Hachard came with his retainers and, finding Ralph there, laid siege to the place, allowing no one to come in to bring Ralph provisions or anything else. Growing impatient after a time, the besiegers felled trees in the nearby orchard, hoping that Ralph would leave and let them occupy the tenements rather than see the destruction continue. After five days they tired altogether of waiting and knocked the house down. Ralph had to run out quickly, he said, in order to avoid being crushed. In the subsequent proceedings at law, the court considered that Hachard's violence was justified if only he could prove that his right to the property was good.[5]

The principle behind the court's attitude appears in a much later case, from 1292. William of Chirington claimed to be the rightful parson of the parish of Chipping Norton in Oxfordshire, which a rival, Richard of Gloucester, had held for the past eleven years. William sued before papal judges delegate and got a favourable judgment. He gathered his supporters, went to Chipping Norton, entered the church, and there took

---

[1] fo. 163. [2] J.I. 1/503 m. 12.
[3] C.P. 40/110 m. 258.
[4] Such cases are very frequent in the records of all periods. For an early example, see *CRR* ii. 40, 43, 45–6 (1201). In J.I. 1/1245 m. 53 (1281) the record expressly states that the seven or eight co-defendants were a group of friends who had come to help the principal defendant take seisin of the property he claimed.
[5] *BNB* no. 287 = *CRR* xiii. 733 (1228).

possession of the parish by execution of judgment, reading out documents, ringing the bells, and receiving professions of obedience from the chaplains of the place: but all of this without any royal officer, for his judgment had been in an ecclesiastical court. Then, since Richard of Gloucester had holed up in the parsonage, William and his men proceeded there. Finding the door locked they seized a cart and used it as an improvised battering-ram to break down the door. William remarked that it was his own door, since the parish with its parsonage was now his, and that if he wanted to break down his own door he was within his rights in doing so. When the door gave way Richard of Gloucester left the house, and another disseisin reached its successful conclusion. Richard prosecuted an action in the King's Bench, but the jury that pronounced on the case said that 'no evil' had been done, and Richard abandoned his suit.[1] Apparently the court accepted the logic of what Chirington had said at the time of the disseisin, that he could without offence break down his own door. In carrying out a lawful disseisin one might enter with violence and damage to the tenements in dispute, for they were the disseisor's own property. The principle is illustrated in other cases of this time and after.[2]

But in the case between Gloucester and Chirington, before the court would accept the jury's finding that 'no evil' had been done it insisted on probing further. The jury had to say, first, that when Chirington and his men came to Chipping Norton they came unarmed; second, that after they broke the door of the parsonage they did not assault Richard of Gloucester's person or drag him out of the house but that he left unharmed and under his own power; and, finally, that in taking over the house Chirington did not appropriate Gloucester's personal property.

Any of those three acts would have been illegal, even in the course of a lawful disseisin. Chirington's case implies as much, and other cases confirm it, at least for the middle years of the thirteenth century and after.

It was permissible to come with a large company to effect a disseisin, but it was against the law for the company to come bearing arms. This may not have been the rule of the older law.

---

[1] *Sel. Cases in K.B.* ii. 72, *Rotuli Parliamentorum* i. 96.
[2] K.B. 27/153 m. 28 (1298), *Eyre of London 1321* p. 327, 22 Ass. no. 57 (1348).

In the 1180s Abbot Samson of St. Edmund's sent eighty armed men to enforce his franchisal rights against the rival claims of the archbishop of Canterbury, without bringing any penalty upon himself in the litigation that followed before the king.[1] In the 1250s Bracton said that the man who wished to make a lawful disseisin could 'gather arms' for the purpose,[2] and the record of a lawsuit of 1250 seems to bear him out.[3] But from at least the 1230s the court rolls bear case after case of Trespass where the plaintiff charges that the defendant entered his lands wrongfully and by force of arms, where the defendant admits entering the lands and justifies this as a proper assertion of his right, but always denies flatly that he or his men either used force of arms or brought any arms to the scene.[4] Evidently the fact that he was carrying out a lawful disseisin would not justify a private person's appearing in arms. A later medieval record shows that even purely verbal threats were against the law.[5]

Violence to the opponent's person was also ruled out; it was illegal to lay any hand upon him. In cases of Trespass in the latter half of the thirteenth century and after, where the plaintiff accuses the defendant of entering on his land and also of beating him, the defendant often replies by justifying the entry on the land but always pleads a uniform and invariable 'Not guilty' to the charge of beating.[6] Apparently it was impossible to justify beating the opponent. The law comes clear in the case of Delisle v. Duramme, from the year 1260. After Hugh Delisle leased a meadow to Henry Duramme a misunderstanding arose (so we may take it) about how long the lease was to run. When Delisle, the lessor, considered that the lease had expired he came with his retainers to resume possession. Duramme resisted, since he held that the term had not yet run out. A light scuffle ensued in which one of Duramme's men,

---

[1] *Chronicle of Jocelin of Brakelond*, pp. 50–2.   [2] fo. 163.

[3] K.B. 26/139 m. 15d.

[4] See these early cases, for example: K.B. 26/117 m. 4d (1237), 26/124 m. 27d (1242), 26/138 m. 18d (1250), 26/145 m. 40 (1251), 26/161 m. 8 (1259), 26/169 m. 34d (1260). For a later example see Y.B. Mich. 11 Ed. III pp. 185–7 (1337). In the case of an illegal disseisin, coming to the scene in arms constituted unlawful violence, aggravating the basic offence, even if the weapons were not used: C.P. 40/131 m. 165 (1300).

[5] *Sel. Cases in K.B.* vii. 50 p. 203 (1411).

[6] For example, K.B. 26/152 m. 9d, 26/155 m. 3 (1254), Y.B. Trin. 6–7 Ed. II no. 1 (1313), *Eyre of London 1321* pp. 133–6.

defending his master's right to hold on to the meadow, hit one of Delisle's men with a stick. Delisle finally withdrew and sued at law. He lost his case, for the court decided that the lease, properly interpreted, had not run out; but Duramme had nevertheless to pay damages for the blow that Delisle's servant had sustained.[1] Even in defence of a good title it was illegal to hit a member of the opposing party.

This ruling fits in well with what else we know about the contemporary law governing violence to the person. If a man had killed or maimed or wounded another there were very few grounds on which he could show that it was justifiable or pardonable.[2] The making of a lawful disseisin was not one of them. In 1223 a man was hanged for a homicide which he apparently committed in the course of an attempt to carry out a disseisin,[3] and the records occasionally show other appeals of felony brought under similar circumstances.[4] In 1329–30 it was reported that 'a man was condemned to death because he participated in a disseisin where someone was killed, even though the jury said that he did not come there with intent to do any wrong'.[5] Neither was simple beating at all easy to justify, unless it was a moderate chastisement of one's child, wife, or servant.[6] In 1260 Geoffrey Sumenur was accused of beating a woman. He was not guilty, the jury said: she was carrying off grain of his and he tried to stop her, she struck at him with her staff, he parried the blow, and the staff rebounded and hit her on the head.[7] This is not a very likely story, but evidently it was the sort of story that the jury had to tell if Geoffrey was to be judged innocent; it was no good saying that he had beaten her because she tried to carry away his goods. Even an attack on one's person would not justify a counter-attack unless it was a case

---

[1] K.B. 26/168 m. 15.

[2] On the limits of justifiable and pardonable homicide see Naomi Hurnard, *The King's Pardon for Homicide*, chapter 3, and P. & M. ii. 478–85. Bracton said, fo. 162b, that one might defend his lands and tenements by any means necessary, even by killing the would-be disseisor if there were no other way, but elsewhere, fos. 120b, 132b, 144b, 155, he comes around to the view that a man may lawfully kill only to save his own life, and this is the law to which the records bear overwhelming witness. As for mayhem, I have seen only one record where it is justified, and the justification there is on the ground that the victim assaulted the defendant with a knife intending to kill him: *BNB* no. 1084 (1225).

[3] *CRR* xi. 509, 598, 599.   [4] Hurnard, op. cit., pp. 199, 340.

[5] Bodleian Library Rawlinson MS. C. 187 fo. 39ʳ.

[6] Hurnard, op. cit., p. 99.   [7] K.B. 26/168 m. 11.

of mortal danger. In 1242 several men approached William of Cantilupe's bailiff to replevy some animals that he had distrained. The bailiff assaulted them and they fought back, beating and wounding him. They were convicted and sent to gaol.[1] Men who were attacked ought to behave as did Robert Symond in 1260. When the bailiff of Orford assaulted him, he and his friends simply held the man back to restrain him, without ever striking him; the law approved and took no penalty from them.[2] The same strict rules prevailed in the early fourteenth century,[3] though they were later relaxed to allow the victims of simple assaults to strike back in self-defence.[4]

Lawful disseisin bore illegitimate offspring, furthermore, if the victor appropriated the chattels of the man whom he ousted. His personal property was no part of the tenements and the law that permitted damage to the tenements in dispute could not be stretched to allow the taking of personal property. The disseisor who wished to stay on the right side of the law must let his opponent take away his wardrobe, his cash-box, his horse, and whatever else was his. This law seems to be attested by a case of 1221,[5] and appears clearly in a number of cases from 1242 on.[6]

Besides these three, one other restriction was enforced, which was not mentioned in the case of *Gloucester* v. *Chirington* because there was no suspicion of its having been violated. It was wrong

---

[1] K.B. 26/124 m. 28. [2] K.B. 26/168 m. 13d.

[3] Y.B. Pasch. 12 Ed. II no. 56 (1319), *Eyre of London 1321* pp. 142–3, 335.

[4] e.g. Y.B. Trin. 43 Ed. III no. 18 (1369), Lincoln's Inn Hale MS. 77 fo. 213b (1384), K.B. 27/538 m. 12d (1395). Any direct admission of beating was avoided even in this period. The plea of self-defence ran in the coy form, 'A. in ipsum B. insultum fecit, et sic malum quod recepit, si quod ei evenit, fuit de insultu suo proprio et in defensionem ipsius B.' Y.B. Mich. 21 Henry VII no. 50 (1505) also reports that one may strike an assailant in defence of his master.

The traditional limits seem to be left behind in a case of 1439 where defendants admitted that in the course of an entry on lands they charged their adversary to withdraw and, when he would not do so, 'manus suas [ei] imposuerunt prout eis bene licuit', C.P. 40/715 m. 640. They were servants of Humphrey Duke of Gloucester and had been making a disseisin in his name. Y.B. Trin. 12 Henry VIII no. 2 (1520) on the other hand, agrees well with the older law: 'Quant al persone dun home, nest loyal a ascun de toucher ceo forcement si issint ne soit que il soit in tant grand peril que il sera peri sil nad aide.'

[5] *CRR* x. 73–5.

[6] K.B. 26/124 m. 4 (1242), 26/145 m. 40 (1251), J.I. 1/1187 m. 8 (1258), C.P. 40/58 m. 53 (1285), Y.B. Trin. 3 Ed. II no. 26 (1310), *Eyre of London 1321* p. 327, 22 Ass. no. 57 (1348).

to carry out a disseisin in the night-time. Several cases that I have seen witness this rule, the earliest of them from 1258.[1]

The study of these restrictions on the ways and means that might be used to effect lawful disseisins carries us some way from the assize of novel disseisin. If a disseisin was unlawful then the fact that it was accompanied by the breach of these rules would increase the damages and the amercement laid on the guilty party in an assize. But if the disseisin was legal no penalty could be laid at the assize for the ways in which it had been carried out. The outraged disseisee had to use other procedures, appeals of felony or actions of trespass.

But however the courts might make procedural distinctions, the law that governed disseisins must have presented itself as a coherent body of doctrine to those who lived under it. A private Englishman of the thirteenth century, considering whether he should attempt a disseisin, could be pretty confident that the law would approve his enterprise if only he could show, in any litigation that might result, that he was truly entitled to hold the land in question. The law insisted that he act without delay, but as one who found himself kept out of his property he would probably want to do that in any case. He proceeded, of course, at his peril. In disputes about lands and tenements the right was seldom all on one side, and if the disseisor failed to establish his superior title in ensuing litigation, no protests about good faith and probable cause would save him from conviction. But for a man confident of his right and quick to act upon it, the law usually left the way open.

The really serious restraints were not on the right to disseise but rather on the methods that might be used. The prohibition against the use or display of weapons and, above all, the prohibition against laying hands on the opponent or any of his party, meant that the disseisin would have to be a somewhat uncertain process of facing out the antagonist. He could not be driven out by direct force. The disseisor would come and enter the property. He could force his way in if necessary. Once there he would conduct himself as the owner, commanding his opponent to leave, moving in his own chattels, living in the

[1] J.I. 1/1187 m. 3 (1258), K.B. 27/41 m. 49 (1278), 27/155 m. 36d, 38 (1298), 27/165 m. 15 (1301); *Casus Placitorum* p. lxxxiii no. 74. *Econtra tamen*, J.I. 1/1245 m. 24 (1279).

house, taking fealties from sub-tenants and distraining them for services due, harvesting the crops if they were ripe. For all these purposes a large company of followers would be useful. Particularly if the opponent found his house occupied by the disseisor and a dozen of his friends, he would probably withdraw to more comfortable quarters and sue at law for his right. Besides, a large force might wreak a little well-calculated havoc in the tenements so that the adversary might withdraw voluntarily rather than see the continued destruction of what, in most cases, he took to be his own.

Those were the methods that could be used within the law. Where the disseisor had clearly superior force, particularly in the number of supporters whom he could muster, such measures would be likely to be effective. But where the forces were somewhat evenly balanced the prospect of success for the disseisor cannot have been particularly good unless he was willing to break the law, for the law did not permit anything like outright warfare. In warfare a commander with forces no larger than his enemy's might capture a place by surprise attack at night, or by turning to advantage the superior equipment, discipline, or prowess of his men, enabling them to strike down their opponents. No such tactics could be used, no such resources could be put into play, by the private Englishman who wished to stay on the right side of the law. Under these circumstances, it would not be rash to guess that a good many disseisors overstepped the bounds. If the disseisin itself was justified, only personal penalties could be laid for the use of illegal methods, and these penalties would not deprive the successful disseisor of the lands that he had obtained by his action except in the extreme case where he committed a felony, such as homicide. Many intending disseisors must have been willing to face the prospect of a conviction for assault and battery if only they could thereby get back into their land. Still, the law set its face against such methods, called them illegal, and would punish their use.

IV

NEW TASKS FOR THE ASSIZE:
THE SECOND HUNDRED YEARS

WHEN it was invented early in Henry II's reign, novel disseisin was designed to be an expeditious action, bringing swift justice.[1] Presumably it worked that way from the first, and certainly it continued to do so all through the thirteenth century. Henry of Bracton wrote, 'This assize waits for no man. It would not be delayed even if the king was on his way to attend and was almost at the door.' He said elsewhere, in soberer language, that the assize resolved disputes 'by summary investigation without great solemnity of law, by short-cut as it were'.[2] The Statute of Westminster II of 1285 declared, 'There is no other writ . . . that gives plaintiffs such quick justice as does the writ of novel disseisin.'[3] Counsel in a case argued in the King's Bench about 1300 echoed these words when he remarked, 'There is no other writ in the king's court that is designed to produce such quick remedy.'[4] In 1316 the justice Henry le Scrope was of the same opinion: novel disseisin was, he said, 'the quickest and speediest action there is'.[5] In an assize of 1290, when the defendant raised technical objections that called for a postponement of proceedings the court overruled them, for particular stated reasons but 'especially because this is an assize of novel disseisin'.[6] The assize should not be delayed unless it was absolutely necessary.

Let us see how fast it could work. A freeholder of Lincolnshire was disseised, apparently of modest tenements, some time between October 1198 and May 1199. He purchased his writ of novel disseisin on or after 27 May 1199; his case came up on 15 July 1199 and he recovered by judgment that same day: within about nine months of the disseisin, then—and it may

---

[1] Above, pp. 17–20.   [2] fos. 183b, 164b.   [3] c. 25.
[4] '. . . cum non sit aliquod breve in curia regis per quod tam festinum fieri debeat remedium', MS. Y, in the case reported on fos. 37ᵛ–40ʳ.
[5] Y.B. Mich. 10 Ed. II no. 5.   [6] 'Annals of Dunstable', p. 350.

have been a great deal less than that—and about a month or a month and a half after he opened proceedings.[1] Some years later, an important Wiltshire landowner suffered a disseisin on 11 November 1207 and recovered by novel disseisin on 15 June 1208, after about seven months.[2] In later generations the action was, if anything, even more efficient. In September or October of 1253 a plaintiff recovered before Henry of Bracton lands of which he had been disseised on 1 August in the same year, only one, two, or three months before.[3] In 1274 Ralph of Hengham gave a judgment of recovery in favour of the bishop of Hereford just 31 days after he had been disseised.[4] John of Mettingham heard, tried, and judged on 15 September 1289 a disseisin allegedly committed on the previous 22 August.[5] In another case, a tenant who was put out of his land on 31 July 1299 recovered by judgment about six months later, on 20 January 1300.[6] In a spectacular case in 1281, the abbot of Ramsey recovered six square miles of marshland against the abbot of Thorney just 12 days after he purchased his original writ.[7]

Of course not all litigants were so fortunate as these. A plaintiff could not recover quickly unless justices of assize came to his county soon after he had been disseised, and that did not always happen. After the disruptions of the 1210s the justices of the new eyres of 1218–22 heard many cases of disseisins committed several years before. There had been little opportunity for the plaintiffs to get justice and they had simply had to wait.[8] Litigants of Northumberland sometimes found that their first chance to sue came when the king travelled through their remote county, perhaps years after they had been disseised.[9]

---

[1] *Rotuli Curiae Regis* i. 446. Cf. pp. 447, 448 for two other similar cases.

[2] *CRR* v. 227.

[3] J.I. 1/1179 m. 8d. Cf. *Somerset Pleas* i. 1452, a similar case in the same year, also before Bracton. [4] J.I. 1/1217 m. 25d.

[5] J.I. 1/503 m. 34. [6] K.B. 27/163 m. 53d.

[7] J.I. 1/1245 m. 39d and K.B. 27/127 m. 53. The abbot of Thorney afterwards made elaborate attempts to get the judgment reversed for error, arguing in part that the proceedings had been carried through in undue haste. But he was unsuccessful.

[8] Above, p. 56. *Eyres of Lincs and Worcs, Eyre of Yorks 1218–19, Eyres of Glos, Warw, Staffs, passim,* or, for example, *Eyre of Yorks 1218–19* nos. 367, 420.

[9] Their difficulties are suggested by *CRR* v. 258 (1208) and K.B. 27/127 m. 58d (1291). But in the latter half of the century the sheriff of Northumberland had some power to hear actions of novel disseisin: above, p. 63.

Through most of the thirteenth century and in the fourteenth, most counties were visited once, twice, or even three times a year by regularly commissioned justices of assize.[1] But even so, if one was disseised soon after the departure of the justices, he might have to wait several months before they came round again. He could expedite matters by getting a special commission to hear his case, but probably it was only the wealthy who found that a practical resort.

Even when a hearing could be obtained soon, judgment might not always follow very quickly. The procedural law of novel disseisin was well designed to abridge delays, but there was nothing to guarantee that a case, once pleaded and tried, might not raise hard issues of substantive law, so that judgment would have to be put off 'for difficulty'. Sometimes the difficulties might be long in the resolution, sometimes they might never be resolved.[2]

Nevertheless, the justices who heard assizes of novel disseisin kept in general to a remarkably high standard of efficiency. On several visits to Somerset in the early 1250s Henry of Bracton heard a total of sixty cases of novel disseisin. In fifty-six of these he gave a final judgment on the merits on the first day the case came up. Only three cases were adjourned for difficulty and only one was thrown out for procedural reasons. This is an extraordinary record: 93 per cent concluded quickly on their merits. There also appear in his rolls a number of other cases where the plaintiffs withdrew or failed to prosecute. Sometimes this was because one of the parties had died, sometimes because the parties had decided to compromise; there are seven where the action *may* have been abandoned because of procedural difficulties. But even if all seven were in fact cases of litigants delayed and frustrated by the law's tangles, the cases decided quickly on the merits would still amount to 84 per cent.[3]

Bracton seems to have been unusually efficient, but others were not far behind him. Holding a general eyre in Northumberland in 1256, Roger of Thurkelby and his associates concluded on the merits and before they left the county 90 per cent of the

---

[1] Above, pp. 61–2 and, for the later period, Pugh, *Imprisonment in Medieval England*, pp. 278–86.

[2] See, for example, Sutherland, 'Peytevin *v.* la Lynde', pp. 543–5.

[3] These statistics are drawn from the records printed in *Somerset Pleas* i. 388–455.

assizes of novel disseisin that were prosecuted before them. Even if a good half of the other cases where the plaintiffs abandoned their suits were broken off for procedural reasons, the court was still giving quick judgments on the merits in 60 per cent of the cases.[1] Back in Somerset again, the several justices who visited the county with commissions of assize in 1270–2 succeeded in giving judgments on the merits on the first day of hearing in 85 per cent of the cases prosecuted. If a full half of the cases not prosecuted failed for procedural reasons, the proportion where they gave quick and substantial justice was still 71 per cent.[2] Nearly the same picture emerges from the rolls in which Ralph of Hengham recorded the work that he did as a justice of assize in 1271–89, mostly in the West Midlands. Of the more than 500 cases that were prosecuted before him, 84 per cent were carried to a judgment on the merits on the day they first came up; 9 per cent were adjourned for difficulty and in 7 per cent the judgment was given on procedural grounds. Hengham's records show clearly that where plaintiffs failed to prosecute it was often because the parties had come to an agreement, for he liked to set down in his roll the terms of their compromises. If we discount these, there remain another 177 cases where suit was begun and dropped. But even if all of these represented failures due to procedural difficulties, Hengham was still deciding 63 per cent of the cases on their merits when they first came up.[3]

Even an adjournment for difficulty did not always mean long delay. There is some reason to believe that the king and the leading justices made a special effort to reach early decisions where the difficulty arose out of an assize of novel disseisin. In May 1275 William Gereberge took out a writ of novel disseisin, which came up before the justices of assize in Hertfordshire the next month. The justices took a verdict at once but decided for certain reasons that they could not proceed to judgment upon it. They ordered a search of records, but when even this failed to show a clear basis for judgment the case was sent into the King's Bench. There judgment was given, with full explanation of how the court resolved the legal difficulties, in late October: about four months after the first hearing and about five months after the plaintiff opened suit.[4] Shortly afterwards, the King's

---

[1] *Northumb Assize Rolls*, pp. 1–67.   [2] *Somerset Pleas* ii. 116–85.
[3] J.I. 1/1217 and 1/1245.   [4] K.B. 27/18 m. 15.

Bench decided early in February 1276 another hard case that had been initiated in late October 1275 and first heard and adjourned for difficulty on 12 November: the judgment came after just three months of litigation.[1] Thirty years later, in 1305, a disseisin was committed on 28 June, and a final judgment given on 3 November.[2] Ralph of Hengham's roll of assizes for 1277–89 shows that of the thirty-seven cases that he had to adjourn out of their counties for difficulty, at least fifteen were decided promptly, some within a few days or weeks, others within three or four months.[3]

In short, we seem to have here a standard of efficiency of which any legal system in any age might be proud. It bespeaks the basic soundness of the system of law and administration, a fundamental health upon which men like Thomas of Weylond and Walter Langton—frauds and oppressors and perverters of justice—could sometimes prey;[4] it exemplifies the 'good government of the thirteenth century' of which Professor Joseph Strayer has written.[5]

Since the assize was so efficient, the leaders of law and government in the late thirteenth century wanted to expand its scope. The statute of 1285 said, 'because there is no other writ in the Chancery which gives plaintiffs such quick justice as the writ of novel disseisin, the lord king, who wants quick justice to be done and delays in lawsuits to be obviated or reduced, grants that novel disseisin shall henceforth apply in more cases', and went on to detail several changes to that effect.[6] This statute was only one expression of a consistent policy. For the truth was that the many compelling considerations which in his own day had restrained the impatient reformism of Henry II and forced him to limit the procedures of the assize to certain kinds of cases only, namely cases of disseisin committed at a recent date,[7] had lost all their importance now a hundred years and more after Henry II's time. The assize was a procedure in the king's court and Henry II could not ride roughshod over the valued rights of feudal courts by making it available for all kinds of suits; now in

---

[1] K.B. 27/20A m. 20, 20d.

[2] Y.B. 33–5 Ed. I p. 29, and MS. Y fos. 17ʳ–17ᵛ.   [3] J.I. 1/1245.

[4] For Weylond see *State Trials of the Reign of Edward I*; for Langton, Alice Beardwood, *The Trial of Walter Langton*.

[5] *Western Europe in the Middle Ages*, p. 198.

[6] Statute of Westminster II c. 25.   [7] Above, pp. 36–8.

Edward I's reign feudal courts had become mere shadows of their former selves and no longer in practice possessed jurisdictions worth caring for. The assize determined disputes by the verdict of a jury or in some other rational way, so that if Henry II had appointed it as a means for the final resolution of disputes of all kinds it would have deprived men of their right to defend their lands and tenements in trial by battle; but by Edward I's time trial by battle was largely disused and altogether disreputable. In Henry II's day it was recognized that in complex cases that might turn for their decision on facts of no recent date the tenant must often be allowed delay to call in a warrantor, but the speed with which the new assize was designed to work would not admit delay for such a purpose and therefore the procedure of the assize could not be used to hear complicated disputes turning on old facts. By the late thirteenth century it was common practice for the defendant at the assize to make good his claim to be warranted through an independent action of warranty of charter. Since he could secure his warranty in that way there remained no reason why an assize should not proceed in a case where the defendant might be entitled to a warranty.[1]

Most of all, the past hundred years had worn away the old feeling that law ought to be slow, that no one should be called summarily to account for his established rights, that legal process should be a form of pressure, gentle at first, pushing men to compromise.[2] The king's courts were manned by professionals now, and these men had a confidence in the exact science of reason as they practised it which made them believe that they could find definite, correct solutions for disputes. It was not too much to call a man suddenly to answer, for he would only receive right and reason, which every man should always stand ready to receive. The courts were not forums for talking out differences, but swift swords for justice; quick justice was the new ideal. Edward I's statutes professed time and again that their purpose was 'to speed justice',[3] to give the people 'quicker justice than they previously got when they were

---

[1] See Note F, p. 218.
[2] Above, pp. 35, 37.
[3] 'pur haster dreit', Statute of Ragman, *SR* i. 44; and several other similar expressions in the same enactment.

wronged',[1] to enable merchants 'to recover their debts speedily
on the day appointed for payment'.[2] A statute of 1293 was made
because 'the king wishes that as far as he is able quick justice be
done to everyone in his kingdom'.[3] In the years from the 1250s
to the 1270s mesne process against defendants in personal actions
was drastically speeded up.[4] In 1285 a new and vastly improved
procedure was given for plaintiffs whose cases rested upon
matters of record in the king's court, such as recorded acknow-
ledgements of debt or final concords. For such plaintiffs, a writ
of *scire facias* would assign the defendant a day when he could
come to court if he wished and show any cause that he had to
show why the plaintiff's rights as they appeared in the record
should not straightway be enforced. If the defendant could
show no good grounds for objection, the court would enforce the
plaintiff's claim; but the court would also enforce it, and without any additional delay, if the defendant simply elected to
stay away on the day appointed. The process by *scire facias* was
given to avoid 'solemnities of court' such as summonses, attach-
ments, essoins, and views of lands in dispute: in short, to hasten
justice.[5] Toward the end of Edward I's reign the justices re-
modelled the action of replevin to let it do the work of the action
contra formam feoffamenti: Replevin gave the plaintiff a quicker
remedy.[6]

The men of the law even worked to speed up novel disseisin,
rapid as it was to begin with. In 1285 the Statute of Westminster
II obviated one source of vexation and delay:

Defendants in novel disseisin should take care in future not to
enter mendacious pleas in bar in order to delay the taking of the
assize, as by saying that an assize was held earlier between the same
parties for the same tenements or saying falsely that a writ of a
higher nature is pending between the same parties for the same
tenement, and vouching rolls and records in proof of these and
other similar pleas. They do this in order to use the delay occasioned
by their vouchers to carry off crops and collect rents and other
profits, to the great damage of the plaintiff. Until now a defendant

---

[1] Statute of Westminster II, preamble.
[2] Statute of Acton Burnell, *SR* i. 53.
[3] *Statutum de Justiciariis Assignatis*, *SR* i. 112.
[4] Sutherland, 'Mesne Process in Personal Actions', pp. 482–94.
[5] Statute of Westminster II c. 45.
[6] Plucknett, *Legislation of Edward I*, pp. 63–75.

who mendaciously pleaded such untrue exceptions suffered no penalty except that when his plea had been tried and found false the court would proceed to take the assize. But the lord king, who hates such prevarications, now decrees that if a defendant pleads the exception in person and then fails, on the day assigned him, to prove it by the matter that he vouched, he be convicted as a disseisor without the assize being taken . . . and if the exception is pleaded by a bailiff, the taking of the assize and judgment for recovery of the tenement and damages shall not be postponed on this account.[1]

The rule was in constant use and probably did a good deal to expedite proceedings.[2]

Many years later, in the bad days about the end of the reign, Edward I's government still found time to enact another reform for the same purpose. It was noted as an abuse that the defendant could defeat a writ of novel disseisin by pleading, in person or by bailiff, that he held the tenement that was being sued for jointly with someone else—his wife in many cases—who was not named in the writ, and by showing a deed of joint feoffment in proof of this. The deed might be an utter fraud and the plaintiff might know it to be so, but the plaintiff could not be allowed to show that his writ was good by traversing the deed, for that would result in a trial of the rights of the alleged joint feoffee, whose rights, however, could not be tried on this occasion because he or she was not named as a party to the action. The plaintiff would have to get a new writ naming the alleged joint tenant. The new writ could not be quashed in the same way, for it had been 'given' the plaintiff by the defendant's own plea; but the quashing of the first writ was an effective way of impeding justice for a time. All this doctrine had been established by a judgment of 1292.[3] Now in 1306 the Statute of Joint Tenants provided that a plea of this sort, if it was to be entered

---

[1] c. 25. This enactment seems to have been occasioned by the case of Hengston v. Kyriole, K.B. 27/92 m. 22 and 27/130 m. 27d. For the old law which allowed bailiffs to plead records in bar and which exacted no penalty when such pleas were found to be false, see Sel. Cases in K.B. i. 140–5 (1280), 161–2 (1282), K.B. 27/20A m. 20–20d (1276), K.B. 26/158 m. 18 (1258). The real difficulty seems to have lain in the receipt of vouchers of records by bailiffs, for whose pleas the principals could not be held responsible. If the tenant personally failed of his record, it seems that judgment would immediately be given against him, without the taking of the assize, even before the statute: K.B. 27/24 m. 16d (1276), J.I. 1/1245 m. 58 (1281).

[2] See Note E, on p. 218.   [3] C.P. 40/96 m. 283, 283d.

at all, had to be entered in person and not by a bailiff, and that when the defendant entered it in person the plaintiff should be allowed to traverse it in order to maintain his writ. The court would adjourn the case and call the supposed joint tenant by *scire facias* to come if he wished to join in defending the deed. If he came and joined in defence the deed would be tried; it would be tried, equally, if he chose to stay away. This new procedure was given because 'it is no new thing that, among other enactments that we have designed in our time, on account of the outrageous wrong that is dealt with in writs of novel disseisin we have provided speedier remedy in those writs than in others'.[1]

The same idealism, the same confidence in right reason, the same impatience with whatever stood in the way of justice account for the readiness of Edward I's government to aggravate penalties against offenders, a tendency that appears in many ways but nowhere more than in their work with the assize. For the defendant who falsely vouched records the Statute of Westminster II provided not only immediate conviction but also double damages and a year in gaol. Under the Statute of Joint Tenants the defendant who falsely pleaded joint tenure would be imprisoned for a year and remain in gaol until he 'ransomed' himself, even if he were acquitted of the principal charge of disseisin. If he were convicted of the disseisin he would also pay double damages. Aside from such special cases, a rule of more general application was laid down in the Statute of Westminster I of 1275. Anyone convicted of disseisin with robbery or with violence, said the statute, should be imprisoned and put to ransom in addition to all the other usual penalties for disseisin. This rule was regularly applied and worked an important change in the assize.[2]

Such was the confident new ideal of justice, impatient of wrong and a little self-righteous, that guided men's thoughts in and about the time of Edward I. From this point of view the speed with which the assize of novel disseisin operated was a reason, not as in Henry II's time for limiting its applicability, but on the contrary for extending it, and for extending it as much as possible.

It was hard for them to effect major changes, however, for they were blessed with only small measure of courage. They

---

[1] *SR* i. 145–6.   [2] See Note G, p. 219.

would not break with any of the received theory of their law. If they had possessed the bold vision of the lawyers of the nineteenth century they would probably have abolished the system of separate forms of action and substituted in all suits for real property a common process based on the procedure of novel disseisin which they liked so well. But they would have looked with horror upon any such proposal. To them, the basics of the law were fixed, even in procedure. The fundamental system of forms of action must stand, and in order to maintain it they must respect the separate theory of each individual action, distinguishing it from the others. So the assize must continue to lie for disseisin alone; it must deal with 'novel' disseisins, being bound by a limitation-date more recent than those set for other kinds of action; it must lie between the original parties, disseisor and disseisee, for to make it available between others would confound it with Entry sur disseisin; it must remain a 'possessory' as distinct from a 'proprietary' remedy, with the possibility reserved of resort to a 'higher' form of action. To expand the scope of the assize while keeping within these bounds was, to say the least, difficult.

Still, if the lawyers of Edward I's time had little courage they had abundant ingenuity. They used their ingenuity to find a way for reform between theory and fact; in the end they and their successors accomplished most of what they could have wished.

A little was gained, to begin with, by expanding the definition of what constituted a free tenement protected by the assize. The gain here was not enormous—there was, for instance, no question of declaring that leaseholders' interests were free tenements and so of making the assize available to protect them—but it was substantial. The Statute of Westminster II of 1285 extended the assize to cover not only common of pasture, as in the past, but also common rights of every kind, in turbaries, fisheries, and the like, in estovers of woods and in rights to collect nuts and acorns and other woodland products: matters which had hitherto been handled by the sheriff.[1] Furthermore, the statute

---

[1] Above, pp. 62–3. Bracton thought that novel disseisin ought to serve for common rights of all sorts, fo. 231, cf. fo. 164b, and in the records of the first half of the century there are occasional suits by the assize for common rights other than pasture: *CRR* i. 385 (1201), v. 264 (1208), vi. 33 (1210), 353 (1212), *BNB* no. 1194 (1236–7), *Yorks Assize Rolls* pp. 45–6 (1251). But these become frequent and regular only after the statute, e.g. C.P. 40/138 m. 1 (1301), Y.B. 30 & 31 Ed. I p. 135 (1302).

continued, the assize could henceforth be used to recover cor-
rodies and annual payments of grain, food, or other 'necessaries'
if these were bound to be paid in some fixed place;[1] and tolls
of all kinds could likewise be recovered, again provided that
they were collectable in some certain place.[2] Finally, the statute
gave the assize for 'offices in fee', such as wardenships of parks,
woods, forests, warrens, chases, and gates.[3]

Plaintiffs who sued for any rights of these kinds had to be
able to claim at least a life-interest, but Edward's legislation
ignored that traditional boundary in extending the definition
of free tenement to some other cases. The same Statute of
Westminster II of 1285, in another of its sections,[4] founded the
process of 'execution by *elegit*'. According to this procedure, a
successful plaintiff who had recovered a debt or been awarded
damages by judgment of the king's court could choose to collect
by having half of the defendant's land turned over to him for him
to hold until he had levied out of its income the sum that was due
him. If while he was holding this land the 'tenant by *elegit*' should
be disseised, the statute allowed him to recover by the assize.
The same remedy was given in the Statute of Merchants, contemporaneous as it was with the Statute of Westminster II.
Special registries for debts were established in mercantile
centres and provision was made for swift execution if the loans
registered there were not repaid on time. If all else failed the
creditor was to have the debtor's lands and tenements—all of
them this time, not just half as in the process of *elegit*—to hold

---

[1] Cases begin to appear in the records just a few months after the statute: K.B.
27/94 m. 1, 8d (1285), J.I. 1/1245 m. 102 (Jan. 1286), 1/503 m. 10 (1287), 36
(1289). Later on, beginning about 1300, the rule developed that the plaintiff in
such cases must show his title by proffering a deed of grant: C.P. 40/121 m. 234
(1297), Y.B. Mich. 1 Ed. II no. 2 (1307), 19 Ed. II p. 654 (1326). It was not strictly
necessary that payments be annual: Y.B. Pasch. 12 Ed. II no. 43 (1319).

[2] Attempts to sue for tolls by novel disseisin in earlier times appear in *Lincs Assize
Rolls* no. 505 (1202), *Pleas 1198–1212* iv. 4128 (1209), and *Somerset Pleas* i. 1274
(1244). After the statute, cases appear, for example, in C.P. 40/102 m. 8od (1293)
and 40/130 m. 154d (1299).

[3] Occasional examples of the assize brought for franchises and offices appear
before 1285: *Rotuli Curiae Regis* i. 142 (1198), *CRR* v. 227 (1208), *Pleas 1198–1212*
iv. 4344 (1209). After the statute cases were very frequent: e.g. Y.B. 21 & 22 Ed. I
p. 577 (1294), MS. Y fo. 22ʳ (1309), fo. 23ᵛ (*c.* 1310), Y.B. Trin. 5 Ed. II no. 30
(1312), *Eyre of Kent* iii. 96 (1313–14), Y.B. Trin. 15 Ed. II p. 468 (1322), Pasch. 20
Ed. III no. 32 (1346). In the fourteenth century the plaintiff was required to show
his title, either by deed of grant or from time out of mind, as several of the above
cases show.   [4] c. 18.

until he had raised from their profits the amount of the loan and his damages. While he held, the assize of novel disseisin would protect the 'tenant by statute merchant' against being put out.[1] Later on, when the similar estates 'by statute staple' were set up under an act of 1353,[2] the assize was naturally extended to protect them as well.

The definition of a free tenement was stretched a little further not by legislation but by judicial decisions. In medieval times lands were sometimes given to a donee to hold for the grantor's lifetime. This was a natural device for a life tenant who wanted to sell his land but had no right to sell for any period longer than his own life, or for a tenant in fee who wanted to sell what interest he could without disappointing his heir. In these cases the purchaser became a 'tenant *pur autrui vie*', 'for another's life'. So too in the less common case where a grantor gave lands for the donee to hold during the lifetime of a third party.[3] Through most of the thirteenth century the law held that these tenants *pur autrui vie* were not freeholders and could not invoke the assize if they were put out.[4] But by the 1280s this law was changed: Ralph of Hengham said in his *Summa Parva* that the tenant *pur autrui vie* could use the assize. It was undoubtedly available, he wrote, if the grantor had been a life tenant, although 'some people still think' that it might not be so if the grantor had been a tenant in fee.[5] Hengham's rulings as a

---

[1] *SR* i. 98–100.

[2] *SR* i. 336–7.

[3] In the 1270s a man and his wife agreed to live apart, and the husband consequently gave some land to one of his wife's relatives to hold as long as she should live. Evidently the donee was to hold to the wife's use. J.I. 1/1245 m. 2d (1279).

[4] Bracton fo. 26b; K.B. 26/191 m. 13 (1269–70).

[5] 'Summa Parva', p. 60. The printed text needs correction: the editor should have followed MS. J and omitted 'non' at n. 3, giving the sense in which I have read the passage. This is proved by the case of La Moigne v. Denesy, which was pleaded some time in 1293–1308 and reported in MS. Y fo. 36ᵛ. There John Delisle, J., ruled as a basis of judgment that where a tenant in fee grants for his own life the grantee has only a term, not a freehold. It was otherwise, Delisle said, if the grantor was a life-tenant, for there the grantor, whose own life estate was a freehold, gave away all that he had, so that it must follow that the grantee, who received what he gave, received a freehold. Serjeant Huntingdon and Justice Howard agreed with this, 'et in Parvo Hengham reperitur concordia'. Elsewhere MS. Y notes, 'cum aliquis dimittit tenementa alicui ad terminum vite dimittentis *nihil sibi retinendo*, transfert liberum tenementum in personam cui dimittitur' (fo. 12), and cites the case of Hasthorpe v. Hasthorpe, C.P. 40/143 m. 115 (1302), where a doweress had granted over for her own life.

justice in the 1270s and 1280s correspond exactly to this doctrine,[1] and it seems to be confirmed by other contemporary
cases.[2] By about the end of the reign all doubt had been removed
and the tenant *pur autrui vie* was regarded as a freeholder
entitled to the assize even if his grantor had held in fee.[3]

Another ambiguity was resolved in the same generous sense,
extending the applicability of the assize. The old device of the
'gage of land' as security for a debt, described by Glanvill and
shown by him to be outside the protection of the assize,[4] fell
out of use after his time and was eventually replaced by the
'common-law mortgage'. In this new type of arrangement the
borrower of money who was required to put up his freehold
as security did so by enfeoffing the lender outright, but with
a provision that the feoffment should be void if the debt was
repaid on time.[5] At first judicial opinion was much divided
about whether the mortgagee who received lands by feoffment
under these circumstances should be treated as a freeholder for
the purposes of the assize while he held on awaiting the repayment of his money. Fleta, writing about 1290, thought that he
could have the assize,[6] and his view is supported by a case of
1275,[7] but the question was still debated without a decision in
1293 and 1296.[8] By 1302, however, it was settled in the mortgagee's favour: he was to be treated as a freeholder.[9]

Besides expanding the definition of a free tenement in these
ways, the men of the law of Edward I's reign also worked to
loosen the old restriction of the assize to 'novel' cases. Already in
the 1220s, as we have seen, the popularity of the assize had

---

[1] In two separate cases of 1279 and 1280 he held that where a doweress had
granted over for her own life the grantee had a free tenement (J.I. 1/1245 m. 28,
37), but in an exactly contemporary case he cautiously suspended judgment about
the status of a tenant *pur autrui vie* whose grantor had the fee (J.I. 1/1245 m. 2d).
By 1285 his own doubts were probably resolved, for in that year the King's Bench,
where he was Chief Justice, held that where a tenant in fee granted *pur autrui vie* the
donee had the freehold, K.B. 27/79 m. 27.

[2] K.B. 26/161 m. 14d (1259), K.B. 27/138 m. 5 (1293), C.P. 40/109 m. 44 (1295).

[3] The King's Bench ruling of 1285, cited in n. 1 above, did not settle the matter
as it ought to have done. But early in the next century we find the doctrine that
the tenant *pur autrui vie* is a freeholder stated generally without regard for any
possible distinction based on the estate of his grantor: MS. Y fo. 29ᵛ (1307–9?),
Y.B. Mich. 7 Ed. II no. 20 (1313), Mich. 14 Ed. II pp. 409–10 (1320).

[4] Above, p. 12. 　　　　　　　[5] P. & M. ii. 120–3, and above, p. 116.
[6] iv. 2. 4. 　　　　　　　　　　　[7] K.B. 27/16 m. 71.
[8] C.P. 40/101 m. 73, K.B. 27/149 m. 41. 　　　[9] Y.B. 30 & 31 Ed. I p. 211.

generated a feeling that it should never be limited to less than seven, eight, or nine years, time enough for suit to be brought in all ordinary cases.[1] The later years of Henry III, and Edward I's reign, saw this feeling carried further. The limitation of the assize to May 1230, which had left about seven years when it was first imposed in 1237, was allowed to stand unchanged until it lay forty-six years back. Then it was moved up, by legislation of 1275 effective in 1276, but moved up only twelve years, to May 1242; the allowance was still thirty-four years, which may impress everyone as a generous definition of 'novel'. But even this advancing of the date was only a final bow to a dying tradition. The common lawyers of Edward I's time, and their successors in the fourteenth century, wanted to make the law 'reason and not will', and to their minds it smacked of 'will'— arbitrariness—for the law to pick some particular date as the limit of an action. They would not undo what had been done, but they wanted no more of it: they left in force for the rest of the Middle Ages the several limitations, for novel disseisin and for other forms of action, that had come into effect in 1276. As these dates receded into history they ceased to matter. In the fourteenth and fifteenth centuries the assize was for practical purposes free of any time-limitation.

When the period within which the assize might be brought was first allowed to run to more than ten years, in the latter part of King John's reign, this development immediately generated the new rule that the current tenant must be named as a defendant along with the disseisor, if these were different persons.[2] Now in the latter half of the thirteenth century, when the limitation first began to be left twenty, thirty, and forty and more years in the past, a similar reaction took place. Men began to argue that the plaintiff's writ must name as defendants not only the original disseisor and the current tenant, but also everyone who had held the tenements since the alleged disseisin, or at any rate everyone who had held them for any considerable length of time. The plaintiff might have released his claims to one of the intermediate tenants, who should be joined as a defendant, then, so that he could plead the release. The current tenant might have been enfeoffed by the intermediate tenant and might therefore be entitled to have a warranty of title from

[1] Above, p. 56.   [2] Above, p. 57.

him, but under the rules of the assize the tenant could vouch him to warranty only if he was a co-defendant; so the law should require him to be made co-defendant.

There was substantial merit in the argument. But if it were accepted it would deny the assize to some plaintiffs, for the more persons required to be named the greater the chance that the assize would become unavailable through the death of one of them. And even if the plaintiff should be permitted to proceed by naming the heir of a deceased intermediate tenant, as was sometimes suggested, his suit would be complicated and the possibilities increased that his prosecution might break down for technical reasons. Because they wanted to keep the assize simple and freely available the leaders of the law set their faces against the new doctrine and saw to it that it was rejected.

Though the matter had been debated since at least 1259,[1] the decisive case was a suit that Earl Gilbert of Clare brought against the abbot of Thornton in 1281. The abbot, as defendant, pleaded that after the alleged disseisin the lands had been held for a long time by one Roger of Lovetot, now deceased, who had enfeoffed his own predecessor. The assize should not proceed, the abbot said, in view of the fact that neither Lovetot nor his heir was joined as a defendant. His objection was overruled, the assize was taken, and the earl recovered.[2] Discussion of the

---

[1] In a case of 1254 the plaintiff's suit was allowed to proceed against his disseisor and the current tenant without naming the intermediate tenant. The defence relied on the plaintiff's release to the intermediate tenant but the current tenant was allowed to plead it himself. J.I. 1/1182 m. 10. In a case of 1259, recited in C.P. 40/78 m. 95 (1289), it was ruled in the Bench after debate that the intermediate tenant need not be named. But all seems in doubt again, and no judgment was given, in a case of 1276, K.B. 27/14 m. 11.

[2] J.I. 1/492 m. 47d. The abbot pleaded that since the alleged disseisin 'Rogerus [de Lovetot] feoffavit . . . predecessorem suum . . . et postea ipsemet hucusque extitit in seisina . . . Unde petit iudicium si assisa ista debeat versus eum procedere desicut predictus Rogerus modo obiit. Preterea videtur sibi alia ratione quod assisa ista versus eum procedere non debet, quia dicit quod si . . . procederet preclusa esset sibi via perquirendi per breve warantie carte versus heredem predicti Rogeri de Lovetot eo quod non nominatur in brevi nec posset versus eum narrare quod pro defectu warantie sue tenementum illud amiserit.' The argument to the nature of Warranty of charter was ingeniously conceived, for the suit by Warranty of charter was supposed to drive the warrantor to enter into warranty in the case pending against the tenant. The warrantor could not plausibly be charged with failing to intervene in an assize of novel disseisin if he had not been named as co-defendant to the assize, for everyone knew that if he was not named as co-defendant he would not be allowed to intervene. But in fact the talk about requiring the warrantor to enter into warranty in the principal suit had been allowed by this time

point continued for some years,[1] but when the issue arose again in a case of 1290 the king and a very full council decided, citing Earl Gilbert's case, that the intermediate tenants need not be named.[2] That judgment settled the matter.[3] The longer limitations that were allowed to operate in the late thirteenth century were not to be offset by this proposed new doctrine.

But of course even with the longer limitations there still remained the old rule that the assize was available only between the original parties, the man ejected against his disseisor. If either of them died, novel disseisin could no longer serve the case. This restriction was never broken through, but the lawyers of Edward I's reign introduced a new rule whose effect was to stretch it as much as possible. The old law had required the principal disseisor to be joined as a defendant, that is to say, the man who had first acquired seisin when the plaintiff was put out. Now it was ruled that it was enough if the plaintiff named as defendants the current tenant and anyone at all who was 'a la disseisine fere', in on the act of disseisin. If the principal disseisor had brought with him a rout of his friends and henchmen, as he often did, the plaintiff could use the assize as long as any single member of that gang remained alive. The survivor did not even have to be at hand so that he could be brought to answer, for the assize would not stay for any man's absence or default; if he was alive and named in the writ, that was enough.[4]

to become a fiction, and Warranty of charter was constantly used to secure compensation for tenants who lost at novel disseisin, against warrantors who had not been named in the writ of assize: above, p. 131; Milsom, 'Introduction', pp. clix–clxiii; and *Sel. Cases in K.B.* ii. 17.

[1] In a case of 1284 the tenant observed that the lands had been held in the meantime by one Robert Walrand, his own feoffor, to whom, as he understood, the plaintiff had released: 'unde dicit quod ex quo predictus Robertus [Walrand qui] per longum tempus tenuit . . . et cui [querens] remisit clamium suum iam obiit, videtur ei quod assisa ista non debet inde fieri, quia [querens] posset a casu . . . si assisa curreret recuperare versus unum id quod alii quietumclamavit, et etiam idem [tenens] posset amittere warantiam suam versus heredem prefati Roberti [Walrand] . . . ex quo verificare non posset quod idem Robertus in vita sua super aliqua disseisina fuit convictus.' The court proceeded nevertheless. K.B. 27/98 m. 23. The issue was raised again, and decided the same way, in C.P. 40/83 m. 36 (1290).

[2] *Select Cases in K.B.* ii. 17.

[3] It followed as a corollary of the judgments of 1281 and 1290 that where an intermediate tenant had held and the plaintiff had released to him the current tenant must be permitted to plead the release in defence: *Eyre of Kent* iii. 139 (1313), Y.B. Trin. 15 Ed. II p. 467, 468–9, 481–2 (1322–3), Mich. 17 Ed. II pp. 500–2 (1323), Mich. 14 Ed. III no. 107 (1340–1). [4] See Note H, p. 220.

Under these circumstances, and always provided that the plaintiff himself did not die, the assize could often be brought even after very long delay. In his case of 1281 against the abbot of Thornton, Gilbert of Clare recovered on a disseisin committed about eighteen years before.[1] In another case, an assize was taken in 1291 on a disseisin allegedly committed in 1256.[2] The action had partly transcended its traditional limitation to recent cases.

While this was being accomplished, the reformers also set about modifying the rule that the assize was merely possessory. By Edward I's time the primary meaning of this was that judgments given in novel disseisin were not definitive, that the defeated party could 'resort' to an 'action of a higher nature' such as a writ of entry or a writ of right and recover after all where he had lost at the assize. As a corollary, it was held that the assize could be used only once as between the same parties on a given set of facts. If John and Henry in the course of a long quarrel disseise one another of the holding by turns, once or twice or several times over, and if John at length finds himself out of possession and brings the assize, that is the only time the assize may be used by either of them to look into and correct the tangle of their dispute up to that time—though of course a new assize may be brought if a new disseisin is committed later on. If the plaintiff 'fails of his action' for any reason he cannot renew his suit by the assize, and it was possible to fail of one's action through a technical error without a trial on the merits.[3] If the plaintiff succeeds and recovers the property, but recovers it on the ground that he was illegally disseised regardless of the merits of his title, still his opponent is not allowed to bring a counter-suit by the assize for any of the earlier disseisins that the plaintiff committed against him, however illegal those may

---

[1] Above, p. 140.   [2] Sutherland, 'Peytevin v. La Lynde', pp. 541–2.

[3] If the plaintiff failed not 'of his action' but merely 'of his writ', as, for example, by naming the wrong township in his writ, he was free to renew his suit by the assize. Bracton discusses the effects of a withdrawal 'from the writ' and again 'from the action', fos. 104, 182b, and his law on this point is illustrated in *Rotuli Curiae Regis* ii. 117, 139 (1199), *CRR* vii. 263–4 (1214), *BNB* nos. 1118 (1234), 1285 (1239–40).

That the plaintiff who had once lost by judgment was prevented from suing again by the assize is shown in these cases: *Rotuli Curiae Regis* i. 370 (1199), *CRR* ii. 122 (1202), iii. 67 (1203), *Northants Pleas* no. 665 (1203), *Eyres of Lincs and Worcs* nos. 91, 299 (1218–19), *Eyres of Beds* iii. 2 (1227), J.I. 1/1245 m. 12d (1279).

also have been. After one try at the assize between them, if either of them wants more litigation he should betake himself to a higher action.[1]

None of this was much to the liking of those who were minded to make more of the assize, but the corollary was especially objectionable, as preventing the assize from doing work that it was clearly qualified to do. In two judgments given in 1290 and 1291 the corollary was swept away. In the first case the King's Bench ruled that a defendant who had lost at novel disseisin could if he liked initiate a counter-suit by the assize to correct earlier disseisins that he had suffered at the hands of the same opponent.[2] In the second it was judged that whenever a plaintiff failed at novel disseisin on account of a technical error, he could renew his suit as many times as he liked until a judgment was given, either for or against him, on the substantial merits of his complaint.[3]

The principal rule, that one could 'resort' from the assize to an action of a higher nature, was founded far too deep in legal theory for the justices to think of abrogating it. But they could rob it of some of its effect, and this they proceeded to do early

---

[1] For all this see Bracton, fos. 226–226b, 294b–295, and cf. the marginal note to *BNB* no. 360. The law is illustrated in *Eyre of Yorks 1218–19* no. 286, K.B. 27/18 m. 48–50 (reciting a case of the 1260s), 27/24 m. 16d (1276).

[2] *Sel. Cases in K.B.* iii. 15. In the 1280s such countersuits had been brought by the assize in a couple of cases, *Sel. Cases in K.B.* i. 140–5 (1280) and K.B. 27/107 m. 24, 27/132 m. 22 (1284–7), but in each case it was later contended that this was an error and the courts reserved judgment whether this was so. After 1290 the new law is illustrated in many cases, e.g. MS. Y fos. 12ʳ, 35ʳ (1302–9), 101ᵛ–102ʳ (1311), Y.B. Mich. 5 Ed. II no. 28 (1311), Pasch. 13 Ed. III no. 12 (1339), Trin. 21 Ed. III no. 15 = 21 Ass. no. 9 (1347), and cf. Y.B. Mich. 6 Ed. II no. 80 (1312), Mich. 11 Ed. II no. 12 (1317). Some complex law was developed about whether the earlier disseisin alleged as the basis for a second assize had or had not been tried in the first assize: Y.B. 18 Ed. II pp. 617–19.

[3] C.P. 40/89 m. 131. John Hunter had been dispossessed of his freehold in Leicestershire, and brought his assize in the court of the verge. The jurors found that he had not been disseised since the king's arrival in the county, so the court of the verge had no jurisdiction and his case was thrown out. Later he brought novel disseisin again before the justices of assize. The defendant objected, but the justices of assize ruled that the new action should proceed because the earlier judgment against Hunter had not been a 'judgment of the freehold'. This ruling was later upheld in the Common Pleas. That it worked a general change in the law is shown in Sutherland, 'Peytevin v. La Lynde', pp. 537–46, and, for later times, in Y.B. Mich. 44 Ed. III no. 60 (1370), 45 Ass. no. 10 (1371). Some refinements of the later law are shown in B.M. Egerton MS. 2811 fos. 214ᵛ–215ʳ, 219ʳ, 253ᵛ, 283ᵛ–284ᵛ, J.I. 1/685 m. 38, 46 (1330), Y.B. Mich. 18 Ed. III no. 17 (1344), 46 Ass. no. 10 (1372).

in the reign of Edward II. In two cases of 1311 and 1313 it was ruled that when the jurors in an assize of novel disseisin resolved particular questions of fact by their verdict, their findings were as good as the findings of any jury in any form of action, and the matters that they pronounced on could not be tried again even in an action of a higher nature. Although resort to a higher action always remained possible in principle, this rule meant that in many cases it was useless for the party to try to avail himself of it.

In the case of 1313, for instance, Geoffrey Scoland had given lands to his bastard son Richard. Richard died in seisin of them and, since he left no issue, rival claims were put forward by Geoffrey's heir Frank Scoland and by the superior lord of the fee. Frank Scoland contended that the gift to Richard had been an entail, which should now revert to him, as the donor's heir, for failure of issue; the lord contended that the gift had been in fee simple, so that Richard had held directly of him as the superior lord according to the rule of the statute *Quia emptores* and he was therefore entitled to have the lands by escheat for failure of heirs. The lord took over the holding, Frank Scoland threw him out, and he brought novel disseisin and recovered: in a carefully reasoned verdict the jurors said that Richard had held in fee simple and not in fee tail and that the lord was therefore in the right. Defeated at novel disseisin, Scoland resorted to a writ of formedon. But he was met by the objection that, although formedon was undoubtedly 'higher' than novel disseisin, nevertheless his claim to the land in this higher action was still founded on the contention that Richard had held in fee tail, that the assize had found that this was not so, and that he therefore ought not to be allowed to proceed. The court seemed to agree and Scoland withdrew.[1]

The most important limitation on the assize was that which confined it to cases of disseisin. The plaintiff had to be able to show that he had been 'seised and wrongfully disseised'. Here again, there was in the late thirteenth century no question of abandoning the rule, for that would have disturbed the whole system of forms of action. But the definitions of who was 'seised and disseised' could be stretched.

The law began to find constructive disseisins in situations

[1] See Note I, p. 221.

where an ordinary observer might not feel that anyone had been ejected. In the beginning the common law had worked with a basic concept of disseisin that was as plain and straightforward as could be: it was a disseisin when a person in occupation of lands and tenements was put out of them against his will. But later on the men of the law came in a practical way to identify disseisin with the kinds of acts which, when they were illegal, could be remedied by the assize, and as this became the characteristic way of looking at the matter and as thoughtful men reflected on its implications, the original basic concept of disseisin became more and more difficult to maintain. The acts that the assize would correct took a number of forms: direct ejectment was covered, surely, but so were the keeping a man out of his holding when he came back from market,[1] harvesting the crop on his land,[2] putting in cattle to pasture,[3] or, in the case of such a tenuous free tenement as a rent, replevying a distress.[4] It was neither necessary nor very easy to think of all these as special cases of putting the occupant out against his will. Furthermore, the law had always recognized that a freeholder was disseised not only where he himself was thrown out but also where anyone was ejected who held in his name. It might be his wife, his bailiff, his serf, his guardian if he was a minor, his termor if he had leased the land out: if you eject any of these you disseise the freeholder.[5] But if the offence of disseisin was always against the freeholder even where he was not the occupant, then it was impossible to hold that the offence consisted in forcing the occupant out. So after about mid century the basic idea that a disseisin had to involve putting someone out against his will was quietly, perhaps unconsciously, dropped. Instead, a disseisin was taken to be any interference with a freeholder's use and disposal of his own. As a remnant of the older and plainer way of thinking there stood only a rule that

---

[1] Bracton fo. 161b.

[2] For example, *Pleas 1198–1202* ii. 462, 503 (1201), *Northants Pleas* no. 448 (1202), *CRR* iii. 160–1 (1204), iv. 237 (1206), vi. 33 (1210), vii. 118 (1214), *Eyre of Yorks 1218–19* no. 1114, *Somerset Pleas* i. 394j (1238).

[3] For example, *Pleas 1198–1212* iii. 907 (1204), *CRR* vi. 43 (1210), 126 (1211), xi. 614 (1223), *Somerset Pleas* i. 1448 (1251).

[4] Above, pp. 51–2.

[5] Bracton alluded to these rules, fo. 161b, but did not discuss them at length for they must have seemed to go without saying. They are illustrated in hundreds of cases.

in order to classify as a disseisin a violation had to be such as to raise in the freeholder a right to an immediate remedy, as if he or his representative had been involuntarily ejected.

In the older style of thought it was not a disseisin if someone who had the management of lands in a freeholder's name, such as his bailiff or guardian or termor, took it upon himself to make a feoffment of the freehold to a stranger. His act was an offence but not a disseisin, for the stranger entered by the voluntary handing-over of the tenements and not by forcing anyone out. In later times, given the new understanding of disseisin, the case was entirely changed. The stranger's entry into the holding put the true freeholder out of control of his own, and the freeholder could take immediate action to oppose it, so it was a disseisin and a case for the assize. Henry of Bracton stated this as firm law[1] and it is illustrated in occasional cases where plaintiffs recovered by the assize because their lands had been granted away by their guardians (1227, 1269),[2] their tenants-at-will (1254, 1280),[3] their tenants *pur autrui vie*, here regarded as termors (1270),[4] and their bailiffs (1284).[5] But doubt remained even in Edward I's reign[6] until the statute of 1275 decreed definitely that it was a disseisin for a guardian to enfeoff a stranger and until the statute of 1285 expressly enacted the same rule for termors and for those who held 'in custodia'.[7] These legislative acts settled both theory and practice. Thenceforth the assize could be used to recover after any tortious feoffment by one who held in the freeholder's name and did not himself possess the freehold.[8] In 1310 Justices Bereford and Stanton

---

[1] fos. 94b, 161b, 166, 273–273b, 285; but cf. fo. 422 for a more cautious statement.

[2] *BNB* no. 1906 (1227), *Derby Assizes* p. 146 (1269); cf. *BNB* no. 1840 (1227), K.B. 26/207 m. 5d (1272).　　　　[3] K.B. 26/151 m. 42d, *Somerset Pleas* iv. 52.

[4] K.B. 26/191 m. 13.　　　　　　　　　　　　[5] J.I. 1/492 m. 85d.

[6] In 1256 a court ruled that it was not a disseisin when a termor granted the freehold, *Northumb Assize Rolls* p. 66. In 1275 the King's Bench was unsure whether a grant in fee was a disseisin when it was made by a creditor who was holding the debtor's lands until he should have levied a certain sum, K.B. 27/14 m. 5.

[7] Statute of Westminster I c. 48, Statute of Westminster II c. 25. The rule in the latter statute concerning feoffments by termors was occasioned by judicial doubts in Roger le Peytevin's case, brought in 1284, Sutherland, 'Peytevin *v.* la Lynde', pp. 529–39.

[8] *Fleta* iv. 1. 10, *Britton* ii. 3. 10 and 11. 13, and these early illustrative cases: C.P. 40/59 m. 4 (1285—guardian), *Sel. Cases in K.B.* ii. 17 (1290—guardian), C.P. 40/106 m. 246 (1293–5—guardian), MS. Y fo. 10ᵛ (*c.* 1300—bailiff). In 1304 Chief Justice Hengham ruled that it was a disseisin under the provisions of the statute of 1285

agreed that the old writs of entry that used to serve such cases were 'not founded on sound principle'.[1] By the same token, the assize was allowed, from around 1300, to serve freeholders whose bailiffs, guardians, termors, or other representatives did anything else that interfered with the freehold, as by asserting a claim to freehold for themselves[2] or by refusing to get out when their rights expired.[3]

Thinking along the same lines, some men came to the conclusion that it was a disseisin to force a freeholder by threats, prison, or pains to make a feoffment, and that it was a disseisin to accept a feoffment from a minor. The former doctrine was accepted in the law: a feoffment made under duress became a case for the assize.[4] After a prolonged flirtation the law rejected the second doctrine in principle and left to other remedies those who made feoffments while they were under age.[5] A minor's feoffment *was* a disseisin, however, in the fourteenth century and after, if he did not make livery of seisin in person, for any authority that he might give to an attorney to do it in his name was simply void on account of his nonage, and the livery carried out without authority was, of course, an actionable disseisin by any standard.[6]

for a stepfather to alienate his stepchild's freehold, though some thought that the statute should not be construed so broadly: Y.B. 32 & 33 Ed. I p. 75. In 41 Ass. no. 7 (1367) an alienation by a 'tenant at will in ancient demesne' was treated as a disseisin.

[1] Y.B. Mich. 4 Ed. II no. 26.

[2] Bracton fo. 44b; K.B. 27/155 m. 28 (1298), MS. Y fo. 6ʳ (c. 1300).

[3] Bracton fos. 39b, 263b; *BNB* no. 1925 (1227); Y.B. 20 & 21 Ed. I p. 423 (1293), K.B. 27/156 m. 77 (1298), Y.B. 33–35 Ed. I p. 389 (1306), *Eyre of Kent* iii. 207 (1313–14), Y.B. 19 Ed. II pp. 659–60 (1326).

[4] The old law, which required a writ of entry for these cases, appears in *Eyres of Beds* iii. 2 (1227), K.B. 27/20A m. 20 (1266–7); cf. *CRR* xii. 344 (1224). The change to the new law is shown by K.B. 26/207 m. 27 (1272), J.I. 1/1245 m. 42d (1280), Y.B. Hil. 15 Ed. III no. 34 (1341).

[5] The old law provided the writ of entry *dum fuit infra etatem* for the recovery of lands given away by minors. In his treatise Bracton stated this law, fos. 273–273b, but as justice in a case of 1251 he held that it was a disseisin to enter by a minor's feoffment, J.I. 1/1178 m. 2d, and in a number of later cases this rule was applied to grants by those who were very young: Y.B. Mich. 4 Ed. II no. 36 (1310; grantor under 14 years of age), *Eyre of Kent* ii. 181–3 (1313–14; under eight years), iii. 87, 145–6 (1313–14; one year old). The point was that such grants were in fact the guardian's deeds, done in the ward's name and with the ward perhaps going through the motions of sealing documents and delivering seisin. The doctrine was, however, wholly rejected in C.P. 40/83 m. 36 (1290), Y.B. Mich. 12 Ed. II no. 80 (1318), and John Rylands Library Latin MS. 180 fo. 42ᵛ (1329–30).

[6] B.M. Egerton MS. 2811 fo. 238ᵛ (1330–1), Y.B. Pasch. 42 Ed. III no. 18 (1368), Pasch. 9 Henry VII no. 7 (1494), Dyer fo. 108 (1554).

The plaintiff in the assize had to have been 'seised and dis-seised'. If the latter concept, of disseisin, could be reformulated to broaden the applicability of the assize, so could the former. The rule in the old law was that no one had a seisin protected by the assize, however good might be his title, unless he had taken genuine control of the tenements. Genuine control might be gained on an instant where a purchaser received full and peaceable livery of seisin under a valid feoffment that worked no wrong to any man,[1] or where one was put in by authority;[2] but in other cases it had to be continued for at least a few days in order to demonstrate its substantiality.[3] Now in the 1270s and 1280s the courts began to rule that any man who had a right to take possession of land could gain a legally effective seisin much more easily than that. He had only to come to the tenements openly and in the daytime, enter them, declare his intention and make a show of taking control, and charge any adverse occupier to withdraw. If he did this, or what amounted to this, he was seised in the eyes of the law. Anyone who then prevented him from having full and peaceable control committed an illegal disseisin, and he could recover by the assize.[4]

This new law generated the ritual performances, often en-livened with bits of slapstick, that lay behind an increasing number of actions of novel disseisin. John of Ruda was only one or two years old when his grandfather died in 1300. His grand-mother Cecily believed that John could claim as his heritage the house and land that had belonged to her late husband but she knew that this would be disputed by his uncle Henry. During

---

[1] Bracton fos. 39b, 43; *Somerset Pleas* i. 1489 (1254), *Yorks Assize Rolls* pp. 103–4, 123 (1260). For feoffments to the prejudice of third parties see above, pp. 93–4, 109–15.

[2] *Eyre of Yorks 1218–19* no. 100.

[3] *CRR* iii. 97–8 (1204), vii. 79 (1214), *Eyre of Yorks 1218–19* no. 401, *BNB* no. 1794 (1222), K.B. 26/182 m. 21 (1268), J.I. 1/1217 m. 18 (1273). The case of 1268 is particularly authoritative. The plaintiff had denounced a fraudulent feoffment made of his land and had ejected the feoffees but had managed to stay in for only three hours or so until one of the feoffees re-ejected him. During his brief stay he had taken no esplees. After full deliberation the king and council judged that his seisin was not such that he could recover by the assize.

[4] K.B. 26/181 m. 20d (1267), K.B. 27/24 m. 23d (1276), J.I. 1/503 m. 26 (1286–9). From a little later the doctrine is fully stated in MS. Y fo. 11ᵛ (c. 1300) and illustrated in Y.B. 33–35 Ed. I pp. 53–5 (1305), MS. Y fo. 15ʳ (1306), 16ᵛ (1300–10), B.M. Egerton MS. 2811 fo. 345ʳ (1330), Y.B. Trin. 14 Ed. III no. 1 (1340), 22 Ass. no. 15 (1348).

the grandfather's funeral, which was held in a neighbouring church, Cecily carried John to the house and set him down by the door. When Henry came back from the funeral he found John there, 'claiming an estate . . . through Cecily's words'. Henry removed him and Cecily sued for disseisin in John's name.[1] Some years earlier, Maud atte Bele came to take over a heritage of hers: finding that the property was held by an adversary so that she could not enter the hall of the principal dwelling, she went by a back way and entered a storeroom (*celerium*), where she managed to stay for about twelve hours and serve herself a meal before she was put out. She sued for disseisin and recovered.[2] In the 1330s a man who claimed ownership of a house came to take possession and discovered that the door was barred against him, so he tried to climb in the window. He was halfway through when his opponent dragged him back out; he sued and recovered by the assize.[3]

The point of setting baby John at the door until uncle Henry came home, of going in the back way when no one was watching, of climbing through the window, and of all the other acts of this kind, was to establish the nominal seisin that the law now regarded as sufficient, so that one could then claim to have been disseised and use the assize to sue for the property. It was necessary to face the opponent out in this way, for no thirteenth- or fourteenth-century 'casual disseisor' was ever invented, in the style of the imaginary 'casual ejector' of the seventeenth century, to enable claimants to avoid the requirement of a real confrontation. The most that the medieval law would concede, and even this came only in the latter part of the fourteenth century, was that if the claimant dared not approach the tenements for fear of death on account of the adversary's threats then it was enough for him to come as close as was safe and there publicly state his claim.[4]

Even so, this redefinition of what it meant to be seised was the decisive breakthrough in the effort to expand the scope of the

---

[1] C.P. 40/134 m. 128d. [2] J.I. 1/503 m. 8 (1287).
[3] 8 Ass. no. 25 (1334).
[4] 38 Ass. no. 23 (1364), 39 Ass. no. 11 (1365), Y.B. Pasch. 49 Ed. III no. 7 (1375). In the fifteenth century the doctrine was broadened a little to allow this kind of seisin-by-declaration where the fear was not necessarily of death but only of bodily assault: Y.B. Pasch. 12 Henry IV no. 5 (1411), Hil. 14 Henry IV no. 2 (1413), Littleton, *Tenures*, paragraph 419.

assize. Where work with the concepts of free tenement, of novelty, of possessoriness, and of disseisin gained bits of legal territory in this direction and that, the new definition of seisin annexed whole provinces and kingdoms. The pattern of litigation for lands and tenements was never to be the same again. For if a claimant to freehold rights who found himself kept out of his property by an adversary would only go to the trouble of taking a nominal seisin then he could use the assize as the vehicle for suing on almost any kind of claim. When his case came up the court and jurors could pass lightly over his attempt to enter and the resistance offered, for these need not be in any doubt: they would be recent facts and the plaintiff who had arranged that they should occur would also have arranged that they should be well witnessed. But the plaintiff's nominal entry into the tenements established a seisin in the eyes of the law only if he had had a good right to take possession and to disseise his adversary: only if he had a 'right of entry', to use the new language of the fourteenth century. The real task of the court and jury would be to determine whether he had the right of entry. Generally speaking, this meant that they had to find out whether he was the true owner of the land, for rights of entry normally went with rightful ownership, as we saw in the last chapter. Usually then, the plaintiff's claim to the property would be tried, and if he could show that he had a good title which also supported a right of entry, he would recover on the strength of it through the procedure of the assize. So a pretending heir, for example, who found himself kept out of his heritage, generally need not betake himself to the assize of mort d'ancestor, with its more dilatory procedure. He could make a formal entry and then charge the adversary with disseisin and recover his right by the assize of novel disseisin. Novel disseisin did the work of mort d'ancestor, and as a result mort d'ancestor sank into obsolescence in the fourteenth century. It was the same for many other forms of action.

From this time on, in fact, the only major limitation on the power of the assize to serve as a comprehensive action for the recovery of freehold rights lay in those fairly numerous cases where the true owner did not have a right to disseise the adverse occupier. The owner might be a married woman whose husband had alienated her land, or an heir in tail whose father had sold the entailed property: in these as in some other cases the owner never had a right of entry. One who had had a right of entry at first might have lost it because he delayed too long, so that the passage of time or the occurrence of some event conferred on his adversary legal protection against his entry.[1]

Accordingly, from the time of the change of doctrine about seisin, around 1280, the law began to wear away at the rules that sometimes denied a right of entry to the true owner. The process was painfully slow, carried on as it was by men whose thinking was bound by received theories, and it was never pushed to completion. But once begun it continued for a hundred years, as deliberate but as powerful too as the flow of a glacier, until by the late fourteenth century the large majority of the rules that could stand in the way of entry by an owner had been set aside. As these rules were eliminated one after another, the ability of the assize to serve as a general action for freehold was increased step by step.

Thus in the early fourteenth century it was often held that a right of entry ought to be recognized, regardless of particular circumstances, wherever anyone had a valid claim that could not be fitted under any of the received forms of action at law. Recognizing a right of entry would make the assize available for the case; in this way, novel disseisin would fill in all the gaps in the system of forms. So if a husband made a feoffment of his wife's lands she could recover after his death by suing in the form of Entry *cui in vita*, but that form could serve only where the wrong consisted in a feoffment and not where the husband had released his wife's right to a rent charge or established a charge on her lands. In such cases, then, it was ruled about 1310, the widow could enter after her husband's death.[2] Similarly it was argued that no lapse of time, no intervention of events, would extinguish a right of entry for breach of condition on a feoffment, for the law provided no means of enforcing conditions in feoffments except by the grantor's entry.[3] An unincorporated group,

---

[1] Above, Chapter III, and especially pp. 100–5, 109–13.

[2] MS. Y fo. 23ᵛ (*c.* 1310); MS. Y fo. 35ᵛ and Y.B. 2 Ed. II no. 70 (1309). The widow 'entered' on a rent owing to herself by making a distraint for payment; on a rent charged against her own lands, by withholding payment. Cf. Y.B. Hil. 8 Ed. II no. 35 (1315).

[3] Scrope, J., *arguendo*, Y.B. Hil. 11 Ed. II no. 3 (1318); cf. 21 Ass. no. 28 (1347), and Littleton, *Tenures*, paragraphs 391–2.

such as the parishioners of a church, could not bring an action at law. If their collective rights were interfered with they could enter to assert their rights, any time, under any circumstances, because otherwise they would have no remedy at all.[1] A century and a half later, Thomas Littleton applied the same reasoning in interpreting a provision of the Statute of Merton.[2]

Under the Statute of Merchants of 1285,[3] it was common practice for the lands of an insolvent debtor to be turned over to the creditor for the creditor to hold until he should have recovered his debt and damages out of the income. When the creditor had taken all that he was entitled to, the lands would pass back to the original owner, who was discharged of the debt. When the time came, the original owner could get the lands back by process of law, calling the creditor into court to render account of the income that he had levied and recovering by execution of judgment if it appeared from the account that the obligation had been fully covered.[4] But although the erstwhile debtor had a suitable means for suing at law, it was thought proper to give him a right of entry too, because the process at law might entail some delay. So as soon as the creditor had in fact levied all that was due him the original owner had a right to enter and oust him. If he took this course, the litigation that resulted would be by novel disseisin. The issue between the parties would still be a matter of accounts, whether the creditor had or had not collected all he was entitled to, but it would be handled through the more efficient procedures of the assize.[5]

---

[1] *Per* Bereford J., Y.B. Trin. 6 Ed. II no. 1 (1312). The issue in this case was not entry upon land but the parallel right to abate a nuisance. Unable to bring suit, the parishioners could not use a nominal entry to bring the assize; they had to make a true and effective entry and leave the adversary to sue.

[2] *Tenures*, paragraphs 107–8.   [3] Above, pp. 136–7.

[4] Y.B. Pasch. 15 Ed. II pp. 465–6 (1322).

[5] K.B. 27/156 m. 71, 76, C.P. 40/123 m. 91, 40/124 m. 80 (1298), Y.B. 2 Ed. II no. 135 (1308–9). It was often debated whether rights of entry should not also be conceded in cognate cases, where execution according to the Statute of Merchants was made in lands that were exempt from execution (Y.B. Pasch. 15 Ed. II pp. 465–6 (1322)), where the estate on which execution was made came to an end (MS. Y fos. 5ᵛ–6ʳ (1298–1304?)), or where the creditor gave an implied release (Y.B. Hil. 15 Ed. III no. 34 (1341)). Some of the same issues arose in connection with tenancies by *elegit*, with mortgages, and with some kinds of conditional feoffments: *Eyre of London 1321* p. 357, Y.B. Mich. 6 Ed. III no. 53 (1332), Pasch. 17 Ed. II pp. 542, 543 (1324), *Eyre of Kent* iii. 126–7 (1313–14), Y.B. Pasch. 21 Ed. III no. 2 (1347).

A much more important development came about in the 1300s and 1310s. The old rule was abandoned that one who had a right of entry must exercise it without delay or else lose it. The new law held that the right could be exercised after ten years, twenty years, or any other lapse of time just as well as on the day when it first arose, and no talk about the owner's negligence, 'tolerance', or 'impotence' in delaying to act would have any bearing on the matter.

Right through the thirteenth century and in the opening years of the fourteenth the old law, familiar from Bracton's time and before, continued to be enforced: every right of entry had to be exercised with reasonable promptness under the circumstances of the individual case.[1] Then it began to be struck down, in a subtle but decisive way, about 1310.

We learn of the development from a case of 1314.[2] An uncle and his nephew fell into dispute about which of them was entitled to the tenements that had belonged to their common ancestor—the uncle's father and the nephew's grandfather— and in the end the nephew threw his uncle out of the property. When the uncle brought an assize for this, the nephew readily admitted that he had disseised him. He did so, he said, with full justification. His own father was the elder brother and his uncle was the younger, so his grandfather's heritage descended by right through his father to himself; as true heir he was entitled to enter and put his uncle out. The uncle answered that however that might be he himself had been seised for ten years before his nephew put him out and seisin for such a long time should be grounds enough for recovery in novel disseisin. This was of course a good traditional stand, and his counsel argued it hard and long, but the justices, Bereford and Inge, would have none of it. The nephew, they said, had 'shown his title of right' when he described the descent from his grandfather through his father to himself. If the uncle wished to pursue his action he would have to set forth a good 'title of right' on his side; the title must be either by descent or by purchase and long

---

[1] Above, pp. 100–4. The continued enforcement of this rule around the end of the century is shown in K.B. 27/9 m. 7d and *Calendar of Inquisitions post Mortem* i. 32 (1274), J.I. 1/503 m. 16d (1288), Y.B. 20 & 21 Ed. I p. 219 (1292), Hil. 10 Ed. II no. 11 and Mich. 11 Ed. II no. 49 (case of before 1294, reported later), 30 & 31 Ed. I p. 123 and J.I. 1/118 m. 5 (1302).

[2] Y.B. Mich. 8 Ed. II no. 6, Hil. 8 Ed. II no. 37.

tenure alone would not suffice. The uncle showed no such title, and so he lost his case by judgment.

The implications of the judgment were revolutionary. A defendant could justify a disseisin by describing his right of entry; long tenure was no sufficient answer on the plaintiff's part, he had to have something more to show if he was to get to the assize; therefore long tenure as such was not protected by the assize. A claimant to lands who once had a good right of entry against the tenant could exercise it any time he liked, early or late, for his opponent could never succeed against him at the assize.

These implications had to be taken with full seriousness, for the judgment of 1314 was not isolated. In that case itself one of the pleaders cited 'John Chamberlain's case' as a precedent and the justices, when they came to give their decision, said that they were observing the rule followed by Ralph of Hengham, the Chief Justice of the Common Bench who had retired in 1309. A similar decision was given just the year before, in 1313.[1] Twenty years later, in 1334, a case arose between two brothers who were disputing which of them was their father's heir.[2] The defendant admitted that he had put the plaintiff out of the holdings but said that he was the elder brother and that he therefore had a right as true heir to take over the heritage. The younger brother replied that he had been seised for twelve years after the father's death, with his elder brother's knowledge and acquiescence, before the elder brother ejected him. But he did not even attempt to rely on his twelve years' seisin for he could tell from the discussion that it would be useless. He pleaded that his elder brother was illegitimate and that he himself, therefore, was the true heir, and on that issue the judgment was left to turn. So again in a case of 1343.[3] Maud Casse, the defendant, pleaded that the plaintiff, Alice Darcy, had earlier granted the tenements to her by fine. Alice replied that she and her late husband had reoccupied the tenements at once after they were 'wrongfully ousted by colour of that fine' and had continued in seisin until her husband died, and she after his time until the disseisin about which she was complain-

---

[1] *Eyre of Kent* iii. 143-4.   [2] Y.B. Hil. 8 Ed. III no. 43 = 8 Ass. no. 5.
[3] Y.B. Mich. 17 Ed. III no. 32. Cf. Y.B. Mich. 19 Ed. III no. 21 and Hil. 21 Ed. III no. 5 = 21 Ass. no. 1 (1345), Y.B. Trin. 22 Ed. III no. 41 (1348).

ing. But Maud remarked that the allegation of re-entry and continuance in seisin was irrelevant, for even if it was true it would not entitle her to recover the lands, and this statement was not disputed. However long Alice had continued in seisin, Maud was entitled to put her out if the fine had indeed made Maud the true owner. From some time around 1310, the law of the land was the law shown in these cases.

The reports show that if a defendant wanted to prevent a plaintiff from recovering on the strength of long tenure alone the defendant had to plead in bar of the assize, setting forth his own title to the tenements and showing how it was superior to his opponent's claim. If the defendant did not plead in bar but let the case go straight to the assize, the jurors should, theoretically at least, give the plaintiff a recovery by their verdict, regardless of any superior title in the defendant, if they found that the plaintiff had been seised for a considerable time before the defendant ejected him. This state of affairs let men suppose as late as the 1330s that the traditional law still stood in principle, that rights of entry must be exercised promptly or not at all.[1]

But if the old law still stood in principle, it was devoid of meaning for those who successfully took seisin of lands and appeared as defendants to the assize, for any defendant could plead in bar if he would only take due care about it. The rule that a bailiff might not enter a plea in bar was no obstacle after 1318, for a statute of that year allowed defendants to appear by attorney,[2] and an attorney could bar the assize just as well as his principal. Neither was there any real difficulty in the rule that in order to plead one's title in bar one must 'give colour' to his opponent. The rule was that the defendant had not only to explain his title, which generated his right of entry, but also to show what claim his adversary relied on and then draw the comparison, showing the superiority of his own title. Before most justices, it was not enough to describe one's right and then say that the opponent 'came and intruded' on the tenements, for to

---

[1] The rule is still spoken of as governing law in MS. Y fos. 101^v–102^r (1311), Y.B. Hil. 11 Ed. II nos. 2, 10 (1318), 18 Ed. II p. 617 (1325), B.M. Egerton MS. 2811 fos. 237^r–237^v, 345^r–345^v (1330), Y.B. Hil. 8 Ed. III no. 43 = 8 Ass. no. 5 (1334). It seems to have been part of the basis for judgment in *Eyre of London 1321* pp. 225–7.

[2] Above, p. 44.

call the opponent an intruder gave him no colour of right at all. One had to say that the opponent was a representative of another branch of one's family who pretended to rights of inheritance—but his right was not good, for his was the junior branch and was excluded from the heritage by the rule of primogeniture; or that the opponent was the heir of a former owner of the tenements, whose rights had, however, been extinguished when that owner granted by final concord to the defendant; or something else of this kind. But where a man who had a well-founded right of entry on lands had failed to act on it for a long time, almost certainly it was because his adversary really *had* had a pretty good colour of right. Very few responsible men of property would delay to seek their remedy if they were opposed by mere lawless strangers. Long delays to act resulted from family tangles, misunderstandings, fallings-out, and changes of heart. So the plea in bar, assigning some colour of right to the opponent, would be simply an account of what had been going on, though of course an *ex parte* account. And if someone had after all neglected for too long to take action against an adversary who had no colour of right at all, he could still enter and oust the man and then, when the opponent brought his assize in reliance on long seisin, give him some fictitious colour, as by saying that he was a cousin belonging to a junior branch of the family who was unreasonably contesting the rights of the senior line, that he was the purported grantee of a reversion but the grant was null for there had never been any attornment, or the like. The opponent could not get to the assize just by saying that he was *not* a cousin or that he did *not* suppose that he had been granted a reversion, unless he would go on to state affirmatively what his right was, and as soon as he did that the plea in bar had served its purpose: the plaintiff could not recover unless he could show that his right was better than the defendant's.[1]

---

[1] For 'giving colour' in novel disseisin see Reeves, *History of English Law*, iii. 229, 590, where the author discusses its use from the later years of Edward III. The use of fictions to give colour seems to go back to the early fourteenth century. In the case of 1314 between uncle and nephew, reviewed above, the colour given the plaintiff was that he was the defendant's uncle, a younger son of his grandfather. Presumably this was true; but the plaintiff refused to acknowledge any family relationship, and in discussion of the pleas Chief Justice Bereford contemplated the possibility that his actual title to the land might have nothing to do with family

Even so, the tying of the new law to pleas in bar was unsatisfactory, for it was the defendant's choice whether to initiate pleadings on a bar and the new law was available, then, only at his option. If a claimant to lands whose opponent had long been in occupation made only a nominal entry and then sued on the technical disseisin that resulted, he would appear in court as plaintiff and his adversary would probably elect to plead straight to the assize and so win on the ground that there was no right of entry against his own long-continued seisin.[1] The claimant would have to attempt not a nominal entry but a true and effective entry, so that he would figure as defendant, not plaintiff, in consequent litigation. But making a genuine entry in the face of resistance was a chancy business and, in any case, not something that the fourteenth-century law wanted to encourage.[2] So in the 1340s it began to be frankly admitted that the ancient rules were abandoned and that, quite apart from forms of pleading, lapse of time never deprived anyone of a right of entry. In 1343 counsel argued as a general principle that when a bastard occupies a heritage 'long continuance in possession will not bar the true heir from entering upon him',[3] and in a case of 1349 the heir's entry was judged lawful even though he was said to have waited for ten years.[4] So too where other issues than rights of inheritance were in question. In 1348 it was judged, over strenuous objection, that where a life tenant had made a tortious feoffment the reversioner was entitled to enter even twenty-two years after the feoffment.[5] In a case of 1350 it was said in argument that the true owner who has been unlawfully disseised may enter and oust his disseisor even after twenty years or any other length of time: 'the question of promptness

---

ties. The alleged relationship could just as well have been pure pleader's fiction. The use of fictitious colour appears in these other early reports: Y.B. Trin. 5 Ed. III no. 1 = 5 Ass. no. 4 (1331), 21 Ass. no. 22 (1347), *London Possessory Assizes* no. 105 (1352). In 1341 it was held that a defendant who had pleaded in bar might be allowed in the course of further pleading to contradict statements that he made as part of his bar: Y.B. Pasch. 15 Ed. III no. 11. Note, however, a case of 1388 in which the parties were allowed to join issue on a traverse of the matter offered by way of colour, Y.B. Pasch. 11 Richard II no. 28, and the editor's comments, Introduction, p. *l*.

[1] *Eyre of London 1321* pp. 157–62 provides an example of a plaintiff caught in these rules.

[2] Below, pp. 166–7.

[3] Y.B. Pasch. 17 Ed. III no. 25.

[4] 23 Ass. no. 5.

[5] 22 Ass. no. 37.

does not arise between the disseisee and his disseisor'. The adversary's counsel agreed, even though he recognized that this was new law: '. . . we have seen that it was once the opinion of the justices that a disseisee might not re-enter upon his disseisor if the disseisor had remained in occupation for ten years. But now the law is otherwise.'[1] So the requirement of promptness was abandoned altogether.

The change was introduced through the technicalities of pleas in bar, but it was not controlled by technical considerations. In the case of 1314 the justices could well have ruled, if they had wished, that long continuance in seisin was a good answer to a plea in bar.[2] As we shall see in a moment, the courts made some exactly analogous rulings in circumstances where they thought it would serve good purposes. In striking down the requirement of promptness the justices knew perfectly well what they were doing and they did it deliberately. Probably they were troubled by the vagueness of the old law that rights of entry must be exercised without delay. The men of the fourteenth century wanted a law of mathematical precision, one that would leave everything to the justices' learning and nothing to their discretion. But the learning of the past offered no firm rules about what length of time would take away a right of entry and so any attempt to resolve the law's vagueness by setting definite time-limits would have called for an especially bold use of discretion. The courts went the other route and, increasingly, refused ever to rule that a given right of entry had been lost by the passage of time. By mid century it was their acknowledged doctrine. It was the same unwillingness to exercise choice with its inevitable strain of arbitrariness that prevented the men of the law from ever advancing the limitation-dates of actions after 1275.[3]

More important, however, was the leading motive in all the developments described in this chapter, the desire to increase the usefulness of the assize. The removal of the requirement of promptness extended rights of entry and the extension of rights of entry made the assize more broadly serviceable. In the case

[1] Y.B. Pasch. 24 Ed. III nos. 12, 33.

[2] So it was done, we are assured, in the court of the borough of Oxford: Y.B. Pasch. 15 Ed. III. no. 20 and Appendix A (1338). And so it had been done in the county of Chester in earlier times: Booth, *Real Actions*, p. 217 (1298).

[3] Above, p. 139.

of 1314 between uncle and nephew, the justices refused to accept the plaintiff's plea that he should recover on his long tenure regardless of right, because they wanted this assize to bring a final adjudication of the parties' rights: '[The defendant] entered as into his heritage . . . and he is of the elder line and you are the younger son, so you must show a title, for the assize could hardly do so if you cannot show one yourself.'[1] Chief Justice Bereford was indignant that the plaintiff should have tried to get a judgment on his long seisin alone, that might run counter to the parties' true rights, and told him when he ruled against him that he would be 'en un bon mercy'.[2] In the similar case of 1334 between two brothers, Serjeant Parving argued that since the defendant had pleaded a bar that raised an issue of right (to wit, which of the brothers was the heir of their common father) the conclusion of this assize would be as definitive as if it were a suit founded on a writ of right.[3] The policy comes into focus in *Stanton* v. *Beauchamp*, a case of 1329–30.[4]

The Nottinghamshire man Henry of Stanton had given land to his mistress Elizabeth Beauchamp. Later, when Elizabeth left him and went overseas, Henry granted the same land to his brother John of Stanton. Elizabeth returned to Nottinghamshire about two years later, waited for another year or so, and then put John of Stanton out of the land. John sued by the assize and the jury found these facts and left judgment to the justices.

The court reasoned that when Henry gave Elizabeth's land to his brother John it was a disseisin of Elizabeth and that both Henry and John were guilty of it. Elizabeth therefore had a perfect right to enter and put John out. The fact that she waited so long to do it could be excused in part on the grounds that she had been overseas and for the rest—for she had delayed a good year after her return—the court would overlook it, for 'if we should decide now that John should recover by this assize, [Elizabeth] would recover in turn against him' by suing on the original disseisin that he committed when he accepted a feoffment of her land from Henry. The justices were not willing thus to give a judgment that would only put the parties to further

---

[1] Y.B. Mich. 8 Ed. II no. 6 (p. 31).
[2] Ibid., p. 29.
[3] Y.B. Hil. 8 Ed. III no. 43 = 8 Ass. no. 5.
[4] B.M. Egerton MS. 2811 fos. 218ᵛ, 222ᵛ–223ʳ.

litigation; they wanted this one assize to set the matter to rest. They decided therefore that Elizabeth's delay did not take away her right of entry and they gave judgment in her favour.

'If we try to make our *possessorium* do the work of a *petitorium* it will soon refuse to do its own proper work; questions of title will be raised in it and decided.'[1] More deliberately than Maitland suspected, this was just what the courts of the fourteenth century were trying to do with novel disseisin. They consciously arranged that this *possessorium* should do the work of a *petitorium* and they accepted the consequence that it would 'refuse to do its own proper work' of protecting established seisin simply as such and even against superior title. They hesitated precisely because they knew so well that they were changing the traditional law, but in the end they went through with it. By mid century they had removed all time-limits on the exercise of rights of entry.

There remained the lesser general restrictions that had been known to the thirteenth-century law. The rule that a man's right of entry was taken away if he opened suit at law was abandoned about 1320,[2] but the courts still felt obliged to enforce the old laws that rights of entry were defeated if the adversary successfully carried through a feoffment to a third party, or if he died seised so that his claim descended on his heir.[3] These two rules were thrown into prominence now by their contrast with the new law that the mere passage of time did *not* destroy a right of entry, and they were equipped with a new fourteenth-century terminology: a right of entry was 'tolled', they said, by a feoffment over to a third party or again by a 'descent cast'.

The former rule, that a feoffment over tolled the right of entry, was preserved because the feoffee ordinarily had a right

---

[1] Maitland, 'Beatitude of Seisin', p. 293.   [2] Above, p. 105 n. 1.

[3] Above, pp. 105. In the fourteenth century, the continued use of the rule that a feoffment over tolled entry is shown, for example, in these cases: Y.B. 30 & 31 Ed. I p. 113 (1302), B.M. Egerton MS. 2811 fos. 237^r–237^v (1330–1), Y.B. Hil. 10 Ed. III no. 7 = 9 Ass. no. 6 and 10 Ass. no. 2 (1336), Y.B. Pasch. 13 Ed. III no. 12 (1339), Pasch. 16 Ed. III no. 34 (1342), Pasch. 24 Ed. III no. 25 (1350), Mich. 50 Ed. III no. 3 (1376). The continued use of the rule that a descent cast tolled entry is illustrated in Y.B. 30 & 31 Ed. I p. 113 (1302), *Eyre of London 1321* pp. 225–7, 341, Y.B. 18 Ed. II pp. 579–80 (1324), 12 Ass. no. 22 (1338), Y.B. Mich. 20 Ed. III no. 103 and Trin. 21 Ed. III no. 10 = 21 Ass. no. 8 (1346–7), Y.B. Pasch. 42 Ed. III no. 18 (1368).

to be warranted by his grantor if he should subsequently lose the tenements on account of any defect in the grantor's title. In order to enforce a warranty by legal action one had to be able to show that he was in seisin when he commenced his suit for enforcement; if one who had a right of entry against the grantor was allowed to enter and oust the feoffee then the feoffee, being out of seisin, would be unable to enforce his warranty.[1] Since no one was entitled to be warranted for his own misdeeds, it was recognized that a feoffment over would not toll a right of entry where the feoffee was a party to the offence that first raised the right of entry. Thus if a bailiff made a feoffment of his principal's freehold it was a disseisin, and the purchaser was guilty of it as well as the bailiff;[2] so the freeholder could enter and eject the purchaser. Similarly, if a life tenant granted over in fee it was a wrong (though not a disseisin) and the purchaser was a party to it and the reversioner was entitled to enter and oust him.[3] Or again, if A is disseised by X and Y, if X takes seisin and holds for some time and later enfeoffs Y, A may enter upon Y regardless of the feoffment, for Y was a party to the disseisin even though he did not straightway acquire his seisin thereby.[4] Only purchasers who deserved to be warranted were protected against entry.

But even holding it in this restricted form, the law was ill at ease with the doctrine. As Maitland conjectured,[5] it probably troubled the leaders of the law that feoffments might be made collusively for the specific purpose of defeating rights of entry. Since the courts were not commonly prepared to inquire into good faith, collusive feoffments could make mockery of the law,

[1] This reasoning appears, for example, in Y.B. 20 & 21 Ed. I pp. 267–9 (1292), Mich. 1 Ed. III nos. 1 and 10 = 1 Ass. no. 13 (1327), B.M. Egerton MS. 2811 fo. 218ᵛ (1329–30), Y.B. Trin. 21 Ed. III no. 20 (1347), Mich. 21 Ed. III no. 16 = 21 Ass. no. 19 (1347), 42 Ass. no. 24 (1369).

[2] Above, p. 146. The Statute of Westminster II c. 25 specifically provided that in such cases the purchaser as well as the grantor should be considered guilty of disseisin.

[3] Above, pp. 113–15. As explained there, until 1348 the courts would protect the feoffee of a life tenant after the life tenant's death, but after 1348 this rule was overcome by the consideration that the feoffee was 'party to the tort'.

[4] 29 Ass. no. 54 (1355), *Sel. Cases in K.B.* vi. 90 (1363). For feoffments that fell under this rule on account of other circumstances, see 9 Ass. no. 7 (1335), *London Possessory Assizes* no. 14 (1342), 118 (1353), 43 Ass. no. 17, 45 (1369), Y.B. Mich. 50 Ed. III no. 3 (1376).

[5] 'Beatitude of Seisin', pp. 296–7.

and since feoffments to the use of the grantor—in which the grantor continued to enjoy the tenements and the feoffee became the owner in name only—were becoming familiar in the fourteenth century, it could be particularly outrageous mockery. In a case of 1324 the justice John of Mutford indicated his dislike of the whole rule;[1] in a discussion in 1347 'it was remarked that one may enter after a feoffment made by his disseisor even if he held against him for ten years', though the reporter doubted that this was true;[2] in 1368 counsel argued that a disseisee might enter upon the tenant even after two feoffments over from the disseisor.[3]

From the first, too, the law held that one who had a right of entry could save it from extinction by a feoffment over if he would exercise it immediately upon the making of the feoffment, before the purchaser had enjoyed a well-established seisin.[4] Chary as they were of attributing any legal effects to the mere passage of time, the fourteenth-century courts may have had difficulty in putting any practical limits on this right to enter 'immediately' after a feoffment over.

It was presumably for these reasons that the entire doctrine that a feoffment over should toll entry was jettisoned early in Richard II's reign. In cases of 1376 and 1383 it was still accepted,[5] but in assizes in London in 1380-2 it was wholly disregarded,[6] and the common-law courts ignored it in cases of 1387-9 and 1391.[7] Once the rule was struck down it never rose again and we hear no more of it. Rights of entry endured regardless of the passage of time and now, in the 1380s, regardless too of feoffments over.

---

[1] Y.B. Hil. 17 Ed. II p. 515.   [2] 21 Ass. no. 28.
[3] Y.B. Pasch. 42 Ed. III no. 18.
[4] Bracton fo. 165b; Y.B. 20 & 21 Ed. I p. 267 (1292), Mich. 8 Ed. III no. 10 = 8 Ass. no. 25 (1334), 9 Ass. no. 15 (1335), Y.B. Pasch. 15 Ed. III no. 11 (1341), Pasch. 17 Ed. III no. 25 (1343), Mich. 50 Ed. III no. 3 (1376).
[5] Y.B. Mich. 50 Ed. III no. 3 (1376), Lincoln's Inn Hale MS. 77 fo. 203 (1383). In the latter case a litigant pleaded that a disseisee had made a lawful entry upon the feoffee of his disseisor, but took care to include the allegation that the original disseisin was done 'by covin' between the disseisor and his feoffee, thus demonstrating that the feoffee was a party to the tort. Evidently he considered that the disseisee would have had no right of entry against the disseisor's feoffee if the feoffee was innocent of wrongdoing.   [6] *London Possessory Assizes* nos. 151, 161, 272.
[7] Y.B. Trin. 11 Richard II nos. 8, 17, Mich. 11 Richard II no. 7 (1387), Pasch. 11 Richard II no. 9 (1388), Hil. 12 Richard II no. 7 (1389), *Sel. Cases in K.B.* vii. 39 (1391).

The other rule, that a descent cast tolled the right of entry, experienced only slightly better fortune. It was maintained partly because the courts felt that they should show some respect for the traditional doctrine that the true owner must act quickly. They would not decide that two years, ten years, or twenty years constituted too long a wait, for it would seem arbitrary thus to pick out a point in the continuum of time. But the death of the tenant was a point given by circumstances, not one chosen by the justices; if time's web was seamless men's affairs were not so and the death of a tenant was a natural discontinuity; if the person entitled to enter delayed until the tenant had died seised, that could be taken as 'remissness' and 'lack of fresh suit'.[1] But these reflections can hardly have seemed compelling, for they were never applied to death and descent on the side of the true owner who was out of possession: his right of entry was not tolled when he died but descended undiminished to his heir.[2]

The decisive reason for keeping the rule lay in the assize of mort d'ancestor. That assize was founded on the principle that where a man's ancestor had died seised of tenements in fee the heir should have immediate possession of the holdings without any inquiry into his ancestor's right. If an owner with a title superior to that of the ancestor should be allowed to enter and oust or exclude the heir because of his superior title, it would squarely contradict that principle and the assize of mort d'ancestor would be destroyed. Mort d'ancestor might be declining as more and more of its business was handled by novel disseisin, but it was nevertheless an ancient and honourable form of action and as such was entitled, according to the ideas of the fourteenth century, if not to full employment at least to life. So the courts did not feel that they could countenance any right of entry against an heir on account of a fault in his ancestor's title.[3]

Though the courts held to this doctrine, they plainly disliked

---

[1] This reasoning appears in MS. Y fos. 12ʳ, 35ʳ (1302–9), where it is attributed to Ralph of Hengham. Cf. B.M. Egerton MS. 2811 fos. 251ʳ–252ᵛ (1330).

[2] Y.B. Pasch. 7 Ed. III no. 36 and Trin. 7 Ed. III no. 42 (1333), Trin. 22 Ed. III no. 41 (1348), Pasch. 42 Ed. III no. 18 (1368), Mich. 50 Ed. III no. 3 (1376). *Econtra tamen*, Y.B. Hil. 21 Ed. III no. 16 (1347). For later evidences and refinements of learning see Bordwell, 'Seisin and Disseisin', pp. 592, 717.

[3] This reasoning appears in a case of 1313–14, *Eyre of Kent* iii. 139 ff.

it, and they did everything they could to vitiate it short of abrogating it in principle. A descent cast would not toll a right of entry for breach of condition,[1] nor a right of entry against a member of a rival branch of one's own family, where the dispute was about the rightful descent of the heritage of the common ancestor.[2] After prolonged hesitation, the law decided that if a claimant to land had a valid document that extinguished the right of his adversary's ancestor, such as a deed of release from the ancestor or a record of a judgment for recovery against him, then he could enter and oust the adversary even if the adversary had come into the land by descent.[3]

Just after mid century the courts struck their heaviest blow against the doctrine. Their dislike of it may have been aggravated in these years by the effects of the Black Death, for the large-scale and sudden mortality of the plague must have meant that many rights of entry were tolled quite unexpectedly, when a tenant in the prime of life died after a few days' illness. At any rate, it appeared in a case of 1351 that a man had acquired lands by illegal disseisin, that he had died in possession of them and so passed them on by descent to his heir, and that after his death the true owner who had been disseised entered and ousted the heir. The entry against the heir was legal, ruled the court, because it had also been found in this case that during

---

[1] Above, pp. 115, 151.

[2] This doctrine first appears in the form that the true heir, or any heir of his, may enter without regard to descents cast from one who came to the lands as heir apparent: *Eyre of Kent* iii. 121 (1313–14), Y.B. Pasch. 15 Ed. III no. 11 (1341), Pasch. 40 Ed. III no. 26 (1366). For its later form see Littleton, *Tenures*, paragraphs 396–7. It derived, presumably, from the old rule in mort d'ancestor that when possession of a heritage was awarded to one who was only an heir apparent—to a younger brother, for instance, when his elder brother was out of the realm and it was not known whether he would ever return—the heir apparent gained only a conditional estate, defeasible if the true heir should appear. Conditions, such as this, perdured without regard to descents cast.

[3] For the early period this doctrine is attested by B.M. Egerton MS. 2811 fo. 219ʳ and J.I. 1/685 m. 38, B.M. Egerton MS. 2811 fo. 270ᵛ (1329–30), Y.B. Mich. 5 Ed. III no. 73 (1331), Hil. 6 Ed. III no. 2 = 6 Ass. no. 1, Y.B. Pasch. 6 Ed. III no. 35 (1332), Mich. 10 Ed. III no. 13 = 10 Ass. no. 23 (1336), but contradicted by Y.B. Hil. 2 Ed. III no. 12 (1328), B.M. Egerton MS. 2811 fos. 270ʳ, 278ʳ, 343ʳ–343ᵛ (1329–30), Y.B. Trin. 9 Ed. III no. 1 = 9 Ass. no. 11 (1335), Mich. 10 Ed. III no. 40 (1336), *London Possessory Assizes* no. 125, Y.B. Hil. 18 Ed. III no. 32 and Trin. 18 Ed. III no. 40, Pasch. 18 Ed. III no. 8 (1344), Hil. 20 Ed. III no. 13 (1346). I have not followed its development in detail after the 1340s, but it is clearly accepted in Y.B. Mich. 10 Henry VI no. 5 (1431), and Pasch. 5 Henry VII no. 12 (1490). Booth, *Real Actions*, pp. 276–7, was not sure whether it was good law.

the disseisor's lifetime, before the descent cast, the true owner had 'protested his claim and constantly raised contention so that [the disseisor] did not have peaceable possession'.[1]

This proved to be a leading case. After 1351, then, a descent cast would not toll the entry of an adversary who had 'protested and constantly raised contention' down to the time of the tenant's death. By 1365 it was held that the 'protest and contention' required for these purposes must consist in attempts to enter;[2] by 1407 it was settled that for the attempts to qualify as 'constant' the most recent of them must have been made within the year last past before the tenant's death[3]—for once the common law had found the courage to define a time-limit. So were laid down the main lines of the doctrine of 'continual claim' which Thomas Littleton described in detail, a hundred years or so after it originated, in his *Tenures*.[4] The rule still held that a descent cast tolled the right of entry, but it was offset to a large extent by the countervailing rule of continual claim.

Thus the removal in the fourteenth century of most of the old limitations on rights of entry brought out the full effect of the decision made in Edward I's reign to recognize merely nominal seisin as a sufficient basis for the assize. By the 1380s novel disseisin had been made into a comprehensive action for litigating about freehold lands and tenements. Any owner who found himself out of his property could use the assize to make good his claim if only he had a right of entry and would go to the trouble of making a nominal exercise of it; and the law had arranged that the owner should almost always have a right of entry. The circumstances in which he had none, and so had to betake himself to some other form of action, were isolated, almost anomalous. There were the three cases in which title was 'discontinued' by certain kinds of tortious feoffments. Widows who wanted to recover lands of their own that their husbands had alienated during the marriage had no right to enter but were thrown on the writ of entry *cui in vita*, with *sur cui in vita* for their heirs if the work of gaining recovery was left to them. If a tenant in tail wrongfully sold the entailed properties, after his death

---

[1] 25 Ass. no. 12.   [2] 39 Ass. no. 11.
[3] Y.B. Mich. 9 Henry IV no. 18. Cf. Y.B. Hil. 14 Henry IV no. 53 p. 36B (1413). The general effect of continual claim is also shown in Y.B. Mich. 14 Henry IV no. 7 (1412).   [4] Book III, Chapter 7.

the heir in tail or remainderman or reversioner was 'put to his action' by formedon, and the case was the same for a new abbot whose predecessor had sold lands belonging to the monastery without getting the consent of his monks as was required to make the transaction good—he had to seek a writ of entry *sine assensu capituli*. Besides the discontinuances there were a few other cases, particularly that of the widow seeking her dower who had no right of entry and had to use the old real actions of Dower, and of the feudal lord who wanted to recover lands on which the services had not been rendered for two years—his action was *cessavit per biennium*. One could not make an entry on an advowson; *quare impedit* was the writ for litigating about that peculiar kind of real property.

Within the broad area that novel disseisin served it had two lively competitors, Replevin and *scire facias*, which matched the assize in efficiency and attracted a great many plaintiffs.[1] Actions of replevin always remained the commonest procedure for litigating about customs, services, and rents but they were restricted to that field and indeed, within the field, to cases where the claimant had a right of distraint. *Scire facias* was the usual resort of a plaintiff who wanted to claim property under a judgment in the king's court that had not yet been executed or under a final concord whose terms remained to be carried out, but unless the litigant had such 'matter of record' to rely on *scire facias* was not for him.

The result was, for litigation about freehold property, a geography of justice in which novel disseisin was the great Middle Empire, covering most of the territory, bordered by the substantial second-rate powers of Replevin and *scire facias*, and fringed with the minor principalities of *cui in vita*, formedon, Entry *sine assensu capituli*, Dower, *cessavit per biennium*, and *quare impedit*. The rest of the old real actions were becoming obsolete and found only occasional users in hostile litigation.

The motive behind the expansion of rights of entry in the fourteenth century was the desire to make the assize more widely available and thereby to smooth the path of litigation in the courts. There was certainly no intent to give men any new licence to right their own wrongs by private force. For just about the same time that rights of entry were being extended

---

[1] For the development of these actions, see above, p. 132.

the law took away from subjects the only methods that had previously been allowed them for forcing true and effective entries against adversaries who resisted. In the thirteenth century, although much was forbidden him, the maker of a lawful disseisin could bring a large body of men to back him up and could damage the tenements as he liked, and the use of these means would often effectively compel his opponent to get out.[1] Now in 1381 a statute made it clear that entries on lands, if they were to keep within the law, must be carried out without large gatherings of supporters and without any sort of violence, 'ne mie a forte main ne a multitude des gentz, einz tantsoulement en lisible et aisee manere'.[2] The statute may have been enacting new law or it may have been declaring what was by that time the understood rule; in any case, what it said held for the future. A report of 1495 confirms that 'if a man comes with more people than he customarily has attending upon him, that is considered [illegal] force'.[3] Where an adversary stood in the way, the only kind of entry that could be made within the rules of the law was a formal, nominal entry, whose effect was not to put the claimant in control but to let him use novel disseisin to try his claim in court.

Whether by accident or by design or by some combination of the two, the law had hit in these developments upon that formula of great ideological consequence which we mentioned in the beginning of this study.[4] The autonomy of freehold rights in land, their subsistence apart from the sanction and aid of the government, was affirmed even more clearly than in the thirteenth century by the increased recognition of the owner's right to enter on his own, without the need for any official authorization. He could take for himself without higher authority what belonged to him apart from any government. The need to preserve peace and quiet was satisfied even more fully than in the thirteenth century by the prohibition of all semblance of private armies and all forms of private violence in connection with entries on land. The acts of private persons in claiming their property must be thoroughly peaceable acts. If this latter rule meant that claimants to lands who encountered opposition

---

[1] Above, pp. 118–25. [2] 5 Richard II Stat. 1 c. 7.
[3] Y.B. Hil. 10 Henry VII no. 2. Cf. the several statutes of forcible entry, cited below, p. 174 n. 1. [4] Above, pp. 3–5.

when they tried to enter had after all to go to court in order to obtain effective possession, still they went to court only to ask aid in removing obstacles to their private entry. The lawsuit was a petition that the king join his power to the subject's exercise of his own right.

There could hardly be a better way of driving home to the nation's freeholders the whiggish doctrine that property belonged to private persons apart from government while to the government pertained a monopoly of the use of force. However often men of the fourteenth and fifteenth centuries may have been able to disregard the law's strict prohibitions upon violent entry, all of this law survived as a permanent part of the English heritage and came eventually, in the modern centuries, to be pretty well enforced. We have here one of the most enduring of the contributions of fourteenth-century constitutionalism, which lived on to become in later times an important correlative, and perhaps in some measure a source, of the thought of men like John Fortescue and John Locke. In this as in the simple convenience and efficiency of the new pattern of judicature that was built on the assize of novel disseisin we have prime exhibits of 'the forward movement of the fourteenth century' which some historians discern through all the well-known troubles and failures of that age.[1]

---

[1] *The Forward Movement of the Fourteenth Century*; Ferguson, *Europe in Transition, 1300–1520*; Knowles, *The Evolution of Medieval Thought*, pp. 333–4.

V

TRESPASS TAKES OVER

THE dominating 'Middle Empire' of judicature over free-hold which had been built up for novel disseisin by the 1380s was never afterwards divided, never lost any of its effectiveness, and was never diminished. On the contrary, it grew considerably as time went on. Thomas Littleton's *Tenures* shows the tendency, in the fifteenth century, to stretch and strain at the limits of rights of entry so as to make them as extensive as possible without going beyond any of the major rules that had been laid down in the fourteenth century.[1] In a later age a bolder line was taken. By legislation of 1540 women whose husbands had alienated their wives' freehold were given the right of entry after their husbands' death (or their heirs could enter if the woman had died), and in this way the statute added to the empire of the assize all the territory formerly reserved for *cui in vita* and *sur cui in vita*. The same statute also provided that a descent cast should no longer toll a right of entry if the descent happened within five years of an illegal disseisin or of the last attempt to enter by way of continual claim. The ambit of the assize was extended to cover suits for 'spiritual' properties, such as parsonages and tithes.[2] In a relative sense, too, and apart from any direct enactment, the juris-diction of novel disseisin increased about this same time, for after the abolition of the monasteries in the 1530s there were no more abbots who might be obliged to sue for recovery of their predecessors' alienations, and after the development around 1500 of the ingenious disentailing device called the common recovery the law no longer provided an effective remedy for alienations by tenants in tail; so that the actions of entry *sine assensu capituli* and of formedon dropped out of use.[3]

[1] See Maitland, 'Beatitude of Seisin', pp. 298–9.
[2] 32 Henry VIII chapters 7, 28, 33.
[3] Maitland, 'Beatitude of Seisin', p. 290.

But it appeared very soon, from the 1380s and even before, that the assize would not be able to manage its large territory alone but would have to share the business with a consortium of other legal procedures, some of them new and others old but newly adapted to this work. Four other forms of action presently stood forth as operating on the same ground, or most of the same ground, as novel disseisin, and competing with the assize to do its work. Intending litigants and their counsel were left with a pretty free choice among the five possible procedures.

The first sharer with novel disseisin was the action of 'entry in the nature of an assize'. This was an invention of the mid 1380s.[1] Writs of entry where the demandant based his claim on a disseisin had of course been familiar for many generations, but in the past they had all been extensions of the assize, not substitutes for it. They charged that the tenant had come to the land through some other person who had committed a disseisin against the demandant or his ancestor—entry sur disseisin—or they sued for a disseisin committed by the tenant not against the demandant but against his ancestor—entry de quibus. The death of the original disseisor or disseisee, or both of them, had prevented such cases from being handled by the assize under the old law before the enlargement of rights of entry, and so the writs sur disseisin and de quibus had had their place in their time. But the new action of entry in the nature of an assize stood just in the place of novel disseisin, for it alleged that the tenant had got into the land by disseising the demandant himself. Anyone who could use the assize could use this new writ; only the procedure was different. The writ of entry ordered that the tenant be summoned, not attached, to appear in the court of Common Pleas, not before justices of assize. If the tenant failed to appear the court would not proceed to trial by default as in the assize but would use instead the procedure common to most real actions, seizing the land in distraint, resummoning the tenant, and continuing on in some circumstances to a judgment for the demandant by default without trial of the principal charge. If the tenant

---

[1] The earliest reports of it are of 1384 and 1385, Lincoln's Inn Hale MS. 77 fos. 216ʳ–216ᵛ, 223ᵛ, and B.M. Add. MS. 34783 fo. 8. In 1388 it was still debatable whether such actions should be permitted, Y.B. Pasch. 12 Richard II no. 15, and argument against them is heard as late as 1421, Y.B. Mich. 9 Henry V no. 4.

came in due time they would plead the case in the Bench and then, ordinarily, send it out to trial at *nisi prius*. For a long time the new procedure attracted only a few litigants, but it survived and in the fifteenth century it gained a modest measure of popularity.

The second substitute was the action of trespass. Instead of charging disseisin and bringing the assize, a plaintiff could charge that the defendant had come onto his land without right, and bring Trespass for it.[1] In a parallel development, Trespass on the case began to be used sometimes instead of the assize of nuisance.[2] Often the writ of trespass would recite that the defendant had committed such-and-such outrages on the land, cutting timber, mowing and carrying off crops, trampling grass, intimidating the rent-paying tenants so that they withdrew from their holdings, and so forth; and it might allege that all the illegalities had been continued, or repeated, over a period of time. When Trespass was used in this way instead of novel disseisin, the defendant would usually reply, either in pleading before the court or else later in trial before the jury, that the land in question was his own freehold, and so the effect of the action would be to try his claim to the property against the plaintiff's, just as in an assize. And just as, in the assize, the disseisin that was complained of might be either an actual ejectment of the plaintiff or else a simple refusal to make way for him when he exercised a right of entry, so also in Trespass the offence for which action was brought could be either a genuine invasion of the plaintiff's property or

---

[1] In Richard II's reign a disseisin could not be treated as a trespass if the plaintiff had been put out of his tenements and kept out for a whole year. The disseisor had a free tenement then, although one that was defeasible by entry or the assize, and could justify himself against any charge of trespass by pleading that he had acted in his own free tenement. Lincoln's Inn Hale MS. 77 fos. 183ᵛ–184ʳ (1382): 'Sire Robert Belknap demaunda de sire Walter Clopton, qe si un home vous disseise et continue sa possession par un an et puis vous entrez sur le disseisour, quel recoverie pour vous pur lez profitz pris en le mesne temps? *Clopton*: Sire, bref de trespas ne poet le disseisi aver, pur ceo qe il fut le franktenement le disseisour al temps de trespas suppose et fait. Quel est bon respons . . . Et . . . non erat dedictum quod dictum erat per Clopton.' Later this doctrine was reversed: C.P. 40/715 m. 338d (1439), Keilwey Mich. 12 Henry VII no. 2 (1496), K.B. 27/952 m. 66 (1499).

[2] Y.B. Mich. 21 Henry VII no. 5 (1505), Pasch. 14 Henry VIII no. 8 (1522), Dyer fo. 195–6 (1561), 319 (1572). The history of this matter is set forth by Baker, *Introduction to English Legal History*, pp. 237–8.

else a mere holding on and continued use after the plaintiff had made a formal entry.[1]

Actions of trespass were 'personal', not 'real', and when they were new in the king's court, back in the middle of the thirteenth century, some people had held that as personal actions they should never be used to try rights of freehold: if it appeared that the true issue between the parties was on the ownership of freehold the case should be thrown out and the plaintiff referred to a 'real' action. But that doctrine, though it was sometimes enforced, was never well established and was presently rejected altogether, so that from Edward I's time it was perfectly normal to adjudicate claims to freehold upon these proceedings.[2] Of course, if the plaintiff won in such an action the court would never give judgment that he be restored to seisin, for in personal actions only an award of damages could be won. This was not a very satisfactory substitute for being restored to one's landed property, and it probably explains why the use of Trespass to litigate about freehold was comparatively uncommon until the latter part of Edward III's reign.

[1] Cases of Trespass of the latter type, based on formal entry alone, appear in Y.B. Trin. 11 Richard II no. 17 (1387), Mich. 13 Richard II no. 22 (1389), K.B. 27/538 m. 57d (1395), C.P. 40/539 m. 386d (1395), 40/715 m. 336, 566 (1439), Y.B. Trin. 22 Ed. IV pp. 13–14 (1482), Keilwey Mich. 12 Henry VII no. 2 (1496), C.P. 40/950 m. 415, 503 (1499), K.B. 27/952 m. 29 (1499), Keilwey Pasch. 20 Henry VII nos. 1, 2 (1505), Mich. 3 Henry VIII no. 4 (1511), Plowden p. 38 (1550), 69 (1551), 142 (1555), 293 (1565), 298 (1566), 516 (1577), Dyer fo. 337 (1574).

[2] Bracton fo. 413. In 1230, 1254, and 1273 the king's court threw out actions of trespass, 'quia advocant terram illam ut suam', 'desicut breve de nova disseisina iacet in hoc casu', 'quia uterque dicit se esse in seisina', and 'quia liberum tenementum non potest per hoc breve de transgressione terminari': BNB no. 378, K.B. 26/151 m. 29, 26/152 m. 9d = Placitorum Abbreviatio p. 142a, K.B. 27/1 m. 18d = Placitorum Abbreviatio p. 262a. But in a case of 1220 the justices were not so sure, CRR ix. 289, and right through the thirteenth century their usual practice was to receive such issues: CRR x. 97–9 (1221), xiii. 733 (1228), K.B. 26/115B m. 20 (1234), 26/124 m. 27d (1242), 26/138 m. 18d (1250), 26/145 m. 8d (1251), 26/156 m. 7 (1261), C.P. 40/5 m. 90d (1274), K.B. 27/103 m. 26d (1287), 27/165 m. 42 (1301). Examples are very common all through the fourteenth century, e.g. Y.B. 18 Ed. II pp. 617–19 (1325), Trin. 6 Ed. III no. 26 (1332), 11 Ed. III pp. 185–7 (1337), Mich. 13 Ed. III no. 88 (1339), Mich. 19 Ed. III no. 79 (1345), Hil. 20 Ed. III no. 13 (1346), Hil. 40 Ed. III no. 10 (1366), Trin. 49 Ed. III no. 2 (1375). As some of these cases show, the King's Bench was for a time reluctant to let the parties plead about the freehold, preferring to receive a general issue of 'not guilty'. The Vieux Natura Brevium, fo. 48b, also observes that issues of freehold cannot be handled at Trespass where the action is originated by bill, but only where it is founded upon a writ.

By bringing novel disseisin one could get both the damages and restoration to seisin. But the progressive extension of rights of entry had by about 1380 in large part wiped out this advantage of the assize. The plaintiff who vindicated his right to the freehold against his adversary in Trespass might, as before, get no more than a judgment for damages, but the fact that he had won his lawsuit almost always showed that he had a right of entry, which he could exercise on his own without any order from the court or any help from the sheriff. He could go to the holding and make his entry and count on it that his opponent would withdraw before him, for it would be a rare adversary who after losing one lawsuit would straightway invite another under the same circumstances by standing in his way.[1] Indeed, it seems that even men who won at the assize or in other real actions usually did not trouble to sue out execution of the judgment restoring them to seisin but simply made their entries on their own with the same confidence as one who had just succeeded in Trespass.[2] Under these conditions, actions for trespass to lands became a major partner with the assize during the last decades of the fourteenth century.

The third partner appeared a little later in the shape of the civil actions for forcible entry. After the reforms of the fourteenth century rights of entry were recognized very freely in those who had good title, but the law's permissiveness in this direction was balanced, as we have seen, by stricter-than-ever limits on the methods that might be used to effect entry. Zealous men seeking what they took to be their lawful property were tempted to avail themselves of the law's new liberality while ignoring its new restrictions, making entries which were lawful if their rights were as good as they claimed but making

---

[1] Particularly if the action of trespass had been pleaded specially, so that it appeared expressly on the record that the freehold was in the successful plaintiff: Y.B. 1 Henry VI no. 11 (1422–3), Mich. 10 Henry VII no. 3 (1494).

[2] Y.B. Trin. 19 Ed. III no. 4 (1345), Trin. 49 Ed. III no. 10 (1375), Mich. 9 Henry VI no. 30 p. 49 (1430), Pasch. 5 Henry VII no. 12 p. 29 (1490), Keilwey fo. 204 (1514), Dyer fo. 107 (1554). In the records of the fifteenth and sixteenth centuries, *scire facias* for execution of judgments for damages is frequent but *scire facias* for execution of a judgment to restore seisin seems rare. Upon indictments of forcible entry, when the defendant was convicted, it was common for the victim of the violence to get a writ ordering the sheriff to restore him to seisin. But this was because proceedings and judgments on the indictments involved no trial of real property rights and therefore could do nothing to affirm a right of entry, but had to do only with illegal violence: below, p. 175.

them with unlawful violence. Consequently, new police measures were needed. They were given by a series of 'statutes of forcible entry' enacted between 1378 and 1429.[1] Legislation of 1381 inveighed against all illegal and violent entries, and prescribed imprisonment and heavy fines for offenders; the act of 1429 added prohibitions against maintenance, decreed that those who were guilty of forcible entry must pay triple damages to the injured party as well as suffering the imprisonment and fine, and provided that all this should be enforced through the assize of novel disseisin or through actions upon special writs of trespass.

The special writs of trespass appear immediately after this latter act, founding actions for 'forcible entry on the statute of 8 Henry VI'.[2] Some years later it was reasoned backwards that if writs could be issued on the statute of 1429 they could also be formed on that of 1381, and thus there was developed the action of 'forcible entry on the statute of 5 Richard II'.[3] The twin civil actions of forcible entry took their place to help in the work that had once been done by novel disseisin alone. The allegation of violence was generally treated as immaterial.[4] The court determined whether the defendant had entered where he had no right of entry, and if they found that he had done so they awarded damages to the plaintiff and sent the defendant to prison.[5] In the action on the statute of 8 Henry VI triple damages could be collected; but since in this action the defendant could if he liked make it a material issue whether he had committed any violence, those who had suffered illegal entry without violence were well advised to use the other writ,

[1] 2 Richard II Stat. 1 c. 6 (1378), shortly afterwards repealed by 2 Richard II Stat. 2 c. 2; 5 Richard II Stat. 1 c. 7 (1381), 15 Richard II c. 2 (1391), 4 Henry IV c. 8 (1402), 8 Henry VI c. 9 (1429).   [2] FNB fo. 248.

[3] *Registrum Brevium* fos. 182b–183. The action appears by 1454: Y.B. Mich. 33 Henry VI no. 42.

[4] FNB nos. 248H, 249D; Y.B. Trin. 9 Henry VI no. 12 (1431), Pasch. 21 Henry VI no. 7 (1443), Pasch. 1 Henry VII no. 4 (1486), Mich. 15 Henry VII no. 12 (1499), Keilwey Mich. 8 Henry VII nos. 2, 3 (1492).

[5] The plaintiff could not get a judgment to restore him to seisin on these writs any more than on other writs of trespass: Y.B. Mich. 22 Henry VI no. 33 (1443), Trin. 10 Ed. IV & 49 Henry VI no. 3 (1470), Mich. 21 Ed. IV no. 2 (pp. 10–11) (1481), Keilwey Hil. 11 Henry VII no. 12 (1496), Mich. 20 Henry VII nos. 6, 11 (1504), Pasch. 1 & 2 Philip & Mary fo. 208 (1555). There was, however, some doubt about this in the 1490s: Y.B. Hil. 10 Henry VII no. 7 (1495), B.M. MS. Royal 17E. vi., K.B. 27/951 m. 33, 38 (1499).

on the statute of 5 Richard II, even though it gave only single damages.[1] In either case, the forcible entry for which the plaintiff sued might, like a trespass or a disseisin, amount to no more than a refusal to make way for the plaintiff when he tried to exercise a right of entry of his own.[2]

Out of these same statutes there also developed the criminal proceeding of indictment of forcible entry, handled by the justices of the peace in the county. This was the fourth action that came to share the work of novel disseisin. A statute of 1391 directed justices of the peace to receive complaints of lands entered and held by force, to hold investigations on the spot with the backing of the *posse*, and to gaol all offenders whom they found.[3] The act of 1429 repeated and reinforced these provisions. The justices of the peace were to use juries to make their investigations and they were not only to punish the guilty by imprisonment but also to restore the victims of forcible entries to their possession. The proceedings on indictments of forcible entry as we can glimpse them in the records and reports seem to be a blend of these statutory directions with traditional procedures. The justices of the peace received indictments from presenting juries, and these were often procured at the suit of a party who had been put out of his land. Those who were indicted were brought before the justices for trial. The proceedings were apt to be swift, for questions of title could not be raised. The essence of the action was the charge of illegal violence and, in contrast with the civil actions of forcible entry, it was here no defence to plead that one had a lawful right of entry: however good his right of entry might be, the defendant should be convicted if he had entered violently. When a conviction was obtained, the defendant was imprisoned and the person who had been dispossessed could have judgment to restore him to the holding if he had procured the indictment.[4]

[1] Littleton, *Tenures*, paragraph 430, Keilwey Mich. 8 Henry VII no. 2 (1492), K.B. 27/953 m. 68 (1499).

[2] Y.B. 10 Ed. IV & 49 Henry VI no. 12 (1470–1), K.B. 27/951 m. 33, C.P. 40/950 m. 498 (1499), Brooke, *La Graunde Abridgement*, Forcible Entry, 22.

[3] 15 Richard II c. 2.

[4] As early as 1396 justices of the peace were using juries of presentment to inquire about forcible entries: *Lincolnshire Sessions of the Peace*, no. 576; *Proceedings before the Justices of the Peace*, p. 14. For restoration of the land, after 1429 and apparently under the statute of that year, see Y.B. Mich. 22 Henry VI no. 33 (1443), Mich. 7 Ed. IV no. 12 (1467), Pasch. 14 Henry VII no. 5 (1499), Pasch. 15

A number of other actions were also turned from time to time to do the work of novel disseisin: Replevin with an avowry for damage feasant,[1] Detinue of charters,[2] or Trespass for taking title deeds;[3] in the 1550s and 1560s some plaintiffs tried to use Account, calling the adversaries who held their lands against them to answer as bailiffs for the income of the estates.[4] But such proceedings ranged from unusual to anomalous. The substantial partners with the assize were Entry in the nature of an assize, Trespass to lands and tenements, Forcible Entry as a civil action, and indictments of forcible entry.

Slowly but steadily in the generations after 1380 and through the fifteenth century these new partners took over most of the business, pushing the venerable assize into retirement. By about 1500 the assize was passing out of use. Trespass, the first of the participants with the assize, proved the most successful and became the commonest means of litigating about common-law rights in lands and tenements.

The comparative roles of these several actions and the decline of novel disseisin before its partners cannot be measured with precision. It is indeed possible to count in the records of the Common Pleas and King's Bench the actions of entry in the nature of an assize and the civil actions of forcible entry, but there are no figures for the other types to compare them with. Indictments of forcible entry were handled by the justices of the peace and whatever records they kept have been lost. Actions of trespass that turned on disputes about rights in land are often indistinguishable in the records from those that were brought for mere lawlessness: in either case it might happen that the defendant would plead a simple 'Not guilty'

Henry VII no. 1 (1500), Keilwey Pasch. 1 & 2 Henry VIII no. 1 (1510), 4 & 5 Philip & Mary fo. 204 (1557–8). Since violence was the essence of the action, a recovery in this form would not prejudice the convicted defendant's title, right of entry, or right of subsequent action: Y.B. Mich. 22 Henry VI no. 33 (1443), FNB fo. 248–9, and cf. 2 Brownlow & Gouldesborough 29 (1611), Booth, *Real Actions*, p. 257, *econtra tamen ut videtur*, Y.B. Mich. 7 Henry VI no. 19 (1428).

[1] e.g. Y.B. Pasch. 43 Ed. III no. 1 (1369), C.P. 40/715 m. 340 (1439), Keilwey Mich. 13 Henry VII no. 3 (1497), Dyer fo. 351 (1576).

[2] Y.B. Pasch. 11 Richard II no. 31 (1388).

[3] e.g. Lincoln's Inn Hale MS. 77 fo. 203 (1383), Y.B. Trin. 11 Richard II no. 8 (1387). But see Y.B. Mich. 43 Ed. III no. 3 (1369), C.P. 40/539 m. 573d (1395).

[4] Brooke's New Cases no. 454 (1554), K.B. 27/1216 m. 108 (1565).

and that the jury would return a general verdict, yielding a formal record that said nothing about the real difference between the parties, for the record did not tell what was said before the jury. As for assizes, the justices who heard them in the counties developed the habit in the first half of the fifteenth century of keeping their records in files rather than in rolls. The files were never turned in at headquarters and, being left in private custody, have perished.[1]

Nevertheless, we can develop a reliable rough impression of what was going on. In the 1430s there were still a few justices of assize who conscientiously enrolled their cases and turned in the rolls; these records are almost the last of their kind.[2] But plaintiffs who obtained writs of novel disseisin in the Chancery had to pay a 'fine' if the property they intended to sue for was of great value, and since the 1390s each fine was recorded together with particulars of the writ for which it was collected.[3] The writs that were fined for in the 1430s show up in those last surviving enrolments of hearings, in so far as they were laid in the counties that are covered by the enrolments, but the enrolments of course set down many other cases as well, where the lands were of comparatively small value and the writ accordingly had not had to be fined for. It appears that the total number of cases heard by the justices stood to that select and wealthy group where fines had to be paid in the proportion of about 21 to 5. Since the writs fined for in Chancery in the 1430s averaged thirty-five a year for the whole kingdom, the

---

[1] *Guide to the Contents of the Public Record Office*, p. 125; *Select Cases in the Exchequer Chamber* i. 186–7 and no. 36. Assizes for lands and tenements in Middlesex, which were ordinarily held in the Common Pleas, are recorded in the rolls of that court only very rarely even in the fourteenth century. Cf. J.I. 1/1454, an assize roll for 1354–60 kept by justices whose commission included Middlesex as well as several neighbouring counties. The roll records numbers of cases for every other county covered by the commission, but not a single Middlesex case.

[2] The rolls are J.I. 1/1542 and 1/1543. The former is for Cumberland, Westmorland, Northumberland, and Yorkshire for the years 1428–37, the latter for Bucks., Beds., Hunts., Cambs., Suffolk, and Norfolk for 1430–9.

[3] These are recorded in the Fine Rolls and in the Hanaper accounts. I am grateful to Mr. Anthony Standen for drawing my attention to them. Comparison of the listed entries with the rolls of the justices of assize shows that fines were paid only for writs that sought large holdings. One entry recording the purchase of a writ of formedon for 6s. 8d. bears a note, 'Non transeat absque meliori fine, quia tenementa valent .xx. li. per annum.' C. 60/236 (1428–9). The writs for which fines were paid, besides novel disseisin, were mostly formedon, Entry, Debt, and Covenant. Trespass rarely appears.

total number of writs taken out must have averaged about 149 a year.[1]

Figures to represent the activity of some of the substitute-actions about the same time may be developed by examining the King's Bench and Common Pleas rolls for Michaelmas term 1439.[2] Since the entire legal year for the central courts contained twenty return days, and since eight of these were in Michaelmas term, we can derive estimates for a year by increasing the Michaelmas figures in the proportion of 20 to 8.

	Michaelmas term 1439	Estimate for a year
Trespass cases known to turn on freehold rights	59	147
Civil actions of forcible entry	3	8
Entry in the nature of an assize	21	52
TOTAL	83	207

About 207 cases, then, for a year; and we must say vaguely that in addition there will be a good many others, of Trespass where the dispute turned on freehold but the record does not

[1] The two assize rolls J.I. 1/1542 and 1/1543 record altogether proceedings in 257 cases of novel disseisin. Of the 257 cases, 61 are founded on original writs whose purchase is recorded in the Fine Rolls. Hence it may be estimated that the total number of writs of novel disseisin purchased stands to the number whose purchase is recorded as 257 is to 61: a proportion of about 21 to 5.

The numbers of writs of novel disseisin fined for in Chancery in the decade of the 1430s were as follows:

1429–30	36
1430–1	48
1431–2	30
1432–3	29
1433–4	31
1434–5	33
1435–6	28
1436–7	30
1437–8	44
1438–9	40
Ten-year total	349

[2] In making these counts I have ignored mere entries of process, since a single suit may generate a large number of such entries in the rolls for many different terms, and have reckoned only entries where the defendants put in an appearance or where a final judgment was given.

show it, and of indictments of forcible entry disposed of in the counties by the justices of the peace. So it appears that in the 1430s novel disseisin still had substantial employment, but that a considerable majority of the cases that it might have handled were already being taken care of through its partner-actions, of which Trespass was the most prominent.

All through the fifteenth century and far into the sixteenth, Trespass went from strength to strength. Actions in this form, identifiable as turning on freehold rights, appear as follows in the King's Bench and Common Pleas rolls for selected terms:

Michaelmas 1395	23
Michaelmas 1439	59
Michaelmas 1499	40
Michaelmas 1565	54

The figure for 1565 is from the King's Bench roll only, without consideration of cases in the Common Pleas. The records also show that indictments of forcible entry found a continuous and important role out in the counties, for the proceedings were sometimes sent into the King's Bench for one reason or another and there they appear often enough to testify to considerable activity:

	Fines against those convicted	Process for appearance	Cases pleaded in King's Bench
Michaelmas 1439	12	8	2
Michaelmas 1499	..	5	1
Michaelmas 1565	4	..	6

But if Trespass and the indictments prospered in this business, the same did not hold for the other actions. Entry in the nature of an assize appears twenty-one times in Michaelmas term 1439, but only once in the rolls for Michaelmas term 1499. The civil actions of forcible entry had their heyday and then declined: there were three in Michaelmas 1439, twenty-six in Michaelmas 1499, but only one in the King's Bench roll of Michaelmas 1565.

And the assize declined. Whereas in the 1430s the Chancery records show an average of thirty-five writs of assize a year that had to be fined for, the fines for some selected years in the century and more that followed were continually fewer and fewer:

1451–2	24
1465–6	14
1475–6	12
1499–1500	8
1525–6	6
1534–5	4
1550	3 or 4

It looks as though by *c.* 1500 the assize was mostly a tradition and a memory. The impression may be exaggerated. Some of the law reports for the early and middle parts of the sixteenth century, which confirm the decline of Entry in the nature of an assize and the flowering and fall of the civil actions of forcible entry, seem to show that the assize was still finding a good deal of use:

	Entry in the nature of an assize	Civil actions of forcible entry	Novel disseisin	Trespass for freehold
Year Books, 1491–1535	9	16	31	65
Dyer, cases of 1536–80	6	4	24	30
Plowden, cases of 1550–75	1	—	7	9
Total	16	20	62	104

But even if the impression given by the reports is right, and the assize still had an active role through the first half of the sixteenth century, its ruin followed not long after. In 1611 Edward Coke lamented that the assize, like the other real actions, had so fallen out of use that the clerks of court no longer knew how to make up the records in due form when these cases did occur, and if he reported two assizes of 1608 it was only in the hope of reviving a branch of legal learning that had been passing away.[1] Nearly a century later George Booth reproduced a little treatise on the rules of pleading in the assize in the hope that the information 'may be useful upon occasion'.[2] Although it was not formally abolished until 1833,[3] the assize was no longer a living part of the law.

[1] Preface to 8 Reports.   [2] Booth, *Real Actions*, p. 262.
[3] 3 & 4 Wm. IV c. 27, 36.

The evidence of the reports is at one with that of the records in showing that for a long period in and around the first half of the sixteenth century it was Trespass that was the most commonly employed action for lands and tenements. But the prevalence of Trespass did not end the developments that we have to trace. In the latter half of the sixteenth century there appeared a fifth new participant in the work which so long before had been done by the assize alone. The action of ejectment came very late upon the scene, but when it came it proved itself more attractive than any of the others and presently took over the bulk of the business.

How it managed this has often been told.[1] Ejectment was a variety of Trespass and by Tudor times it had a long history, extending back to the thirteenth century. But it had never been of any use to freeholders, for it was designed to serve termors, those who took land on lease for fixed periods and whose estates therefore did not rise to the dignity of freehold. If while his lease was running the termor was put out of the holding by a stranger, he could use this writ to sue and collect damages. After 1498 the courts would give him judgment to recover the remainder of his term as well as his damages.

As we have seen, novel disseisin and its substitutes on the civil side could be used to sue for any claim to freehold that supported a right of entry. One simply exercised the right of entry, let oneself be rebuffed, called the rebuff a disseisin or a trespass or a forcible entry, and sued for it by the assize, Entry in the nature of an assize, Trespass, or Forcible Entry. In the sixteenth century it occurred to some lawyer whose name is lost to history that an extension of this procedure would also make Ejectment available to sue for freehold. The claimant to the freehold could exercise his right of entry, make a lease for a term of years to a friend, have the friend make another entry by virtue of his lease, let him be rebuffed, call it an ejectment, and bring the action of ejectment. The friend would be the nominal plaintiff, for he was the termor who had been 'put out' of the leasehold, but the whole effect of the suit would be to try the pretending freeholder's right of entry, just as in novel disseisin and the others.

Once this extension of the old procedure had been devised,

[1] For example .by Simpson, *Introduction to the History of the Land Law*, pp. 135 ff.

N

anyone who wanted to could choose to bring Ejectment in place of novel disseisin or any of the older substitutes for it. Ejectment was a little extra trouble, because of the need for a lease and for a second entry by the lessee, but litigants reckoned that it repaid their pains, for the action became very popular and grew with the passing years until it replaced Trespass as the freeholder's characteristic remedy.

Its rise coincides almost exactly with the half-century from 1550 to 1600. James Dyer reports a case heard in the King's Bench early in 1550 that first shows its deliberate employment to bring suit for freehold. One Newdigate entered upon lands in which he claimed freehold right and made a lease to a termor. The termor was put out and brought Ejectment for it, and Dyer describes the resultant lawsuit as Newdigate's attempt to make good his claim to the freehold.[1] From the years and decades that follow, the reporters tell of more and more such cases,[2] and if we sample the records, Rastell's *Entries* gives four cases dated from 1558 to 1576[3] and the King's Bench roll for Michaelmas term 1565 reveals, along with fifty-four actions of trespass that are seen to turn on freehold rights, ten suits in Ejectment that were arranged in order to try claims to freehold.[4] Then at the end of half a century of development, Edward Coke said in reporting Alden's case of 1601 that 'for the greatest part titles to lands were being tried in actions of ejectments', and Lord Ellesmere wrote at about the same time that the action of ejectment had 'almost utterly overthrown all actions real that be possessory, as assizes of novel disseisin and writs of entry'.[5] The position of Ejectment as the usual

[1] Dyer fo. 68.

[2] Dyer fos. 237 (1565), 266–7 (1567), 300 (1571), 324 (1573), 334 ff. (1574), 337 (1574), 339–41 (two cases, 1574–5), 348 (1576), 357–8 (two cases, 1577), 374 (1580), Plowden p. 223 (1561), 459 (1574), 504 (1576), 530 (1577), 2 Leonard 200 (1584). [3] Title 'Ejectione firmae', nos. 12, 14, 15, 16.

[4] K.B. 27/1216 m. 43, 71, 107 (cf. 108), 137, 148, 180d, 216, 220, 223, 227. There are a good many other suits in Ejectment that appear to be on true leases. In these ten cases the evidence that the lease was given simply for the purpose of bringing an action is that the ejectment followed immediately on the making of the lease, sometimes on the same day, sometimes a few days later. Comparison of the cases on membranes 107 and 108 also shows that the lessor himself entered on the tenements the same day that he made the lease. In the case on membrane 148 there was a plea in bar and issue joined whether the plaintiff's lessor had disseised the defendant.

[5] 5 Reports, Alden's Case; Baker, *Introduction to English Legal History*, p. 167.

action for real property was never afterwards disturbed, but only confirmed and strengthened by all subsequent developments.[1]

Such was the course of development over two centuries and more in the large legal territory that was first brought together under novel disseisin. What shaped the development has been a mystery to modern observers, for no contemporary was considerate enough to set down for posterity an explanation of the reasons why plaintiffs and their counsel decided in increasing numbers to attempt Trespass or, for a time, one of the other alternative remedies rather than suing by the assize, or of why men later found it in their interest to turn away from Trespass to Ejectment. The mystery only seems to deepen when one first looks at the records and reports, for right through to the end, even in the reign of Elizabeth I and after, the assize still appears to be working well for those who care to bring it. Proceedings were, it is true, a good deal less rapid than in the days of the assize's youth in the thirteenth century, but in return for having to proceed at a slower pace plaintiffs could now expect that the judgments, once rendered, would be definitive. It is not obvious that Trespass and the other alternative actions of this age were any faster.[2]

Plaintiffs at novel disseisin sometimes suffered on account of the rule in Magna Carta, that the assize must be heard in the county where the land lay. It was doubtless frustrating to have to begin proceedings out in the county before the itinerant justices of assize in a case where, as sometimes happened, the plaintiff knew that his opponent was going to demur on a point of law or (more commonly) plead matter triable by record or by a jury in another county; for under those circumstances the justices on circuit would regularly send the case back to Westminster where ordinary civil litigation originated anyway without this extra trouble and delay. Even if a case could proceed all the way to its conclusion in the county, the plaintiff might find that he was badly served by the methods of record-keeping used by justices of assize. In general they made

---

[1] Simpson, *Introduction to the History of the Land Law*, pp. 137–41, 143.

[2] The indictments of forcible entry were presumably more expeditious, but we know rather little about them.

no formal enrolments until the case was concluded, and this meant that if for any reason the case should be discontinued and then resummoned the defendant could if he liked plead a wholly new defence after the resummons, for the proceedings down to the discontinuance would not be 'of record'.[1] But these factors cannot have been what determined men to avoid the assize. Assizes for tenements in Middlesex were heard in the Common Pleas or occasionally in the King's Bench[2] and were therefore free of these peculiar problems of jurisdiction and recording, but the use of the assize for Middlesex holdings declined at least as much and as early as its use for lands in other parts of the kingdom.[3]

Professor Milsom has conjectured that the Statute of Forcible Entry of 1381 might have abridged the usefulness of the assize.[4] That legislation prohibited even peaceable entries where there was no right of entry, on pain of imprisonment and ransom at the king's pleasure. Litigants who wanted to make formal entries in order to qualify themselves to sue by the assize may, Professor Milsom believes, have been deterred from doing so. It was hard to be fully sure of one's right; and if the right was in fact not good then by entering one would make oneself liable to the penalties of the statute. According to this hypothesis, men therefore avoided making entries, were unable to use the assize, and had in consequence to turn to other forms of action.

But this cannot be a true explanation of the decline of the assize. The substitute-actions on the civil side depended as much as the assize on formal entries, and such entries were commonly made in connection with them. Ejectment, eventually the most successful of all, could never be used to sue for freehold at all unless the claimant made a formal entry. If anyone feared the statute of 1381, his unwillingness to attempt an entry would have thrown him back on one of the old real actions that novel disseisin had replaced, mort d'ancestor, ael, cosinage, or a writ of entry; but these actions continued to

---

[1] *Select Cases in the Exchequer Chamber* i. no. 15 (1430–1), cf. no. 36 (1460–1).

[2] FNB fo. 177, Y.B. Hil. 11 Richard II no. 3. (1388).

[3] The Fine rolls for the years 1425–39 record the purchase of 488 writs of novel disseisin for which the county is indicated. Of these, only eight were laid in Middlesex.

[4] *Historical Foundations*, pp. 135–6.

decline after 1381 as before. In fact there is no evidence and little likelihood that the statutory provisions were ever enforced in such a way as to discourage nominal entries. Indictments of forcible entry were concerned only with violence, and civil actions under the amending statute of 1429 could not succeed unless there had been violence. The civil actions on the statute of 1381 were late-comers and even they probably did not lay any very frightening penalties against one who made a formal entry without violence. The 'breach of peace' of which he might be convicted if his entry was not congeable was no more than a fiction, and the unwarranted entry of which he was guilty would be understood as a routine proceeding intended to expedite litigation.

Cases of novel disseisin were sometimes held up on technical points of pleading, but this was no peculiarity of theirs; it was equally likely to happen, as far as I can judge, in the other competing forms of action.[1] The artificialities of colour in pleading, which Maitland feared might have done the assize to death by their overwrought complications,[2] cannot have worked any harm. Giving colour and replying to a colourable plea were usually simple matters in the developed practice of the fifteenth and sixteenth centuries, involving no more than the routine use of some fictions well known to any pleader.[3] Colour had been used from the first in Entry in the nature of an

---

[1] See, for instance, the following records: Y.B. Mich. 7 Henry VII no. 3 (1491), Pasch. 13 Henry VII no. 8 (1498), Trin. 15 Henry VII no. 19 (1500), Pasch. 14 Henry VIII no. 1 (1523), Trin. 26 Henry VIII no. 17 (1534), Mich. 27 Henry VIII no. 8 (1535), Dyer fo. 107 (1554).

[2] 'The pleadings in assizes become at least as complicated and "colourable" as the pleadings in other actions, perhaps more complicated and "colourable" because there is a fixed question for the jurors which has to be evaded. And so the assizes fall into the ruck of "real actions".' 'Beatitude of Seisin', p. 295.

[3] For the earlier history of colour, see above, pp. 155–6; for learning of the later period, Y.B. Mich. 11 Henry VII nos. 7, 8 (1495), Trin. 11 Henry VII no. 8 (1496). Logically, giving colour was no more than a variety of confession-and-avoidance. The defendant admitted that the plaintiff had been in seisin and had been put out. In the fifteenth century and after the standard form for making the admission was: 'After the death of A, the plaintiff, claiming by virtue of a deed of feoffment from A, by which deed, however, no seisin ever passed in A's lifetime, entered upon the tenements and was ousted by B, upon whom the defendant later entered as well he might.' The defendant explained why 'he might well enter' by describing his own title. The plaintiff did not reply to the matter offered by way of confession for it was fictitious and non-traversable. He traversed points of the defendant's title or else set up his own title in reply.

assize[1] and by the latter part of the fifteenth century it was practised in Trespass and in the civil actions of forcible entry as much as in novel disseisin. In all these actions it was managed under most of the same rules;[2] where the rules differed the differences tended rather to favour the assize in the sight of plaintiffs.[3]

A handful of cases can be found, however, in which defendants at the assize were allowed, without restraint by the court, to plead with the deliberate object of wrapping the suit in technicalities and complexities, and these may do something to explain why the assize fell from favour. Particularly where there were several defendants, they might bedevil the plaintiff by offering, each of them, a number of separate defences for different parts of the property being sought. In a case in Cambridgeshire in 1437, for instance, there were six defendants. Five of them declared together that they were joint tenants of the property and then each proceeded in his turn to plead in bar in defence of his interest. This did not produce a mere five pleas in bar, for these defendants knew how to do far better than that: each of them offered separate pleas for various fractional shares of his interest. Then the sixth defendant joined in, claimed to be the sole tenant of everything, and put in his own defence. They left the plaintiff to sort his way through this heap of pleas if he could, evidently hoping that he would make some technical mistake. A point of pleading did indeed arise out of it all, and the case had to be adjourned to the Common Pleas.[4]

I know of no reason why the same tactics could not have been used in Trespass or Forcible Entry or Entry in the nature of an assize. It may be that they sometimes were. But the few examples that I have seen are all in records of assizes, and these methods were apparently characteristic enough of the assize that William Rastell took care to illustrate them in two of the

---

[1] Y.B. Mich. 11 Richard II no. 7 (1387).

[2] See, for instance, Y.B. Mich. 19 Henry VI no. 42 (1440), Pasch. 10 Ed. IV & 49 Henry VI no. 12 (1470), Mich. 10 Henry VII no. 15 (1494), Hil. 15 Henry VII no. 6 (1500), Trin. 27 Henry VIII no. 19 (1535), Brooke's New Cases nos. 76, 525.

[3] Y.B. Pasch. 10 Ed. IV & 49 Henry VI no. 20, p. 79 (1470), *Select Cases in the Exchequer Chamber* ii. no. 44 p. 143 (1490), Y.B. Hil. 10 Henry VII no. 10 (1495), Mich. 26 Henry VIII no. 2 (1534).

[4] J.I. 1/1543 m. 29-31. Other examples appear in this same roll, m. 28-9, 32, and in J.I. 1/1542 m. 10. For a later instance see K.B. 27/949 m. 30 (1499).

models for enrolments of novel disseisin that he provided in his *Collection of Entries*.[1] Edward Coke presumably had this practice in mind, and may have had Rastell's book before him, when he wrote in 1611 that the assize had been rendered unpopular because of 'feigned and over-curious pleadings'.[2]

But though it goes some way, this factor cannot go very far to explain the disuse of the assize, for such pleading was never typical or even common. I have seen no more than six or seven examples among some hundreds of cases that I have examined from the last centuries of the assize. A second factor was probably of much greater weight. Novel disseisin was a real action, in which the successful plaintiff got an express judgment for the recovery of his tenements. As a real action it was subject to a number of special rules on which defendants could often capitalize to create difficulties that had nothing to do with the merits of the plaintiff's claim. From time to time all sorts of unusual obstacles could be thrown in the way,[3] but a few tricks were unhappily characteristic. Since Edward I's reign the law had provided that when one sued for recovery of lands of which a married woman was seised and brought his action, as he always must, against both the woman and her husband, if the man defaulted at any time the lady could be 'received' to defend on her own.[4] Nothing that the husband had done would be to her prejudice, neither the default itself nor anything that he had pleaded on his behalf or on hers down to the time of the default. In the assize as in other real actions, men and their wives often used these rules to make cruel sport of the plaintiff. The husband would plead for them both and join issue on some special matter and get an adjournment for its trial, whether by jury or in some other way. If it appeared that the trial was likely to go against them, the husband would absent himself on the day assigned and his wife would appear and be received and start all over again with a new line of defence. The original defence might or might not have been put in in good faith: sometimes

---

[1] fos. 59, 62.

[2] Preface to 8 Reports, 'fictas et curiosas nimis in placitando agitationes'.

[3] e.g. 46 Ass. no. 10 (1372), or Wikes's case, Y.B. Hil. 46 Ed. III no. 20, 45 Ass. no. 12, 46 Ass. no. 5, Y.B. Mich. 48 Ed. III no. 17, 49 Ass. no. 1 (1371–5); or Y.B. 1 Henry VI no. 5 (1422–3).

[4] Statute of Westminster II c. 3 (1285), T. F. T. Plucknett in Y.B. 5 Ed. II pp. xl–xli.

it rested on matters that the couple knew were entirely false but which they pleaded because they could delay the plaintiff in this way without losing anything themselves.[1]

Almost as much trouble arose from the simple rule that the assize, like every other real action, must name the current tenants of the property as defendants. Especially when the subtleties of entry and re-ouster were brought into play, as they so often were, the law itself might be left in doubt, on a given set of facts, as to who was the tenant of the freehold.[2] Apart from these uncertainties, the plaintiff often found when he brought his suit against a man who had disseised him and who appeared still to be the tenant, that the opponent had changed his estate since the disseisin and was holding jointly with his wife or with someone else whom the plaintiff had not named as a co-defendant, and could prove it by producing deeds of joint feoffment or, better still, evidence of final concords.[3] The plaintiff would have to begin his suit again with a new and corrected writ. Worse still, by the end of the fourteenth century lawyers had developed considerable skill in arranging for their clients complicated changes of estate whose purpose was to frustrate opponents altogether by making it wholly impossible for them to find out who was legally in seisin. The feoffment to uses was effective for this purpose as for so many others. Statutes of 1377 and 1402 countered by providing that when this was done the plaintiff could bring the assize against his disseisor as tenant, alleging that he had been the legal tenant and had ceased to be so only because he made a feoffment over to persons unknown for the purpose of obstructing the plaintiff's proceedings, and had continued all the while to receive the income from the property.[4] But even so, when a plaintiff availed himself of the statutes all the special facts that he alleged to bring his case under their terms could be disputed and would have to be established by the verdict of the assize.[5]

---

[1] e.g. J.I. 1/1543 m. 9 (1435), C.P. 40/950 m. 153 (1499), Keilwey no. 107.

[2] 43 Ass. no. 6 (1369), 44 Ass. no. 26 (1370), J.I. 1/1542 m. 3, 9 (1428-30), Dyer fo. 141, Keilwey Trin. 22 Henry VII no. 3 (1507).

[3] Above, pp. 133-4. The difficulty is illustrated again and again. For example, Y.B. Trin. 44 Ed. III no. 28 (1370), C.P. 40/539 m. 276 (1395), J.I. 1/1543 m. 21d (1438-9).

[4] 1 Richard II c. 9, 4 Henry IV c. 7.

[5] e.g. J.I. 1/1543 m. 17d (1432), C.P. 40/950 m. 417 (1498).

Entry in the nature of an assize was also a real action and shared all these impediments with the assize itself. But it was not so with Trespass and the civil actions of forcible entry or with Ejectment when it came into use for freehold. In the eyes of the law these were all personal actions, and the raising and resolution of issues about freehold in the course of litigation upon them did not depend on joining the legal tenant of the freehold as a party. Nothing was in fact more common than to bring the action against the freeholder's servant or someone else who 'justified in his right'.[1] All potential problems about receipt of the wife, joint tenancies, and unknown feoffees to uses were avoided from the outset.

Another important advantage of the partner-actions, and the third contributor to the eventual ruin of the assize, had to do with the award of damages to the successful plaintiff. Damages, and costs along with them, were given on exactly the same principles in the assize and in the other actions. The triple damages that were awarded in Forcible Entry on the statute of 1429 were also given, by virtue of the same statute, in cases at the assize where it was found that illegal violence had been used in perpetrating a disseisin.[2] But in novel disseisin there was an old rule that the damages had to be assessed by the recognitors of the assize and by no other jury and, along with this, a second rule that prohibited any judgment being given in the principal matter, for recovery of the tenements, until the damages had been assessed.[3] When the principal matter of a case was settled

---

[1] e.g. Y.B. Trin. 40 Ed. III no. 12 (1366), Pasch. 46 Ed. III no. 9 (1372), Lincoln's Inn Hale MS. 77 fo. 271b (1387), 273b (1398), C.P. 40/539 m. 508d (1395), 40/715 m. 336, 480 (1439), Y.B. Trin. 10 Ed. IV & 49 Henry VI no. 8 (1470), K.B. 27/952 m. 31, 27/953 m. 55, C.P. 40/950 m. 498 (1499), Y.B. Trin. 15 Henry VII no. 13 (1500), Mich. 21 Henry VII no. 42 (1505), Dyer fo. 134 (1556), Plowden p. 298 (1566). Ejectment, in particular, could be brought for trial of freehold against a termor (Plowden p. 459 (1574)), a servant (2 Brownlow & Gouldesborough p. 223 (1607), 1 Brownlow & Gouldesborough p. 143 = Yelverton p. 144 (1608)), or ultimately against anyone at all, whether a real person or fictitious, as 'casual ejector': Simpson, *Introduction to the History of the Land Law*, pp. 138–9.

[2] 8 Henry VI c. 9. Several examples appear in the two surviving assize rolls of the 1430s: J.I. 1/1542 m. 25, 1/1543 m. 5d, 13, 19, 23, 37d. For a later example see Y.B. Hil. 14 Henry VII no. 5 (1499).

[3] C.P. 40/108 m. 113 (1295), Y.B. Mich. 9 Ed. II no. 15 (1315), Pasch. 8 Ed. III no. 15 (1334), Pasch. 22 Ed. III no. 7 (1348). The latter refinement established itself only in the 1290s and was not known before that time: *CRR* i. 249 (1200), v. 141, 160 (1208), K.B. 27/18 m. 15 (1275), 27/125 m. 65d (1290).

not by the verdict of the assize but in some other way (through trial by jury in another county, for instance, or through inspection of records at Westminster, or through judgment upon a demurrer, which usually involved a reference to Westminster for deliberation) it was tiresome in the extreme to have to get the recognitors resummoned in the next session of the justices of assize before damages could be assessed and a judgment given: so tiresome that plaintiffs who found themselves thus situated often waived their claims to damages in order to get immediate judgment.[1] The problem did not arise in any of the other civil procedures that substituted for novel disseisin. In those actions, if the principal matter was determined by a jury of a county other than that in which the land lay, that jury would also assess the damages;[2] and if it was determined without a jury, judgment would be given at once and an order would issue to the sheriff to inquire about damages.[3]

Then, too, it was important that once damages and costs had been assessed, collecting them was easier in Trespass and Forcible Entry. Any defendant who was convicted in these proceedings was automatically held to have broken the king's peace whether he had actually committed any violence or not. Because he had broken the king's peace he was ordered to prison. To get the order rescinded, or to get out of gaol if the order was actually executed, he had to pay a fine to the king, but he was not allowed to arrange this until he had first satisfied the plaintiff for his damages and costs.[4] Prison is a powerful inducement. Against defendants who were good for the sums awarded this seems to have been the quickest way there was for enforcing payment. As for others who could by no means pay, it probably gave some plaintiffs a kind of satisfaction to see them languish behind bars.

A defendant convicted in the assize might also be ordered to prison, and if this was done then, until the end of the Middle

---

[1] In addition to some of the cases cited in the previous note, see 43 Ass. no. 11 (1369), Y.B. Trin. 44 Ed. III no. 31 (1370), Pasch. 13 Richard II no. 6 (1390).

[2] 44 Ass. no. 4 (1370). Booth, *Real Actions*, p. 279, says that this rule held for the assize as well. But he cites no authority, and is contradicted by Y.B. Pasch. 8 Ed. III no. 15 (1334), Pasch. 22 Ed. III no. 7 (1348).

[3] Y.B. Mich. 12 Richard II no. 25 (1388), C.P. 40/715 m. 306, 334, 466, 707, 566d, 426d (1439), K.B. 27/953 m. 65, 409 (1499).

[4] Y.B. Hil. 50 Ed. III no. 8 (1376), Lincoln's Inn Hale MS. 77 fo. 202 (1393).

Ages, the plaintiff enjoyed all the same advantage in coming by his damages and costs. But in the assize imprisonment was awarded only when it was expressly found that the defendant had committed disseisin to the accompaniment of violence or robbery.[1] In this action there was no fiction about the breach of peace: it had to be real, and therefore most convicted defendants did not go to gaol. Even for those who did, it was ruled in 1499 that after conviction at the assize they could fine with the king and be released without regard to whether they had satisfied the plaintiff.[2] So to collect damages and costs most plaintiffs before 1499 and all of them after that time had to rely on the processes of *fieri facias*, by which the sheriff took and sold the defendant's chattels and turned the proceeds over to the plaintiff, *levari facias*, by which the sheriff took the defendant's revenues for the plaintiff's account, or *elegit*, by which the plaintiff received half the defendant's lands to hold until their income should cover the sum that was due. The justices of assize, who gave the judgments for damages and costs, could grant these processes of execution only in the county in which the tenements lay, for their commissions were for one county at a time. However great the wealth the defendant might have in other counties, it could not be touched by their orders. The plaintiff could circumvent these difficulties by prosecuting a separate action of debt for the sums awarded him by judgment, for actions of debt were brought in the Common Pleas which had jurisdiction over the whole kingdom and the judgments were enforceable by imprisonment.[3] But that was a roundabout procedure, and quite unnecessary if one began in the first place with Trespass or Forcible Entry.

Getting the damages and costs was of central importance. In the thirteenth century the judgment for damages in the assize may have seemed an adjective matter, for the main thing in those days was to get oneself restored to seisin of the

---

[1] Above, p. 134.

[2] Y.B. Hil. 14 Henry VII no. 5 = Pasch. 13 Henry VII no. 4 = Pasch. 15 Henry VII no. 1. The court stated explicitly that this was a rule for the assize and not for Trespass. Cf. Hil. 11 Henry VII no. 11 (1496), where the point was argued but not decided. The rule seems pretty clearly to have been an innovation: see J.I. 1/1543 m. 35, 44d (1432), Y.B. Mich. 18 Henry VI no. 2 = K.B. 27/714 m. 122 (1439), Y.B. Pasch. 33 Henry VI no. 16 (1455).

[3] Brooke's New Cases no. 25. For execution in Debt, see Plucknett, *Concise History*, pp. 368–9.

land by judgment. But now in these latter times, when successful plaintiffs generally entered on their own, counting on the adversary to give way because he had already been struck with one judgment for damages and because he knew that he would doubtless be struck with another if he gave further trouble, the award of damages was the law's principal sanction. The advantage of the partner-actions over the assize was therefore considerable, as using more flexible procedures for assessment and, in the case of Trespass and Forcible Entry, more stringent process for execution.

The fourth reason why litigants turned away from the assize was that the partner-actions on the civil side were always decided upon single points of process and single issues for trial, whereas in novel disseisin it was common for the plaintiff to be required to win on each of a series of issues before he could gain his judgment. When there existed these alternative forms where one could gain the victory by proving either A or B it seemed foolish to litigants and their counsel to use the assize where they might have to prove both A and B.

There was, for instance, the simple case in which the defendant failed to appear in court on the first day appointed for hearing. In the assize they would use the ancient procedure, designed by Henry II to ensure quick justice, of holding the trial in his absence. But usually there would be at least a short adjournment before the trial, for in this later age the recognitors of the assize did not commonly trouble to report on the first summons; experience had shown that too often their services were not needed on that day, which was likely to be devoted to pleadings. When the trial was held after an adjournment, the defendant who defaulted at first could come in and present his case to the assize, arguing against the plaintiff's arguments and opposing his own evidences to what the plaintiff showed on his side. His default deprived him only of the right to plead in bar.[1] In either case, with or without a late-coming defendant, the charge to the assize would be to find (1) whether the plaintiff was seised of a freehold, (2) whether the defendant wrongfully disseised him, and (3) whether the defendant was the tenant of the land. If they found for the plaintiff on these three points, he won.

---

[1] Y.B. Hil. 13 Ed. II p. 402 (1320), Plowden p. 403 (1570).

This procedure contrasted favourably enough with that in Trespass and Forcible Entry, where there could be no trial or judgment against a defendant who had not appeared at all and where the plaintiff consequently had to enter into wearisome proceedings to force him to appear. But the process in Entry in the nature of an assize was more attractive. There they used the rules common to most real actions. If the defendant (technically he was the 'tenant') did not come on the first day the case was put off to another day and notice of the adjournment was served on him. If he chose not to appear on that second day either, the plaintiff (technically, the 'demandant') would recover without any trial at all. If he did come on the second day, the plaintiff could choose to make an issue of his earlier default, and the court would try whether the default was or was not contumacious. If it was found to be contumacious, the plaintiff recovered without any further trial of any other issue. It is true that the trial of these defaults, when issue was taken on them, was by compurgators brought in by the defendant, so that the plaintiff's chance of winning was not very good. But it was the plaintiff's choice whether to let the case turn on that point, and if he chose to do so it was only a single issue, whereas in novel disseisin he would have to win on each of three several points. Those who brought actions of entry in the nature of an assize thought well enough of their chances that it was fairly common for them to take issue on a default.[1]

If his opponent defaulted after once putting in an appearance in the case, the plaintiff had an even greater advantage if he had chosen one of the substitute-actions on the civil side. In all of them, Entry in the nature of an assize, Trespass, and Forcible Entry, the default concluded the matter and the plaintiff would get his judgment thereupon, for the defendant was convicted of contempt by the court's own record so that no trial was necessary.[2] In novel disseisin, however, the judgment

---

[1] For example, C.P. 40/715 m. 1, 120, 124, 306, 334, 466, 620, 566d, 426d, 339d, 1d (1439), 40/950 m. 264d (1499).

[2] In Entry in the nature of an assize an adjournment would be given and the defendant notified before judgment was rendered upon a default after appearance. But the judgment for the plaintiff would almost certainly follow, because defaults after appearance were not easily 'healed'. In Trespass and Forcible Entry judgment for the plaintiff would be given as soon as the default was made: Rastell, *Entries*, fo. 631, K.B. 27/952 m. 29 (1499), 27/1216 m. 272 (1565).

under most circumstances would be that trial proceed by the assize, which would have to find for the plaintiff on the three points already mentioned.[1]

In any form of action, if the defendant came to court in due time he could enter pleas 'in abatement', pleas tending to show that the plaintiff's suit should not be allowed to proceed for the present, or not in this form of action, or not on the basis of the original writ before the court. In actions generally, and in all the civil actions that substituted for novel disseisin, it was a rule that if the defendant pleaded in abatement some matter that called for trial by jury (misnomer of the township, for example), and if the plaintiff stood his ground and joined issue on it so that a trial by jury actually had to be held, then the whole outcome of the case would rest on the trial of that issue alone, even though it concerned a preliminary matter and did not touch the main substance of the plaintiff's case. If the plaintiff won in that trial, he recovered by judgment.[2] But in the assize this was not so. The defendant could plead in abatement matter triable by the assize, and could in fact plead several distinct matters of that kind if he liked, saying for instance that the township was misnamed, and that the plaintiff who was suing alone had no right except jointly with his wife, and that none of those who had been named as defendants was the tenant of the land. He could then go on and conclude that 'if it be found' for the plaintiff on all these points, still he had done no wrong and committed no disseisin. The case would go to trial, and in order to succeed the plaintiff had to win favourable verdicts on all the pleas in abatement and on the final general

[1] Y.B. Mich. 12 Ed. II nos. 4, 43 (1318), Hil. 12 Ed. II no. 47 (1319), Pasch. 12 Ed. II no. 58 (1319), B.M. Egerton MS. 2811 fo. 232 (1330–1), Y.B. Pasch. 7 Ed. III no. 36 and Trin. 7 Ed. III no. 42 (1333), Hil. 14 Ed. III no. 42 (1340), Mich. 18 Ed. III no. 17 (1344), 21 Ass. no. 23 (1347), Y.B. Pasch. 22 Ed. III no. 7 (1348), 22 Ass. no. 11 (1348). The exceptions, where judgment could be given in the assize directly upon a default, were those in which the default implied that the defendant had 'failed of his record' under the provisions of the Statute of Westminster II c. 25: above, pp. 132–3.

[2] This rule was clearly established in later centuries: Chitty, *On Pleading*, i. 455, 458, and the cases cited there. For the period with which we are here concerned, it is illustrated in these cases: Y.B. Trin. 50 Ed. III no. 13 (1376), Lincoln's Inn Hale MS. 77 fos. 208ᵛ (1383), 216ʳ–216ᵛ (1384), Y.B. Mich. 12 Richard II no. 25 (1388), Hil. 12 Richard II no. 13 (1389), Mich. 3 Henry IV no. 12 (1401), Pasch. 22 Henry VI no. 31 at the end (1444), Trin. 2 Ed. IV no. 1 (1462), Long Quinto Mich. 5 Ed. IV pp. 90, 139 (1465).

issue, 'no wrong, no disseisin'.[1] In the assize, the only restriction
on the defendant's freedom thus to multiply issues was that
after his pleas in abatement triable by the assize he might not
plead in bar but must always take the general issue, 'no wrong,
no disseisin'.[2] Even this restriction could be partly evaded,
for most assizes were brought against several co-defendants, the
current tenant together with those who had made the disseisin
or aided in making it. Only the tenant was allowed to plead in
bar, raising issues about the title to the property;[3] the others
had to take the general issue. But since they were going to
conclude with the general issue anyway, they could prefix it
with many kinds of pleas in abatement triable by the assize,
which would thus be accepted by the court while the tenant
remained free to plead in bar.[4]

The fact that most assizes were brought against more than
one defendant also yielded another opportunity to multiply
issues for trial. If the defendants liked, several of them could
assert that they were the tenants of the land, each for himself
and to the exclusion of the others. Each would 'answer as
tenant' and would offer a defence of his own, one of them perhaps pleading the general issue and the others putting forth

---

[1] Examples of this procedure are very common in all periods. See, for instance,
Eyres of Glos, Warw, Staffs no. 521 (1221), Bracton fos. 211–211b, Y.B. Mich. 5 Ed.
II no. 28 (1311), Trin. 9 Ed. III no. 2 (1335), J.I. 1/1542 m. 8 (1430), C.P. 40/950
m. 114 (1499). Gilbert of Thornton in his treatise written in the late 1280s said of
novel disseisin, 'si partes in . . . exceptionibus dilatoriis que non tangunt actionem
neque assisam nisi breve tantum velint facere iocum partitum quod unus amitteret
si ita sit, et si non quod lucretur alius [*sic*], hoc iusticiarii permittere non debent,
quia exceptio accipi non debet pro peremptoria.' Harvard Law Library MS. 77
fo. 56. In some cases at least the same rule applied even to pleas in abatement not
triable by the assize: see C.P. 40/950 m. 153 (1499), a lamentable case in which
the tenants held up proceedings for nearly four years on the plea that the lands in
question were ancient demesne and so not under the jurisdiction of the courts of
common law. When the plaintiff won on this issue he only got judgment that the
assize should proceed.

This whole matter was discussed, and the comparison drawn between the assize
and other actions, by Chief Justice Belknap in 1376, Y.B. Hil. 50 Ed. III no. 23.

[2] Y.B. Trin. 50 Ed. III no. 13 (1376), Brooke's New Cases no. 525, Keilwey no.
59, expressing a doctrine that seems consistently to be followed in the cases of this
period. In the early fourteenth century some authority held that pleas in abatement
triable by the assize could be followed by a plea in bar provided that the plea in
bar also led to a principal issue triable by the assize: Y.B. Mich. 12 Ed. II no. 1
(1318).

[3] Y.B. Trin. 8 Ed. III no. 8 (1334), Trin. 11 Ed. III pp. 121–2 (1337), Mich. 18
Ed. III no. 14 (1344).

[4] e.g. J.I. 1/1543 m. 17d, 28–9, 32 (1432–8); Rastell, *Entries*, fo. 65.

different pleas in bar. The plaintiff was obliged to answer only one of the pleas, the one entered by the defendant whom he took to be the true tenant, and he could ignore everything that was said by the others. But he had to pick the right defendant, the one who really was the tenant, and when the pleading was finished and the case came to trial the first question on which the assize had to pronounce was whether he had chosen correctly: another issue, then, on which he had to win before his case could proceed to trial of the principal matter.[1]

If in a case of the assize none of these tricks was played, but the true tenant of the land duly appeared and put in a forth-right defence, his defence would usually consist of a plea in bar in which he set out his own claim to the property to rebut the plaintiff's suit. The consequent pleadings between the parties would generally yield, here as in other forms of action, a single issue—'Is the plaintiff the tenant's villein or not?', 'Did the plaintiff's ancestor give this property to the tenant with warranty?', 'Was this land included among the holdings that the tenant purchased through a final concord?', and so forth. In almost any other action the determination of that chosen issue in the plaintiff's favour would settle the case and the plaintiff would recover at once.[2] But in novel disseisin after a finding for the plaintiff the court often had to go on and require the assize to say whether the plaintiff had been seised of a free tenement and disseised by the defendant. After winning on the issue that the parties had joined, the plaintiff could still lose on these further points.[3]

The law sometimes required this further inquiry 'of seisin and disseisin' and sometimes did not. There were rules govern-ing the matter, into which we need not descend in detail, for they were not entirely clear and the courts did not always act consistently.[4] But their effect was that the further inquiry had

---

[1] Examples of this subterfuge, which could be practiced in a large number of variations, are common from the early fourteenth century. See, for instance, Y.B. Pasch. 12 Ed. II no. 45 (1319), Hil. 12 Ed. III p. 411 (1338), 42 Ass. no. 1 (1368), Y.B. Trin. 44 Ed. III nos. 28, 30 (1370), Pasch. 13 Richard II no. 3 (1390), *London Possessory Assizes* no. 194 (1410), J.I. 1/1542 m. 18d (1434), 1/1543 m. 28–9 (1437), 32 (1438); cf. Brooke's New Cases no. 418 (1552), Dyer fo. 244 (1565).

[2] Rastell, *Entries*, fo. 677 ff.

[3] For example, Y.B. Mich. 40 Ed. III no. 34 (1366), 44 Ass. no. 6, Y.B. Trin. 44 Ed. III no. 29 (1370).

[4] Above, pp. 73–4.

to be made in a large share of cases. In the 1420s and after, the proportion became higher than ever because of a new device discovered by those who pleaded in defence. In constructing a plea in bar the defendant very often had to proceed by acknowledging that he had indeed put the plaintiff out of the land. It did not amount to an actionable disseisin, the defence would say, because the tenant had a right of entry: and he would then go on to describe the title that gave him his right of entry. When special pleading took this form, a finding for the plaintiff on the single issue that emerged from the pleadings was sufficient to give him his recovery and no inquiry of seisin and disseisin was needed, for the tenant had admitted in his pleading that the plaintiff had been in the lands and that he had put him out.

But in the 1420s counsel pleading this style of defence hit upon a new trick. Since an 'ouster' of the plaintiff had to be acknowledged, they said that it had been done by some other person—picking a name from the air—and that the tenant afterwards got to the lands by putting that person out.[1] The defendant thus avoided admitting that he had ejected the plaintiff and the plaintiff, even if he won on the special issue that was joined, was left with the burden of proving by the verdict of the assize that the defendant had disseised him.[2] This device of the 'double ouster' was accepted by the courts and became standard practice. It was used only in the assize. In Trespass and Entry in the nature of an assize and Forcible Entry the whole case must come to rest on a single issue anyway and so in pleading to that issue one might just as well admit other points.[3]

[1] For the form of the plea, see above, p. 185 n. 3. The earliest example that I have seen of this form is in a report of 1428, Y.B. Mich. 7 Henry VI no. 14. In the assize rolls J.I. 1/1542 (1428–39) and 1/1543 (1430–9) it is invariably used.

[2] St. Germain, *Doctor and Student*, c. 53: '. . . if the tenant by his pleading confessed an immediate entry upon the plaintiff . . . then if the title were after found for the plaintiff the tenant by his confession were attainted of the disseisin. And because it may be that though the plaintiff have good title to the land that yet the tenant is no disseisor, therefore the tenants use many times to plead in such manner . . . to save themselves from confessing an ouster. . . .' Where the double ouster was pleaded and the issue was found for the plaintiff, inquiry was also made 'of seisin and disseisin': e.g. J.I. 1/1543 m. 35d, 41, 47 (1434–8), K.B. 27/949 m. 30 (1499); Rastell, *Entries*, fo. 59.

[3] e.g. C.P. 40/715 m. 499, 566d, 631, 634, 640, 678 (1439), Y.B. Trin. 26 Henry VIII no. 17 (1534); Rastell, *Entries*, fo. 631–2.

The plaintiff in novel disseisin was likely, then, at every turn to bear a heavier burden of proof and to run a correspondingly greater risk of defeat. His opponent was allowed to defend himself with two sticks; sometimes with three or more. As counsel observed in 1375, 'More is to be inquired of in the assize . . . but in [Trespass] there will be only one issue.'[1] If we ask why the assize was subjected, almost alone among actions at law, to these peculiar and disadvantageous rules, the answer is clear and is one of the ironies of history. The early popularity of novel disseisin had begotten the rule that it must be heard by justices on circuit in the county.[2] There the jurors could easily appear, ready to serve the court. Since they were there at hand, there was no reason why several issues should not be received to be tried by their verdict. Truth would out—or so the law held when it submitted a point for trial by jury—and there would be no extra delay—the assize could as soon speak on two or three issues or more as on one.[3] In other civil actions the circumstances were different. In the fourteenth century and after they were all heard in the central courts at Westminster, where no jury of the county was present and none could easily be brought, unless in Middlesex cases; trial was at *nisi prius*. The justices who went out on circuit into the counties with their commissions of *nisi prius* technically had no jurisdiction over the cases in which they held trials and so could give no judgments at all upon the verdicts that they received. That left them powerless to decide that a preliminary issue had been found for the plaintiff and that they should therefore move on to inquire of a consequent issue. If series of issues were to be handled through their offices they would have to be tried one at a time in successive circuits with reference back in between to the court that had jurisdiction of the case. That would entail unreasonable delay, and therefore the courts carefully excluded such series and insisted that each case be brought down to a single issue only. As a result, these actions rose in popularity at the expense of the assize.

In addition to the four that we have now reviewed at some length, one final factor weighed in the balance against novel disseisin. Trespass, the earliest of the partners in point of time

---

[1] Y.B. Trin. 49 Ed. III no. 2.   [2] Above, pp. 59–62.
[3] Cf. the rule in actions of attaint, Keilwey Mich. 20 Henry VII no. 3 (1504).

and always the chief in volume of business, had a wider applicability than the assize. The plaintiff in the assize, who charged
that he had been disseised, had to be a freeholder. The plaintiff
in Trespass, who charged that his land had been entered, his
crops trampled, his trees felled, or whatever, could be a freeholder, termor, tenant-at-will, or anyone else who had good
possession in the eyes of the common law.[1] Novel disseisin sued
for lands and tenements; Trespass served that function but
was also the vehicle for many purely personal actions. It was not
much to set off against all this that novel disseisin could sue for
rents seck, rights of common, and freehold in offices, which were
beyond the reach of Trespass.[2] The greater scope of Trespass
recommended it in practice. If a practitioner of the law trained
himself thoroughly in handling cases at the assize he would also
need in the ordinary course of his work to be master of proceedings in Trespass, for there was so much that Trespass could do
that the assize could not. But, on the other hand, if he knew
Trespass well he could dispense with building and maintaining
his expertise in novel disseisin for he would not often be com-
pelled to bring the assize in a case that Trespass could not
serve. If he made it his custom to recommend Trespass for his
clients wherever possible, he could manage all his ordinary
business out of a smaller fund of learning. This would render
his work easier and would help to insure against mistakes.

If these that I have suggested were indeed the decisive factors
that led to the disuse of novel disseisin, then they suggest a
general observation. Maitland's conjecture that '[the] assize
must have been very badly handled', that it 'deteriorated' in the
late Middle Ages,[3] is wide of the mark; for the characteristics

[1] Not, however, a tenant at sufferance or, before the statute of 1535, *cestui que
use*: Keilwey Pasch. 17 Henry VII nos. 2, 8, Mich. 18 Henry VII no. 2 (1502).
Econtra tamen, Y.B. Hil. 21 Henry VII no. 4 (1506).

[2] Above, pp. 50–2, 135–6. For the exclusion of suits for rights of common from the
ambit of Trespass, see Y.B. Trin. 10 Henry VII nos. 1, 5, 22 (1495); *econtra*, K.B.
27/1216 m. 247 (1565). But Replevin had always been available for such cases,
and Trespass could be used on the other side, by the lord of the soil who wished to
resist claims to common rights over his land.

Novel disseisin survived longest as a means of suing for offices: Dyer fo. 149
(1557), 8 Coke, Jehu Webb's Case (1608) and Earl of Rutland's case (1608),
1 Brownlow & Gouldesborough pp. 26–9, 2 Brownlow & Gouldesborough
pp. 223 (1610), 268 (1610), 328 (1610). In 1610 an attempt was made to turn
Trespass on the case to this purpose, 2 Brownlow & Gouldesborough p. 330.

[3] 'Beatitude of Seisin', pp. 291, 295.

that turned plaintiffs away from the assize in and about the fifteenth century were, most of them, nothing new. The technique of putting up in defence a smokescreen of 'feigned, dilatory, and curious pleadings', which so struck Edward Coke, first appears in the fifteenth century, but it was probably the least of the disadvantages of the assize. The difficulties that arose out of novel disseisin's status as a real action were old. Since King John's day it had been necessary to name the tenant among the defendants,[1] and the subleties and sub-terfuges of 'receipt' had grown up soon after 1285. When concealment of legal title came to be practised in the fourteenth century, statutes were made to bring novel disseisin abreast of the development, and they were at least partly effective. So too of the disadvantages connected with the award and collection of damages. The stubborn rule that damages must always be assessed by the recognitors of the assize, and that this must be done before judgment could be given in the principal, was set in the 1290s; and the methods available in the fifteenth century for enforcing payment of the damages were just those that had been used under Henry III and his son, only improved a little by the possibility of resorting to an action of debt, newly equipped as this was, since 1352, with the sanction of imprisonment for those who did not pay after judgment.

In just the same way, the custom of using the jurors of the assize to inquire of all sides of the plaintiff's case before giving him a favourable judgment was at least as old as Henry of Bracton, who in his treatise in the mid thirteenth century urged the practice on his fellow justices in the form in which he knew it.[2] And as for the greater generality of Trespass, the ambit of novel disseisin and the variety of cases that it could cover were far wider under Richard II and after than ever before.

'La consigne n'a pas changé . . . C'est bien là le drame!'[3] The law was working its way through to newer and higher standards, partly in the speed of litigation but even more in its simplicity and flexibility. The assize, burdened with the precedents of so many past years, could not keep up. Its partner-actions, all of them, decided cases on single issues, and once the plaintiff had won they proceeded straightway to give judgment,

---

[1] Above, p. 57.   [2] Above, pp. 68–74.
[3] Antoine de Saint-Exupéry, *Le Petit Prince*, p. 50.

ascertaining his damages in whatever way was most con-venient. Most of them, being actions of trespass or born out of Trespass, had the drastic process of imprisonment to extract quick payment of damages from the convicted defendant. The trespassory actions tried the title to freehold without figuring as real actions and so without caring whether the defendant had the freehold. They could also try all the other estates known to the common law, and, in the case of Trespass itself, could handle a wide range of personal actions besides. Their take-over of the business that had once been done by the assize repre-sented not the deterioration of the assize, for there was none, but rather a genuine measure of progress in the administration of justice.

The eventual replacement of Trespass by Ejectment does not need so much explanation. Ejectment was a variety of Trespass and the two actions were heard in the same courts and under most of the same rules of procedure; they did not differ from one another nearly so much as they both differed from the assize, and it must have required very little to incline plaintiffs and their counsel to prefer one of them over the other. Two factors, neither of them matters of great weight, seem sufficient to account for the prevalence of Ejectment.

The first was that peculiar bit of play-acting that one had to go through to enable him to use Ejectment as a vehicle for trying freehold: the nominal entry by the pretending freeholder, the lease of a term to a friend or henchman, the nominal entry of the termor who was resisted and then sued in Ejectment. It was all no doubt a troublesome piece of pantomime, but it was worth the trouble for not only did it make Ejectment available but it carried with it a further positive advantage. The true plaintiff who had arranged it all in order to make good his claim to the freehold was, strictly speaking, no party to the resultant action. Since he was not a party, a failure would not bar his claims in the future: whenever he might think it oppor-tune he could open a new suit, and the adverse judgment in the earlier proceedings would not prejudice him. In the seventeenth and eighteenth centuries the law rightly regarded this as an abuse and in time moved to remedy it.[1] But from the partisan viewpoint of the plaintiff it was of course an advantage.

[1] Simpson, *Introduction to the History of the Land Law*, pp. 139–40.

This is shown by the conduct of a litigant of the 1560s named Butler.[1] In 1567 he brought an action of Ejectment for freehold, using of course the device of a lease to a termor who appeared as the nominal plaintiff. He lost the action, but two years later, in 1569, he decided that it would be worth while to try again. This time he was advised, for some reason, to use novel disseisin instead of Ejectment. So he made another nominal entry to enable him to bring the assize. But instead of waiting to be rebuffed, in the traditional manner, and then founding his action on that event, he used his nominal entry to grant an estate for life to a friend, and when the adversary refused to get out of the lands it was the friend who regarded himself as disseised and brought the assize.

Butler was using the same procedure with the assize that he had used with Ejectment. In the one case the lease was for a term because the plaintiff in Ejectment had to be a termor, in the other case it was for life because the plaintiff in novel disseisin had to be a freeholder, and a life tenant qualified as such. But there was no need for this roundabout procedure in the assize; as far as the law was concerned Butler could have sued in his own name. Obviously, he valued for its own sake the advantage that came from having someone else appear as the nominal plaintiff.

Still, the procedure of entry and grant to a nominal plaintiff, though it was more natural in Ejectment because there one could not proceed without it, could also be used with the assize, as this case proves. I know of no reason why it could not have been employed in connection with Trespass.[2] So it is not likely by itself to have won Ejectment its increasing popularity as against Trespass. A second feature was probably more important, namely, that upon winning a favourable judgment in Ejectment the plaintiff got not only damages, as in Trespass, but also specific recovery of the tenement. The termor, as plaintiff, got judgment that the property should be returned

[1] Dyer fos. 266–7, 283–4.
[2] Actions of trespass appear commonly enough in which the plaintiff, being a termor or the holder of some other estate less than a freehold, sets up the freehold right of his grantor against the defendant's adverse claim to freehold; e.g. Y.B. Hil. 10 Ed. IV & 49 Henry VI no. 3 (1471), 1 Brownlow & Gouldesborough pp. 228–9 (1613). It is possible that some of these may have been arranged on purpose to try the grantor's claim to the freehold, just as in Ejectment.

to his possession for the remainder of his term. When the termor obtained possession the freeholder who granted him his term automatically came into seisin.

This was only a marginal advantage for Ejectment. If it had been anything more, Trespass and the civil actions of forcible entry, which gave only damages, would never have been able to do what they did to drive novel disseisin out of use, for the assize of course had always given specific recovery. But in a marginal way it was an advantage, and probably enough to secure men's preference for Ejectment. It meant that after getting judgment one could have the sheriff put him back in the land, under an order from the court, if he found the sheriff's help convenient. And it meant that if the victor executed judgment by himself, making his entry on his own, he could be very sure that his opponent would withdraw and make way for him, for his right of entry was expressly warranted by the judgment that he—or, strictly speaking, his termor—should have the land. The adversary could have no hope at all that the law might support him if he offered resistance. The value that plaintiffs attached to specific recovery is shown by the fact that when they made their leases to the termors who would be the nominal plaintiffs in Ejectment they made them for longish terms. Seven years was common. They wanted to be certain that when the litigation was concluded and time came to give judgment the term would still be running, for of course the specific recovery that Ejectment afforded was given for the balance of the term and would not be given at all if the term had expired when judgment was rendered.

In the seventeenth century Ejectment was improved by the development of elaborate fictions.[1] Repellent as these are to modern sensibilities, they were extraordinarily useful and they assured that Ejectment should retain ever after the place that it had won as the usual form of action for lands and tenements. In particular, they made it unnecessary for the plaintiff actually to go through the motions of making an entry, leasing the land, and having his termor enter and be put out. The era of the formal entry and ouster, which had begun in the late thirteenth century as a means of extending the range of the assize, was thus at length brought to an end.

[1] Simpson, *Introduction to the History of the Land Law*, pp. 138–9.

BIBLIOGRAPHY
OF BOOKS AND DOCUMENTS
CITED IN THE NOTES

ADAMS, G. B., *The Origin of the English Constitution*. New Haven, 1912.

'Annals of Burton', *Annales Monastici*, ed. H. R. LUARD, i. 181–510. (Rerum Brittanicarum medii aevi scriptores, vol. 36, pt. 1.) London, 1864.

'Annals of Dunstable', ibid., ed. H. R. LUARD, iii. 1–420. (Rerum Brittanicarum medii aevi scriptores, vol. 36, pt. 3.) London, 1866.

BAKER, J. H., *An Introduction to English Legal History*. London, 1971.

BEAN, J. M. W., *The Decline of English Feudalism, 1215–1540*. Manchester and New York, 1968.

BEARDWOOD, ALICE, *The Trial of Walter Langton, Bishop of Lichfield, 1307–1312*. (Transactions of the American Philosophical Society, new series, vol. 54, pt. 3.) Philadelphia, 1964.

BLACKSTONE, WILLIAM, *Commentaries*, ed. J. Chitty. 4 books. London, 1826.

Bodleian Library Rawlinson Manuscript C. 187, containing reports of the eyre of Northamptonshire of 1329–1330: see GULIELMUS D. MACRAY, *Catalogi codicum manuscriptorum Bibliothecae Bodleianae*, partis quintae fasc. secundus, coll. 88–9.

BOOTH, GEORGE, *The Nature and Practice of Real Actions*. London, 1701.

BORDWELL, PERCY, 'Seisin and Disseisin', *Harvard Law Review*, xxxiv (1920–1), 592–624, 717–40.

Borough Customs, ed. MARY BATESON. 2 vols. (Publications of the Selden Society, vols. 18, 21.) London, 1904, 1906.

BRACTON, HENRY OF, *De Legibus et Consuetudinibus Angliae*, ed. G. E. WOODBINE: vols. i and ii, translated, with revisions and notes, by S. E. THORNE. Cambridge, Massachusetts, 1968. vols. iii and iv. New Haven and London, 1940, 1942.

Bracton's Note Book, ed. F. W. MAITLAND. 3 vols. London, 1887.

British Museum Additional Charter 5153, containing a transcript of the rolls of the eyre of London of 1276: see *Additions to the British Museum Manuscripts, 1841–1845*, p. 55.

British Museum Additional Manuscript 35116, containing law reports of c. 1310: see *Catalogue of the Additions to the Manuscripts in the British Museum 1894–1899*, pp. 168–9.

British Museum Additional Manuscript 34783, containing pleas of the fourteenth and fifteenth centuries: see *Catalogue of the Additions to the Manuscripts in the British Museum, 1894–1899*, p. 85.

British Museum Egerton Manuscript 2811, fos. 209–352, containing reports of the eyres of Nottinghamshire, Derbyshire, Northamptonshire, and Bedfordshire, 1329–1331: see ibid., pp. 559–60.

British Museum Manuscript Royal 17 E. vi, containing an abridgement based on the Year Books of 1 Edward III–33 Henry VI: see G. F. WARNER and J. P. GILSON, *Catalogue of Western Manuscripts in the Old Royal and King's Collections*, ii. 260.

Britton, ed. F. M. NICHOLS. 2 vols. Oxford, 1865.

BROOKE, ROBERT, *La Graunde Abridgement*. In aedibus R. Tottelli, 1586.

Brooke's New Cases: *Ascuns Novell Cases de les ans et temps le Roy H. 8, Ed. 6. et la Roygne Mary, escrie ex la graund Abridgement compose par Sir R. Brooke*. London, 1604.

BROWNLOW, RICHARD, and JOHN GOULDESBOROUGH, *The Reports*. 2 parts. London, 1675.

CAENEGEM, R. C. VAN, *Royal Writs in England from the Conquest to Glanvill*. (Publications of the Selden Society, vol. 77.) London, 1959.

Calendar of Documents Relating to Ireland Preserved in Her Majesty's Public Record Office, London. 1285–1292, ed. H. S. SWEETMAN. London, 1879.

Calendar of Inquisitions Miscellaneous (Chancery) Preserved in the Public Record Office, vol. i. Prepared under the superintendence of the Deputy Keeper of the Records. London, 1916.

Calendar of Inquisitions post Mortem and Other Analogous Documents Preserved in the Public Record Office, vol. i. Prepared under the superintendence of the Deputy Keeper of the Records. London, 1904.

Calendar of the Cases for Derbyshire from Eyre and Assize Rolls, ed. C. E. LUGARD. Barnston, Cheshire, 1938.

Calendar of the Close Rolls Preserved in the Public Record Office. Edward I, A.D 1272–1279. Prepared under the superintendence of the Deputy Keeper of the Records. London, 1900.

Calendar of the Patent Rolls Preserved in the Public Record Office. Henry III, A.D. 1232–1247. Prepared under the superintendence of the Deputy Keeper of the Records. London, 1906.

Calendar of the Roll of the Justices on Eyre, 1227, ed. J. G. JENKINS. (Publications of the Records Branch of the Buckinghamshire Archaeological Society, vol. 6.) Printed for the Society, 1945.

Casus Placitorum and Reports of Cases in the King's Courts, 1272–1278, ed. W. H. DUNHAM. (Publications of the Selden Society, vol. 69.) London, 1952.

Chancery: Fine Rolls, 1 John to 23 Charles I, 553 rolls in the Public Record Office, London: see *Guide to the Contents of the Public Record Office*

i. 19–20 and, for the details of the individual rolls, *Lists and Indexes* xxvii. 52A–B, 53–6.

CHENEY, C. R., *Hubert Walter*. London, 1967.

CHITTY, J., *A Practical Treatise on Pleading*. 2 vols. London, 1809.

Chronica monasterii de Melsa, auctore Thoma de Burton, ed. E. A. BOND. 3 vols. (Rerum Brittanicarum medii aevi scriptores, vol. 43.) London, 1866–8.

Chronicle of Jocelin of Brakelond, The, ed. H. E. BUTLER. London and New York, 1949.

Civil Pleas of the Wiltshire Eyre, 1249, ed. M. T. CLANCHY. (Publications of the Wiltshire Record Society, vol. 26.) Devizes, 1971.

Close Rolls of the Reign of Henry III Preserved in the Public Record Office. A.D. 1227–1231. Printed under the superintendence of the Deputy Keeper of the Records. London, 1902.

Close Rolls of 'the Reign of Henry III Preserved in the Public Record Office. A.D. 1254–1256. Printed under the superintendence of the Deputy Keeper of the Records. London, 1931.

Code: *Codex Iustinianus*, recognovit et retractavit PAULUS KRUEGER. (Corpus Iuris Civilis, vol. 2.) 14th edition, Weidmann, 1967.

COKE, EDWARD, *Les Reports*. 11 parts. London, 1672.

Court of Common Pleas: Plea Rolls, 1 Edward I to 38 Victoria, 4135 rolls in the Public Record Office, London: see *Guide to the Contents of the Public Record Office* i. 137 and, for the details of the individual rolls, *Lists and Indexes* iv. 34–59.

Court of King's Bench: Curia Regis Rolls, 5 Richard I to 56 Henry III, 234 rolls in the Public Record Office, London: see *Guide to the Contents of the Public Record Office* i. 117 and, for the details of the individual rolls, *Lists and Indexes* iv. 1–4, 4A.

Court of King's Bench: Placita coram Rege, 1 Edward I to 13 William III, 2149 rolls in the Public Record Office, London: see *Guide to the Contents of the Public Record Office* i. 117–18 and, for the details of the individual rolls, *Lists and Indexes* iv. 5–17.

Court Rolls of the Abbey of Ramsey and of the Honor of Clare, ed. W. O. AULT. New Haven and London, 1928.

Crown Pleas of the Wiltshire Eyre, 1249, ed. C. A. F. MEEKINGS. (Publications of the Records Branch of the Wiltshire Archaeological and Natural History Society, vol. 16.) Devizes, 1961.

Curia Regis Rolls Preserved in the Public Record Office. Printed under the superintendence of the Keeper of Public Records. 14 vols. London, 1922–61.

Digest: *Iustiniani Digesta*, recognovit THEODORUS MOMMSEN, retractavit PAULUS KRUEGER. (Corpus Iuris Civilis, vol. 1.) 20th edition, Weidmann, 1968.

DYER, JAMES, *Les Reports*. London, 1672.

Earliest Lincolnshire Assize Rolls, A.D. *1202–1209, The*, ed. DORIS M. STENTON. (Publications of the Lincoln Record Society, vol. 22.) Lincoln Record Society, 1926.

Earliest Northamptonshire Assize Rolls, A.D. *1202 and 1203, The*, ed. DORIS M· STENTON. (Publications of the Northamptonshire Record Society, vol. 5.) Northamptonshire Record Society, 1930.

Early Registers of Writs, eds. ELSA DE HAAS and G. D. G. HALL. (Publications of the Selden Society, vol. 87.) London, 1970.

Early Yorkshire Charters, vol. ii, ed. W. FARRER. Edinburgh, 1915.

Eyre of Kent, The, eds. F. W. MAITLAND, L. W. VERNON HARCOURT, and W. C. BOLLAND. 3 vols. (Publications of the Selden Society, vols. 24, 27, 29.) London, 1909–13.

Eyre of London, 14 Edward II, A.D. *1321, The*, ed. HELEN M. CAM. 2 vols. (Publications of the Selden Society, vols. 85, 86.) London, 1968, 1969.

EYTON, R. W., *Court, Household, and Itinerary of King Henry II*. London, 1878.

FERGUSON, W. K., *Europe in Transition, 1300–1520*. Boston, 1962.

'Fet Asaver', *Four Thirteenth-Century Law Tracts*, ed. G. E. WOODBINE, pp. 53–115. New Haven and London, 1910.

FITZHERBERT, ANTHONY, *La Nouvelle Natura Brevium*. London, 1581.

Fleta: Commentarius Iuris Anglicani:
Prologue, Books I and II, eds. H. G. RICHARDSON and G. O. SAYLES. (Publications of the Selden Society, vol. 72.) London, 1955.
Books III–VI, editio secunda multis erroribus purgata. London, 1685.

FLOWER, C. T., *Introduction to the Curia Regis Rolls, 1199–1230*. (Publications of the Selden Society, vol. 62.) London, 1944.

The Forward Movement of the Fourteenth Century, ed. F. L. UTLEY. Columbus, Ohio, 1961.

Glanvill: *Tractatus de legibus et consuetudinibus regni Anglie qui Glanvilla vocatur*, ed. G. D. G. HALL. Thomas Nelson and Sons, 1965.

GRATIAN, *Decretum*, editio Lipsiensis secunda, post A. L. RICHTERI curas . . . instruxit A. FRIEDBERG. (Corpus Iuris Canonici, pars prior.) Leipzig, 1879.

Great Roll of the Pipe, The:
12 Henry II. (Publications of the Pipe Roll Society, vol. 9.) London, 1888.
13 Henry II. (Publications of the Pipe Roll Society, vol. 11.) London, 1889.
14 Henry II. (Publications of the Pipe Roll Society, vol. 12.) London, 1890.
15 Henry II. (Publications of the Pipe Roll Society, vol. 13.) London, 1890.
16 Henry II. (Publications of the Pipe Roll Society, vol. 15.) London, 1892.
21 Henry II. (Publications of the Pipe Roll Society, vol. 22.) 1897, reprinted 1929.

23 Henry II. (Publications of the Pipe Roll Society, vol. 26.) London, 1905.

32 Henry II. (Publications of the Pipe Roll Society, vol. 36.) London, 1914.

Guide to the Contents of the Public Record Office, vol. i. London, 1963.

HALL, G. D. G. Review of R. C. van Caenegem's *Royal Writs*, in *English Historical Review*, lxxvi (1961), 315–19.

Hanaper Accounts, Edward I to 1660, in the Public Record Office, London: see *Guide to the Contents of the Public Record Office* i. 52 and, for the details of the individual rolls, *Lists and Indexes* xxxv. 147–52.

Harvard Law Library Manuscript 77, containing Gilbert of Thornton's treatise on the laws of England: see T. F. T. PLUCKNETT, 'The Harvard Manuscript of Thornton's Summa', *Harvard Law Review*, li (1937–8), 1038–56.

History of Wiltshire, A, vol. v, eds. R. B. PUGH and ELIZABETH CRITTALL. (The Victoria History of the Counties of England.) London, 1957.

HOLT, J. C., 'The Assizes of Henry II: the Texts', in *The Study of Medieval Records: Essays in Honour of Kathleen Major*, eds. D. A. BULLOUGH and R. A. STOREY, pp. 85–106. Oxford, 1971.

HURNARD, NAOMI, *The King's Pardon for Homicide before A.D. 1307*. Oxford, 1969.

Institutes: *Iustiniani Institutiones*, recognovit PAULUS KRUEGER. (Corpus Iuris Civilis, vol. 1.) 20th edition, Weidmann, 1968.

JENKS, EDWARD, *A Short History of English Law*. 4th edition, London, 1928.

John Rylands Library Latin Manuscript 180, containing reports of the eyre of Northamptonshire of 1329–1330: see M. R. JAMES, *A Descriptive Catalogue of the Latin Manuscripts in the John Rylands Library at Manchester* i. 306–7.

JOLLIFFE, J. E. A., *Angevin Kingship*. London, 1955.

JOÜON DES LONGRAIS, FRÉDÉRIC, *La Conception anglaise de la saisine*. (Études de droit anglais, vol. 1.) Paris, 1925.

—— 'La portée politique des réformes d'Henry II en matière de saisine', *Revue historique de droit français et étranger*, 4ᵉ série, xv (1936), 540–71.

'Judicium Essoniorum', *Four Thirteenth-Century Law Tracts*, ed. G. E. WOODBINE, pp. 116–42. New Haven and London, 1910.

Justices Itinerant: Eyre Rolls, Assize Rolls, etc., 1201 to 1482, some 1620 documents in the Public Record Office, London: see *Guide to the Contents of the Public Record Office* i. 123–6 and, for the details of the individual rolls, *Lists and Indexes* iv. 125–92.

KEILWEY, ROBERT, *Relationes quorundam casuum . . . qui temporibus . . . Regis Henrici Septimi et . . . Regis Henrici Octavi emerserunt . . . Necnon relationes nonnullorum casuum per . . . G. Dalison . . . et G. Bendloes*. London, 1633.

KIRALFY, A. K. R., *A Source Book of English Law*. London, 1957.

KNOWLES, DAVID, *The Evolution of Medieval Thought*. Baltimore, 1962.

LEONARD, WILLIAM, *Reports and Cases*. 2 parts. London, 1658.

Liber Assisarum: *Le Livre des Assises et Pleas del Corone . . . en temps du Roy Edward le Tiers*. London, 1679.

LIEBERMANN, FELIX, *Die Gesetze der Angelsachsen*. 3 vols. Halle an der Saale, 1898–1916.

Lincoln's Inn Hale Manuscript 77, containing law reports of the reign of Richard II: see G. F. DEISER in Y.B. 12 Richard II, pp. xvii–xxvii.

Lincoln's Inn Hale Manuscript 135, fos. 5–133ᵛ, containing Gilbert of Thornton's treatise on the laws of England: see S. E. THORNE, 'Gilbert de Thornton's Summa de Legibus', *University of Toronto Law Journal*, vii (1947), 1–23.

Lists and Indexes, vol. ix: *List of Sheriffs for England and Wales*. Public Record Office, London. Reprinted. New York, 1963.

LITTLETON, THOMAS, *Treatise of Tenures*, ed. T. E. Tomlins. London, 1841.

LOENGARD, JANET S., *Free Tenements and Bad Neighbors: The Assizes of Novel Disseisin and Nuisance in the King's Courts before the Statute of Merton*. Unpublished dissertation, Columbia University, 1970.

London Eyre of 1244, The, eds. HELENA M. CHEW and MARTIN WEINBAUM. (Publications of the London Record Society, vol. 6.) London Record Society, 1970.

London Possessory Assizes: A Calendar, ed. HELENA M. CHEW. (Publications of the London Record Society, vol. 1.) London Record Society, 1965.

MAITLAND, F. W., 'The Beatitude of Seisin', *Law Quarterly Review*, iv (1888), 24–39, 286–99.

MANSI, G. D., *Sacrorum conciliorum nova et amplissima collectio*. 29 vols. Editio novissima, Florence, 1759–88.

MILSOM, S. F. C., *Historical Foundations of the Common Law*. London, 1969.

—— 'Introduction' to Pollock and Maitland's *History of English Law* (2nd edition reissued, Cambridge, 1968), 1. xxiii–lxxiii.

—— 'Select Bibliography and Notes', in Pollock and Maitland's *History of English Law* (2nd edition reissued, Cambridge, 1968), 1. lxxv–xci.

Mirror of Justices, The, eds. W. J. WHITTAKER and F. W. MAITLAND. (Publications of the Selden Society, vol. 7.) London, 1893.

MORRIS, W. A., *The Early English County Court*. (University of California Publications in History, vol. 14 no. 2.) Berkeley, 1925.

Munimenta Gildhallae Londoniensis, ed. H. T. RILEY. 3 vols. (Rerum Brittanicarum medii aevi scriptores, vol. 12.) London, 1859–62.

NICHOLS, J. F., 'An Early Fourteenth-Century Petition from the Tenants of Bocking to their Manorial Lord', *Economic History Review*, ii (1929–30), 300–7.

Novae Narrationes, eds. ELSIE SHANKS and S. F. C. MILSOM. (Publications of the Selden Society, vol. 80.) London, 1963.

Patent Rolls of the Reign of Henry III Preserved in the Public Record Office. A.D. 1216–1225. Printed under the superintendence of the Deputy Keeper of the Records. London, 1901.

Patent Rolls of the Reign of Henry III Preserved in the Public Record Office. A.D. 1225–1232. Printed under the superintendence of the Deputy Keeper of the Records. London, 1903.

Placitorum Abbreviatio. Record Commission, 1811.

Pleas before the King or his Justices: vols. i and ii, *1198–1202*; vols. iii and iv, *1198–1212*: ed. DORIS M. STENTON. (Publications of the Selden Society, vols. 67, 68, 83, 84.) London, 1948–67.

PLOWDEN, EDMUND, *Les Commentaries ou Reports.* London, 1684.

PLUCKNETT, T. F. T., *A Concise History of the Common Law.* 4th edition, London, 1948.

—— *Legislation of Edward I.* Oxford, 1949.

POLLOCK, F., and F. W. MAITLAND, *The History of English Law before the Time of Edward I.* 2 vols. 2nd edition reissued, Cambridge, 1968.

POWICKE, FREDERICK MAURICE, *King Henry III and the Lord Edward.* 2 vols. Oxford, 1947.

—— *The Thirteenth Century, 1216–1307.* Oxford, 1953.

Proceedings before the Justices of the Peace, Edward III–Richard III, ed. BERTHA PUTNAM. London, 1938.

PUGH, RALPH B., *Imprisonment in Medieval England.* Cambridge, 1968.

RALPH OF HENGHAM, 'Summa Parva', *Radulphi de Hengham Summae*, ed. W. H. DUNHAM, pp. 51–71. (Cambridge Studies in English Legal History.) Cambridge, 1932.

RAMSAY, J. H., *The Angevin Empire.* London and New York, 1903.

RASTELL, WILLIAM, *A Collection of Entries.* London, 1670.

REEVES, JOHN, *History of the English Law*, ed. W. F. Finlason. 3 vols. London, 1869.

Regesta Regis Stephani ac Mathildis Imperatricis ac Gaufridi et Henrici Ducum Normannorum, 1135–1154, eds. H. A. CRONNE and R. H. C. DAVIS. (Regesta Regum Anglo-Normannorum, vol. 3.) Oxford, 1968.

Register of the Abbey of St. Benet of Holme, The, ed. J. R. WEST. 2 vols. (Publications of the Norfolk Record Society, vols. 2, 3.) Fakenham and London, 1932.

Registrum omnium Brevium. London, in aedibus Ianae Yetsweirt, 1595.

RICHARDSON, H. G. 'The Marriage and Coronation of Isabelle of Angoulême', *English Historical Review*, lxi (1946), 289–314.

—— and G. O. SAYLES, *The Governance of Medieval England from the Conquest to Magna Carta.* Edinburgh, 1963.

—— —— *Law and Legislation from Aethelberht to Magna Carta.* Edinburgh, 1966.

Rôles gascons, edd. FRANCISQUE-MICHEL and CHARLES BÉMONT. 3 vols. in 4. (Collection de documents inédits sur l'histoire de France, vol. 29.) Paris, 1885–1906.

'Roll of the Justices in Eyre at Bedford, 1202', ed. G. H. FOWLER, *Publications of the Bedfordshire Historical Record Society*, i (1913), 133–247.

'Roll of the Justices in Eyre at Bedford, 1227', ed. G. H. FOWLER, ibid. iii (1916), 1–206.

'Roll of the Justices in Eyre, 1240', ed. G. H. FOWLER, ibid. ix (1925), 75–143.

Roll of the King's Court in the Reign of King Richard I, A. (Publications of the Pipe Roll Society, vol. 24.) London, 1900, reprinted 1929.

Rolls of the Justices in Eyre . . . for Gloucestershire, Warwickshire, and Staffordshire, 1221, 1222, ed. DORIS M. STENTON. (Publications of the Selden Society, vol. 59.) London, 1940.

Rolls of the Justices in Eyre . . . for Lincolnshire 1218–19 and Worcestershire 1221, ed. DORIS M. STENTON. (Publications of the Selden Society, vol. 53.) London, 1934.

Rolls of the Justices in Eyre . . . for Yorkshire in 3 Henry III (1218–19), ed. DORIS M. STENTON. (Publications of the Selden Society, vol. 56.) London, 1937.

Rotuli Curiae Regis, ed. FRANCIS PALGRAVE. 2 vols. Record Commission, 1835.

Rotuli Hundredorum. 2 vols. Record Commission, 1812, 1818.

Rotuli Litterarum Clausarum, ed. T. D. HARDY. 2 vols. Record Commission, 1833, 1844.

Rotuli Parliamentorum, vol. i. [London, 1767.]

RUFFINI, FRANCESCO, *L'actio spolii: studio storico-giuridico.* (R. Università di Torino, Istituto di Esercitazioni nelle Scienze Giuridico-Politiche, Memoria 6). Torino, 1889.

SAINT-EXUPÉRY, ANTOINE DE, *Le Petit Prince.* Paris, 1965.

ST. GERMAIN, CHRISTOPHER, *The Doctor and Student*, ed. WILLIAM MUCHALL. Cincinnati, Ohio, 1874.

SALTMAN, AVROM, *Theobald, Archbishop of Canterbury.* (University of London Historical Studies, vol. 2.) London, 1956.

Select Cases in the Court of King's Bench, ed. G. O. SAYLES. 7 vols. (Publications of the Selden Society, vols. 55, 57, 58, 74, 76, 82, 88.) London, 1936–71.

Select Cases in the Exchequer Chamber, ed. M. HEMMANT. 2 vols. (Publications of the Selden Society, vols. 51, 64.) London, 1933, 1948.

Select Cases of Procedure without Writ under Henry III, eds. H. G. RICHARDSON and G. O. SAYLES. (Publications of the Selden Society, vol. 60.) London, 1941.

Select Charters and Other Illustrations of English Constitutional History, ed. WILLIAM STUBBS. 9th ed., revised by H. W. C. DAVIS, Oxford, 1913.

SIMPSON, A. W. B., *An Introduction to the History of the Land Law*. Oxford, 1961.

Somersetshire Pleas, ed. C. E. H. C. HEALEY and LIONEL LANDON. 4 vols. (Publications of the Somerset Record Society, vols. 11, 36, 41, 44.) Somerset Record Society, 1897–1929.

Some Sessions of the Peace in Lincolnshire, 1381–1396, ed. ELIZABETH KIMBALL. 2 vols. (Publications of the Lincoln Record Society, vols. 49, 56.) Printed for the Society, 1955, 1962.

State Trials of the Reign of Edward I, 1289–1293, eds. T. F. TOUT and HILDA JOHNSTONE. (Publications of the Royal Historical Society, Camden Third Series, vol. 9.) London, 1906.

Statutes of the Realm, The. 11 vols. in 12. London, 1810–28, reprinted 1963.

STENTON, DORIS M., 'England: Henry II', *Cambridge Medieval History*, v. 554–91. Cambridge, 1926.

—— *English Justice between the Norman Conquest and the Great Charter, 1066–1215*. Philadelphia, 1964.

STENTON, F. M., *The First Century of English Feudalism, 1066–1166*. Oxford, 1932.

STRAYER, J. R., *Western Europe in the Middle Ages*. New York, 1955.

STUBBS, WILLIAM, *The Constitutional History of England*. 4th edition, Oxford, 1896; 6th edition, Oxford, 1903.

SUTHERLAND, D. W., 'Mesne Process upon Personal Actions in the Early Common Law', *Law Quarterly Review*, lxxxii (1966), 482–96.

—— 'Peytevin *v.* la Lynde', ibid. lxxxiii (1967), 527–46.

THORNE, S. E., 'English Feudalism and Estates in Land', *Cambridge Law Journal*, 1959, pp. 193–209.

—— 'Livery of Seisin', *Law Quarterly Review*, lii (1936), 345–64.

Three Early Assize Rolls for the County of Northumberland, ed. WILLIAM PAGE. (Publications of the Surtees Society, vol. 87.) Published for the Society 1891.

Three Rolls of the King's Court in the Reign of King Richard the First, A.D. 1194–1195. (Publications of the Pipe Roll Society, vol. 14.) London, 1891.

Three Yorkshire Assize Rolls for the Reigns of King John and King Henry III, ed. C. T. CLAY. (Publications of the Yorkshire Archaeological Society, Record Series, vol. 44.) Printed for the Society, 1911.

VACARIUS, *Liber Pauperum*, ed. FRANCIS DE ZULUETA. (Publications of the Selden Society, vol. 44.) London, 1927.

Le Vieux Natura Brevium. London, in aedibus Richardi Tottelli, 1584.

WILLIAM OF MALMESBURY, *Historiae novellae libri tres*, ed. WILLIAM STUBBS. (Rerum Brittanicarum medii aevi scriptores, vol. 90 pt. 2.) London, 1889.

WOODBINE, G. E., 'The Origins of the Action of Trespass', *Yale Law Journal*, xxxiii (1923–4), 799–816, and xxxiv (1924–5), 343–70.

Year Books:

20–22 Edward I, ed. A. J. Horwood. 2 vols. (Rerum Brittanicarum medii aevi scriptores, vol. 31, pts. 1, 2.) London, 1866, 1873.

30–35 Edward I, ed. A. J. Horwood. 3 vols. (Rerum Brittanicarum medii aevi scriptores, vol. 31, pts. 3–5.) London, 1863–79.

1–12 Edward II, eds. F. W. Maitland, G. J. Turner et al. 23 vols. (Publications of the Selden Society, vols. 17, 19, 20, 22, 26, 31, 33, 34, 36–9, 41–3, 45, 52, 54, 61, 63, 65, 70, 81.) London, 1903–64.

13–19 Edward II, in Les Reports des Cases argue et adjudge in le Temps del Roy Edward le Second . . . solonqe les ancient manuscripts ore remanent en les maines de Sir Jehan Maynard, pp. 392–685. London, 1678.

1–10 Edward III: Le Premier Part de les reports del cases en ley que furent argue en le temps de le . . . Roy Edward le Tierce. London, 1679.

11–20 Edward III, eds. A. J. Horwood and L. O. Pike. 15 vols. (Rerum Brittanicarum medii aevi scriptores, vol. 31, pts. 6–18.) London, 1883–1911.

21–39 Edward III: Le Second Part de les reports des cases en ley que furent argues en le temps de le . . . Roy Edward le Tierce. London, 1679.

40–50 Edward III: Les Reports del cases en ley que furent argues a quadragesimo ad quinquagesimum annum de . . . Roy Edward le Tierce. London, 1679.

11 Richard II, ed. Isobel D. Thornley. (Publications of the Ames Foundation.) London, 1937.

12 Richard II, ed. G. F. Deiser. (Publications of the Ames Foundation.) Cambridge, Massachusetts, and London, 1914.

13 Richard II, ed. T. F. T. Plucknett. (Publications of the Ames Foundation.) London, 1929.

Henry IV and Henry V: Les Reports del cases en ley que furent argues en le temps de . . . les roys Henry le IV et Henry le V. London, 1679.

1 Henry VI, ed. C. H. Williams. (Publications of the Selden Society, vol. 50.) London, 1933.

2–20 Henry VI: La Premiere Part des ans du Roy Henry le VI. London, 1679.

21–39 Henry VI: Les Reports des cases contenus in les ans vingt-premier et apres en temps du Roy Henry le VI, communement appelles The Second Part of Henry the Sixth. London, 1679.

1–9 Edward IV: Les Reports des cases en ley que furent argues en temps du Roy Edward le Quart. London, 1680.

Long Quinto 5 Edward IV: Les Reports des cases en ley en le cinque an du Roy Edward le Quart, communement appelle Long Quinto. London, 1680.

10 Edward IV and 49 Henry VI, ed. N. Neilson. (Publications of the Selden Society, vol. 47.) London, 1931.

11–22 Edward IV: Les Reports des cases en ley que furent argues en temps du Roy Edward le Quart. London, 1680.

Edward V, Richard III, Henry VII, and 1–27 Henry VIII: Les Reports des cases en les ans des roys Edward V, Richard III, Henrie VII, et Henrie VIII. London, 1679.

Yelverton, Henry, Les Reports . . . de divers speciall cases en le court del Bank le Roy. 2nd edition, London, 1674.

NOTES

A. If the defendant vouched a judgment of a court that was not his own feudal court, he would be allowed delay to bring in the record. For example, where he vouched his lord's feudal court, *CRR* i. 400, 458 (1201), ii. 168, 272 (1203), iii. 29, 69, 79 (1203), 132–3 (1204), *Lincs Assize Rolls* no. 1384 (1206), *Eyres of Beds* iii. 328 (1227), and cf. Bracton fo. 205b; or the county court, *Rotuli Curiae Regis* ii. 21, 24, 118–19 (1199), *CRR* iii. 132–3, 139–40 (1204), iv. 158 (1206), v. 141 (1208), vi. 383 (1212); the hundred court, *CRR* vii. 141, 167–8 (1214); or the king's court or the king's express order, *PRS* xiv. 73 (1194–5), *Rotuli Curiae Regis* i. 84 (1194), 370 (*c.* 1199), *CRR* i. 28–9 (1204–5), *BNB* nos. 1297 (1224), 401 (1230), 829 (1233). *PRS* xxiv. 243–4, a case that seems to belong to 1192, hints at a more rigorous law, requiring the defendant to produce on the spot the suitors even of his lord's court, but the record is of doubtful interpretation. For its date, cf. *Pleas 1198–1212* iii, p. xciv.

Delay might also be granted for the voucher of a final concord in the king's court, *CRR* i. 187 (1200), *BNB* no. 976 (1224). In 1202, for some reason that does not appear, the court gave an adjournment in order to bring a special jury to try the defendant's allegation that the plaintiff was a serf, *CRR* ii. 93.

The proof that the defendant was required to offer on the spot or with minimum necessary delay was only prima facie proof. If he produced the suitors of his court to witness a judgment against the plaintiff, or relatives of the plaintiff's to testify that they were serfs, he had done enough for that one day; if in reply the plaintiff traversed the record of the defendant's court, or maintained that he was free even though his kinsmen were serfs, adjournments could then be given as necessary for trial of the issue by jury or by compurgation: *Rotuli Curiae Regis* ii. 58–9, 117 (1199), i. 174–5 (1198–9), *CRR* i. 186, 249 (1200), 187 (1200), *Lincs Assize Rolls* no. 1384 (1206). Where the record of a court was traversed, the king's justices even seem to have contemplated allowing trial by battle, but there is no record in which battle was actually awarded: *Rotuli Curiae Regis* ii. 22–3 (1199), *CRR* i. 156 (1200), *Northants Pleas* no. 809 (1203), *Lincs Assize Rolls* no. 1384 (1206).

B. That feudal lordship was very effective and powerful is argued especially by F. M. Stenton, *The First Century of English Feudalism*, pp. 41–82, 102, and by S. E. Thorne, 'English Feudalism and Estates in Land', pp. 193–209. For contrary views, see Richardson and Sayles, *Governance*, pp. 36–41, and van Caenegem, *Royal Writs*, pp. 25–6. For the case of a tenant who had to invoke King Stephen's help because his lord was absent on crusade, *c.* 1150, see *Regesta Stephani* nos. 546–7.

Professor Milsom believes that if we assume a very powerful and pervasive feudal lordship in the twelfth century it will help to explain the peculiar character of the action of right: 'Introduction', pp. xxx–xxxvi; *Historical Foundations*, pp. 106–14. In an action of right the demandant put forth his claim by stating that some ancestor of his had at some time in the past been seised of the holding 'in demesne as of fee'. Defence by the tenant against the claim had always, as it seems, to take the form of a denial of this statement. Therein lies the enigma. There were obvious sorts of circumstances in which all that the demandant declared might be true and yet the tenant might have the better right to the land. One of his ancestors might have had a yet older seisin, and a better seisin therefore, because it was older, than the demandant's ancestor. The demandant's ancestor, having been seised 'in demesne as of fee', might have subinfeudated to the tenant. Why then was the tenant always restricted to a denial of the declaration and never allowed (if we may borrow terms from a later age) to confess and avoid it?

Professor Milsom suggests that we may make sense of this strange rule if we suppose that actions of right were almost always heard in feudal courts and that the words of the demandant's claim, though formally addressed to the tenant, were effectively directed against the lord. If everything in the demandant's count was true, if his ancestor had indeed been seised as he said, then perhaps that proved conclusively that the demandant was entitled to hold of this lord. Confession and avoidance were logically possible for the tenant but not for the lord; 'the right must be good against anybody within the lordship and against the lord himself'.

These reasonings are a superb example of how to think about historical problems, but it is not clear that the conclusion is one in which we ought to rest. For if logic was to govern the matter, surely there was room for the lord to 'confess and avoid' just as there would be for the tenant. The demandant's ancestor, having been seised in demesne as of fee, might have surrendered to the lord. He might have forfeited his holding. The lord might have given the land to the tenant by way of recognition of an older and 'higher' right than what the demandant's ancestor had had: in that case the demandant might be entitled to compensation from the lord, but he could hardly pretend, as he did in this action, a right to recover these particular acres out of the hand of the tenant.

C. 1, 2. For these limitations, see above, pp. 9–10.

3. The limit was the coronation of Richard I, 3 September 1189. It first appears in use in the plea rolls of the autumn of 1194, *PRS* xiv. 65, *Rotuli Curiae Regis* i. 35–6. Since these are the earliest surviving plea rolls we cannot tell how long before autumn 1194 the limit may have been set.

4. The limit was the second coronation of Richard I, 17 April 1194. It was first used in Easter term 1198, *Rotuli Curiae Regis* i. 140, *CRR* i. 34.

5. The limit was the Michaelmas before King John's coronation, 29 September 1198. John was crowned on 27 May 1199 and the limit was already in use in July 1199, *Rotuli Curiae Regis* i. 446, hence it must have been set in or close about June 1199. The oldest surviving original writ of novel disseisin, dated 4 August 1199, observes this limit: Doris Stenton, *English Justice*, pp. 40–1.

6. The limit was King John's coronation at Canterbury, 25 March 1201. It was first used in a plea heard in June 1202, *Lincs Assize Rolls* no. 72. For problems connected with the terminology of this limitation, see Richardson in *English Historical Review* lxi (1946), 310 n. 1 and *Early Registers of Writs* p. xxxv n. 4.

7. The limit was the return of King John from Ireland, 26 August 1210. It was first used in pleas heard in January 1219, *Eyres of Lincs and Worcs* no. 319, *Eyre of Yorks 1218–19* nos. 108, 185, 199. It must have been set when the regency government was planning the eyres that began at the end of 1218.

8. The limit was the coronation of Henry III at Westminster, 17 May 1220—not his first coronation in 1216 as stated by Maitland, P. & M. ii. 51, Powicke, *Henry III and the Lord Edward* ii. 770, and van Caenegem, *Royal Writs*, p. 261 n. It was first used in a plea heard under a commission of 30 January 1229, *Patent Rolls 1225–1232* pp. 282–3 and *CRR* xiii. 2011, and it appears in other pleas heard in Easter and Trinity terms 1229, *CRR* xiii. 2276, 2279, xiv. 455, 460, 461. It continued until the new limitation was set in 1237, *Calendar of Patent Rolls 1232–1247* pp. 176–7. Bracton's model writ of attaint supposes this limiting term for the assize, fo. 291. For problems connected with the terminology of the limitation see *Early Registers of Writs* p. xxxv n. 6.

9. The limit was Henry III's departure from England on his Breton campaign, 1 May 1230. The decision to set the new limit was taken early in 1237 and the limit began to be used in writs on the following Whit Sunday, 7 June 1237; *Calendar of Patent Rolls 1232–1247* pp. 176–7, *Annals of Burton* p. 252, *BNB* no. 1217. Bracton, writing in the 1250s when this limit was in use, cites it as Henry's *return* from Brittany, which was on 28 October 1230, about six months after his departure (fo. 179). There is no evidence in the records to support Bracton, not even in his own assize rolls, J.I. 1/1178 and 1/1182. His statement looks like a confused mixing of the limit of the 1220s, King John's return from Ireland, with the limit in use when he was writing his treatise, King Henry's departure for Brittany. Most of the records of assizes of novel disseisin collected in *Bracton's Note Book* were from the 1220s.

10. The limit was the first crossing of King Henry III to Gascony, 9 May 1242. It was defined in the Statute of Westminster I of 1275, c. 39, *SR* i. 36, to be used from St. John's Day in the following year, 24 June 1276.

11. 32 Henry VIII c. 2, *SR* iii. 747. The statute was enacted in 1540 but provided that its new limitation should not come into force until 1546.

Whenever the limit was advanced ample time was allowed for prosecuting under the old limitation actions that were pending when the date was moved up. The majority of the assizes taken in the nationwide eyres of 1218–22 were taken under the old limitation to March 1201 even though the date had been moved up about the time when the eyres began at the end of 1218. But writs bearing the old limit were expected to be prosecuted at the first opportunity: *CRR* viii. 36.

D. Janet Loengard, *Free Tenements and Bad Neighbors*, pp. 272–311. She believes that the change may have been introduced in the latter part of King John's reign. In 1282 the king's court refused to give any remedy where the owner of the soil had made small invasions of rights of common by enlarging his garden 'as well he might' or by creating a quarry: J.I. 1/1245 m. 76. In 1285 the Statute of Westminster II, c. 46, ruled that novel disseisin should not lie where pasture-land subject to common rights was taken to build a windmill, sheepfold, or cowbarn, or to make necessary enlargements of courtyards and curtilages. Fleta, Britton, and Ralph of Hengham, all c. 1290, say that only the viscontiel writ of nuisance lies for houses, orchards, gates, sheepfolds, windmills, watering-ponds, ovens, cowbarns, and enlargement of courtyards or curtilages—that is to say, for nuisances created by these operations: *Fleta* iv. 1. 20, *Britton* ii. 11. 14, Ralph of Hengham, 'Summa Parva', p. 60. Cf. the verses (in an accentual hexameter) in MS. Y fo. 217ʳ, from c. 1310

> Stagno, fossato, sepe, viis, aqua diversa
> Hiis datur assisa. Mercatum, feria Banco.
> Domus, virgultum, molendinum, ovileque, porta,
> Gurgites, et furna, vicecomes placitet illa.

Similar verses appear in *Registrum Brevium* fo. 199. They mean that the assize in the king's court is available for nuisances created by millponds, banks or hedges, for interference with rights of way, and for nuisances resulting from diversion of a watercourse; that nuisances created for established markets and fairs by the setting up of new markets and fairs in the vicinity may not be pleaded by the assize but must be heard in the central courts pursuant to other writs (FNB 409, Bracton fo. 235; *econtra tamen, Fleta* iv. 1. 17, 28. 13, and *Britton* ii. 11. 14); and that the sheriff alone can hear nuisances created by houses, orchards, mills, sheepfolds, gates, watering-ponds, and ovens. A statute of 1382, 6 Ric. II c. 3, provided that plaintiffs might thenceforth have writs returnable before the king's justices for these formerly 'viscontiel' nuisances; cf. *Registrum Brevium* fos. 199–199b. For a detailed account of proceedings before a sheriff in 1376 see Y.B. Hil. 50 Ed. III no. 23.

E. Final judgment was given on special matter alone in these cases, for example: *PRS* xiv. 40 (1194–5), *Rotuli Curiae Regis* i. 313–14 (1199), *CRR* i. 72 (1199), *Pleas 1198–1212* iii. 932 (1204), *BNB* no. 1950 (1221), *Eyres of Beds* iii. 328 (1227), K.B. 27/24 m. 16d (1276), C.P. 40/80 m. 78d (1289), MS. Y fos. 35ᵛ–36ʳ (c. 1300), 6–6ᵛ (c. 1300), Y.B. 19 Ed. II pp. 659–60 (1326), B.M. Egerton MS. 2811 fo. 279ᵛ (1330), 23 Ass. no. 11 (1349), 40 Ass. no. 31 (1366), 43 Ass. nos. 11, 43 (1369), 44 Ass. no. 6 (1370), Y.B. Trin. 45 Ed. III no. 34 (1371), Pasch. 13 Ric. II no. 6 (1390). Bracton fos. 192b–193 and the Statute of Westminster II c. 25 (1285) mention cases in which the courts went on and inquired of the points of the writ, and the practice is illustrated in many later cases, e.g. Y.B. Mich. 15 Ed. II pp. 451–2 (1321), Mich. 21 Ed. III no. 2 (p. 59), no. 38 = 21 Ass. no. 20 (1347), 23 Ass. no. 18 (1349), Y.B. Mich. 40 Ed. III no. 34 (1366), 48 Ass. no. 1 (1374), Y.B. Pasch. 11 Ric. II no. 7 (1388), J.I. 1/1542 m. 2 (1428), 1/1543 m. 35d (1434), 47 (1435), 41 (1438), K.B. 27/949 m. 30 (1499), Keilwey Mich. 6 Henry VIII no. 3 (1514), Rastell, *Entries*, fo. 59.

As these cases show, there was a tendency to follow the rule that further inquiry should be held on the points of the writ if the defendant did not acknowledge in the pleadings that he had ousted the plaintiff, and if the special issue joined on the pleadings was tried by the jurors of the assize. This rule was supported by the Statute of Westminster II c. 25 (1285), which prescribed that there should be no inquiry on the points of the writ where the defendant had vouched records by way of special proof and then failed to produce them. In cases to which it applied, the statute was always followed, e.g. K.B. 27/125 m. 65d (1290), C.P. 40/108 m. 113 (1295), Y.B. 3 Ed. II no. 30 (1310), Mich. 16 Ed. III no. 45 (1342), Trin. 44 Ed. III no. 31 (1370). But in other cases the practice of the courts was never wholly consistent. The vagueness that enveloped this subject is best revealed in a case of 1330, where after a finding for the plaintiff on a special issue the court made further inquiry on the points of the writ 'for good measure' ('a bien estre'): John Rylands Library Latin MS. 180 fo. 31. Cf. the debates reported in Y.B. 18 Ed. II pp. 587–8 (1325) and B.M. Egerton MS. 2811 fo. 278^r (1330). The confusion continued to the very end: see Booth, *Real Actions*, pp. 212 ff., 278, 284, 288.

Bracton held, fo. 212b, that the defendant's bailiff speaking for him at the assize could not join in a 'jeopardy', any more than he could compromise or confess (above, p. 45). In later times, and partly under the influence of the Statute of Westminster II c. 25, this was developed into the rule that a bailiff could never plead 'in bar'. The rule as Bracton knew it is illustrated in *BNB* no. 1206 (1236–7), and the later rule in K.B. 27/92 m. 22 and 27/130 m. 27d (1282–92), MS. Y fos. 37^v–40^r (1298–1307). The later development constituted a large extension of Bracton's principle, since pleading in bar did not always mean entering into 'jeopardy', and it was presumably this extension which by weakening the bailiff's power to speak for the defendant made it necessary in 1318 to admit attorneys for the defence (above, p. 44).

F. For the exclusion of vouchers to warranty in the early days of the assize see above, p. 19. Bracton wrote as though they were somewhat freely admitted in his time (fos. 175b, 177b, 178b) but the records contradict him for they show only rare and apparently anomalous cases: *Rotuli Curiae Regis* i. 153–4 (1198–9), *CRR* vi. 376 (1212), K.B. 26/121 m. 34d (1240–1), 26/191 m. 13 (1270), *Somerset Pleas* iv. 86–7 (1280). In the course of the thirteenth century, however, the rule developed that the tenant of lands sued for at novel disseisin might vouch a co-defendant, one who was 'named in the writ' along with him, if that person was present in court and willing to warrant. Such a voucher would cause no delay. The rule is well attested for the 1290s and after (Y.B. 20 & 21 Ed. I p. 5 (1292), C.P. 40/119 m. 127 (1297), 40/130 m. 122 (1299), K.B. 27/156 m. 30–1 (1298), Y.B. Mich. 4 Ed. II no. 36 (1310), Pasch. 15 Ed. II pp. 464–5 (1322), Mich. 18 Ed. III no. 17 (1348), FNB fo. 178 E) but in some form it seems to go back to about 1270, and perhaps even to the 1250s. Gilbert of Thornton, writing in the late 1280s, said that the tenant might vouch his co-defendant; that if the case was heard by justices in eyre they might compel the person vouched to enter into warranty ('secundum quosdam' in one of the manuscripts); but that justices commissioned for the assizes alone had no power to require him to warrant if he would not do it voluntarily (Harvard Law Library MS. 77 fos. 50ᵛ, 51; Lincoln's Inn Hale MS. 135, fo. 54ᵛ). Just so, before justices of assize in 1253 one Reginald vouched his co-defendant Ralph, 'et . . . Radulfus, requisitus si velit . . . Reginaldo . . . warantizare, dicit quod bene vult . . . warantizare et sponte sua ei warantizat', J.I. 1/1179 m. 4; Ralph of Hengham's roll for the early 1270s shows three cases where a co-defendant is vouched 'and willingly warrants' and one case where he 'is present and warrants', J.I. 1/1217 m. 3, 9, 12, 17d; in Hengham's later roll of 1279–89 several defendants 'are present and warrant', J.I. 1/1245, m. 2, 74, 108d; and in other cases of 1287 and 1288 the defendant 'is present and freely warrants', J.I. 1/503 m. 9, 14d. That no one might be vouched who was not named in the writ appears definitely from cases of 1240–1 (K.B. 26/121 m. 34d) and 1281–4 (J.I. 1/492 m. 47d, discussed below, p. 140) and is implied in the case that Roger le Peytevin opened in 1281, Sutherland, 'Peytevin v. la Lynde', pp. 533–4.

The defendant could secure through a separate action of warranty of charter the warranty that was not allowed him in novel disseisin itself. Cases appear from as early as 1206 in which Warranty of charter is used in this way, but they are rare in the first half of the century. I have seen only four examples: *CRR* iv. 66 (1206), ix. 250 (1220), xiii. 27 and 170 (1227), K.B. 26/116A m. 9 (1236). After mid century they became more numerous and by the 1280s the procedure is clearly standard: K.B. 26/145 m. 44, *Yorks Assize Rolls* pp. 63–4 (1251), *Northumb Assize Rolls* pp. 15–16, 55 (1256), C.P. 40/78 m. 95 (1259), K.B. 26/169 m. 44 (1260), *Derby Assizes* pp. 126–7 (1269), C.P. 40/17 m. 109d (1276), *Sel. Cases in K.B.* ii. 17 and *Somerset Pleas* iv. 254, 350 (1280), Sutherland, 'Peytevin v. la Lynde', p. 534, n. 36 (1281), J.I. 1/492 m. 47d (1281–4), 50, 87d (1282), and very frequent examples from all later times; Gilbert of Thornton speaks of it in his treatise in the late 1280s, Harvard Law Library MS. 77 fos. 50ᵛ and 51ʳ. From 1285 Warranty of charter could be brought by one who simply feared that he might be impleaded: the plaintiff had to allege that he was being sued but that was a fiction and the action was concluded, if the plaintiff was successful, with a simple acknowledgment of the warrantor's obligation: C.P. 40/60 m. 60d, 98d (1285). This was not permitted in 1280: *Somerset Pleas* iv. 104–5.

When the plaintiff succeeded in Warranty of charter he gained a claim, if he should ever lose his lands under circumstances that entitled him to the warranty, to be compensated out of all the lands that his warrantor held on the day when the writ of warranty of charter was sued out, even if the warrantor had afterwards alienated them: J.I. 1/492 m. 87d (1282), Y.B. Pasch. 10 Ed. II no. 29 (1317).

G. Statute of Westminster I c. 37. Bracton, writing some twenty years earlier, said that one who robbed in the course of an illegal disseisin should be gaoled and ransomed (fos. 186b–187), and the 'Casus et Judicia', contemporary with Bracton, said that the defendant would be imprisoned if he committed the disseisin by night, *Casus Placitorum*, p. lxxxiii. There is almost no evidence that this was actually done before the time of the statute of 1275. In the early thirteenth century it was common to imprison the convicted defendant in order to secure the payment of his amercement, and a plaintiff who failed might be sent to gaol for the same cause: e.g. *Northants Pleas* no. 870 (1203), *CRR* vi. 329, 396 (1212), *Eyre of Yorks 1218–19* no. 312, *Eyre of Bucks 1227* nos. 242, 388, 433, *Somerset Pleas* i. 474 (1242–3), *Wilts Civil Pleas 1249* nos. 139, 140. This practice is not found in later times. In the 1220s and after, if not before, gaol and fine were used as punishment for mendacious pleading or for fraudulent dealings out of court: e.g. *Eyres of Glos, Warw, Staffs* no. 1417 (1222: a successful plaintiff caused the serjeant who made execution to put him in seisin of more than he had recovered the judgment), *BNB* no. 1840 (1227: a guardian arranged fraudulent by conveyances in order to disinherit his ward), *Somerset Pleas* i. 1280 (1244: the defendant pleaded a forged document), K.B. 26/151 m. 42d (1254: a tenant-at-will granted over an estate of freehold), J.I. 1/1182 m. 6 (1254: a feoffor got hold of and destroyed the deed by which he had made the gift), K.B. 26/189 m. 12 (1269: the defendant took a feoffment from a minor), m. 12d (1269: the defendant traversed his father's deed, which was tried and found good). But from before 1275 I have seen only two cases of imprisonment for disseisin with violence, *Eyres of Lincs and Worcs* no. 940 (1221), and *Somerset Pleas* i. 569 (1242–3). Very few records make any reference to whether the disseisin was committed peaceably or otherwise, and where they do tell of this matter they do not always show that violent disseisors were sent to gaol: *Eyres of Lincs and Worcs* no. 256 (1219), *BNB* no. 1284 (1239–40). Violent disseisin would be punished by stiffer amercement than peaceable disseisin: Bracton fo. 186b.

After 1275 imprisonment and fine are, as the statute prescribed, always awarded for disseisin *vi et armis* or disseisin aggravated by robbery: e.g. J.I. 1/1245 m. 27d (1279), *Somerset Pleas* iv. 109–10 (1280), K.B. 27/127 m. 53 (1281), 27/81 m. 19 (1284), *Sel. Cases in K.B.* ii. 41 (1288), K.B. 27/135 m. 29d (1293), 27/129 m. 45d (1291), 27/136 m. 35 (1293).

H. Bracton does not discuss the matter, for it was no issue to him; he assumes that the 'first and principal disseisor' will always be named and he takes trouble to say so only in connection with some cases where for special reasons doubt might arise: fos. 164, 171b, 178, 203b–204, 218b. In 1219–20 an assize of novel disseisin had to be abandoned and an action of Entry sur disseisin substituted for it because the disseisor had died. But as the disseisor in this case was the earl Marshal it is hard to believe that he did it alone, and as the disseisin was supposed to have been done within the past ten years it is hard to believe that none of those who helped him had survived him. Naming the helpers as defendants was evidently not enough to support the assize. A case of 1227 seems to illustrate the same law, *Eyre of Bucks 1227* no. 475, and so do two assizes heard by Henry of Bracton in the early 1250s, where the plaintiffs failed because the principal disseisors, by whom the current tenants had entered, were dead; no concern was shown for the possibility that one of the other defendants—there were others in

each case—might have been 'a la disseisine fere', for evidently that would
not maintain the assize. J.I. 1/1182 m. 6, 8. The old law is stated clearly,
when it was already becoming obsolete in the late 1280s, by Gilbert of
Thornton in his treatise, Lincoln's Inn Hale MS. 135 fo. 54ᵛ: '. . . tenet assisa
. . . quamdiu principalis disseisitor qui sibi appropriaverit rem disseisitam
et illam tenuit superstes fuerit.'

The new law, that the principal disseisor need not be named but that it
was enough to join anyone who had participated in the disseisin, is adum-
brated in a case of 1280, J.I. 1/1245 m. 37, but first appears clearly in Earl Gilbert of Clare's case of 1281 against the abbot of Thornton, cited above, p. 140.
In that case the principal disseisor had been one Ranulf of Amundeville,
who was dead when Earl Gilbert brought his suit. But a number of small
fry had participated in the act, Brother John of Horbling, Roger of Skerling,
Simon Carpenter, John and Nicholas Cappe, and others. The earl named
them as the disseisors and recovered when they were convicted by the assize.
From later years the rule is abundantly illustrated, e.g. C.P. 40/142 m. 10
(1302), MS. Y fos. 4ʳ–4ᵛ, 12ʳ, 35ʳ (early 1300s), *Eyre of Kent* iii. 126–7 (1313).
In a case of about 1310 counsel argued, 'Par la comune lei si ne puet home
nent user lassise de novele disseisine apres la mort le principal disseisour,
einz fut chace a son bref dentre. Et pur ceo meschief eschuire si est ordine
par la novele lei que tant com il y ad disseisour et tenant apres la mort le
principal disseisour que assise seit meintenu.' MS. Y fo. 33.

I. *Eyre of Kent* i. 158–84, ii. 186–200, iii. 119–20. The other decisive case,
that of 1311, is Y.B. Pasch. 4 Ed. II no. 19. There the demandant's right to
resort from novel disseisin to formedon was denied by the court because
formedon was, according to Chief Justice Bereford, not really a writ of
right and only a little 'higher' than the assize. The demandant could, said
Bereford, resort to a writ of right, 'e tendre sute et dereisne', and 'offer suit
and proof'. In formedon the demandant offered only 'suit' without 'proof'.
Bereford's reasoning was that the demandant might yet bring a writ of
right because in that action trial would be by battle or by the verdict of a
grand assize that might if it liked find for the demandant by a flat assertion
of his 'greater right', without descending into details: hence, whether by
battle or by grand assize, the demandant might recover without anyone's
directly contradicting the verdict that had been rendered in the assize. But
no action could be allowed expressly to undo the findings of the assize.

The doctrine laid down in these cases held good thereafter: Y.B. Pasch.
42 Ed. III no. 24 (1368), 46 Ass. no. 5 (1372). Its novelty in 1311–13 is
shown by the vigour and apparent confidence of the arguments that the
opposing counsel initially brought against it in the cases of those years.
The old law, that whatever was done at novel disseisin was done without
prejudice to suits higher in the right, is expressed by Bracton, fo. 113b, cf.
fos. 267, 290, and may be illustrated in *Rotuli Curiae Regis* ii. 129 (1199).
From well before the time when Bracton wrote, however, the courts may
have distinguished between judgments at novel disseisin based on verdicts
of the assize taken as an assize on the original issue of illegal disseisin and
those based on verdicts of the assize taken as a jury by consent of the parties

to try an issue that emerged from the pleadings: the former could be un-done by resort to a higher action, but no higher action must be allowed to retry issues settled by the verdict of the assize 'taken as a jury'. Such a doctrine, though evidently strange to Bracton, is suggested by *CRR* xiv. 610 (1230). From this point of view, the innovation in Scoland's case of 1313 was that what estopped him of his action of formedon was not the findings of an assize taken as a jury but the special verdict of an assize taken as an assize.

INDEX